Seeking Success and Confronting Failure

Reimagining Ireland

Volume 145

Edited by Dr Eamon Maher,
Technological University Dublin – Tallaght Campus

Seeking Success and Confronting Failure

The British Army's Campaigns in Ireland and Northern Ireland, 1919 to 2007

Geoffrey Sloan

PETER LANG
Oxford · Berlin · Bruxelles · Chennai · Lausanne · New York

Bibliographic information published by the Deutsche Nationalbibliothek.
The German National Library lists this publication in the German National
Bibliography; detailed bibliographic data is available on the Internet at
http://dnb.d-nb.de.

A catalogue record for this book is available from the British Library.

Library of Congress Cataloging-in-Publication Data
Names: Sloan, G. R. (Geoffrey R.) author
Title: Seeking success and confronting failure : the British Army's campaigns in
    Ireland and Northern Ireland 1919-2007 / Geoffrey Sloan.
Other titles: British Army's campaigns in Ireland and Northern Ireland 1919-2007
Description: Oxford ; New York : Peter Lang, [2025] | Series: Reimagining Ireland,
    1662-9094 ; volume 145 | Includes bibliographical references and index.
Identifiers: LCCN 2025025008 (print) | LCCN 2025025009 (ebook) |
    ISBN 9781803748160 print | ISBN 9781803748238 epdf | ISBN 9781803748245 epub
Subjects: LCSH: Great Britain--Relations--Ireland | Ireland--Relations--Great Britain |
    Great Britain. Army--History--20th century | Great Britain--History,
    Military--20th century | Northern Ireland--History, Military
Classification: LCC DA47.9.I75 S58 2025 (print) | LCC DA47.9.I75 (ebook)
LC record available at https://lccn.loc.gov/2025025008
LC ebook record available at https://lccn.loc.gov/2025025009

Cover image: Cheri Hunston, Wildwood Arts.
Image Courtesy of the National Army Museum.
Cover design by Peter Lang Group AG

ISSN 1662-9094
ISBN 978-1-80374-816-0 (Print)
ISBN 978-1-80374-823-8 (ePDF)
ISBN 978-1-80374-824-5 (ePub)
DOI 10.3726/b22438

© 2025 Peter Lang Group AG, Lausanne (Switzerland)
Published by Peter Lang Ltd, Oxford (United Kingdom)
info@peterlang.com – www.peterlang.com

Geoffrey Sloan has asserted his right under the Copyright, Designs and Patents Act, 1988,
to be identified as Author of this Work.

All rights reserved.

All parts of this publication are protected by copyright.
Any utilisation outside the strict limits of the copyright law, without the permission
of the publisher, is forbidden and liable to prosecution. This applies in particular to
reproductions, translations, microfilming, and storage and processing in electronic
retrieval systems.

This publication has been peer reviewed.

TO

Professor John Vincent (1943–1990) - Inspiring Teacher.

Professor Colin Gray (1943–2020) - Outstanding Colleague and Friend.

Contents

Preface ix
Acknowledgements xxi

CHAPTER 1 The Operating Codes – Echoes from Two Campaigns 1
CHAPTER 2 A Slow Burning Fuse 23
CHAPTER 3 Fire and Water: Fighting an Insurgency 59
CHAPTER 4 Tactics, Operations, and Lost Victories 91
CHAPTER 5 Assessing the Assessors – Operation Banner 139
CHAPTER 6 Successes and Failure: A Judgement on
           Operation Banner 177
CHAPTER 7 Conclusions 215

Bibliography 229
Index 239

Preface

This book will challenge the accepted judgements concerning the British Army's two counter-insurgency campaigns in Ireland and Northern Ireland. The first is regarded as an exemplar of sub-optimal military effectiveness, which resulted in defeat. The second is regarded as a stalemate or an honourable draw[1] depending on interpretation.

During the twentieth century and in the early years of the twenty-first century, the British Army, uniquely among European armies, fought two domestic counterinsurgency/terrorist campaigns. They were not expeditionary counterinsurgencies such as the recent operations in Iraq and Afghanistan, as they both occurred within the jurisdiction of the British state. This distinction is important as it meant Britain was in an advantageous position in terms of the ability to generate domestic support and acquire and interpret intelligence. In addition, the strategic calculus, political stakes, and options open to a sovereign power are different from a state which has foreign military forces deployed inside its territory. In both campaigns, the British state was obliged to defend the political integrity of its sovereign area. This represented a key national interest, by contrast, deploying the army abroad was and is a choice, not a necessity.

There is a geographic dimension that requires qualification. The first campaign took place when the British state was geographically synonymous with the British Isles: The United Kingdom of Great Britain and Ireland. It lasted from 1919 to 1921. The British Army produced an assessment of its own performance in 1922. It was a five-volume report titled: *'A Record of the Rebellion in Ireland 1920–1921'*. It was classified as secret and not declassified until 2012, some 90 years after it was written.[2] In sequence, the volumes were titled 'Operations', 'Intelligence', 'Law', 'Training and Administration', while the fifth volume consisted of

---

1   This was a phrase of one favoured by successive generations of civil servants in the Northern Ireland Office.
2   The complete set of volumes can be found in the National Archives at WO 141/94.

reports from Divisions and Brigades.³ The last three volumes represent a new source on the effectiveness of the British Army, in conjunction with the Royal Irish Constabulary, and the Dublin Metropolitan Police in fighting a rebellion that was led by a coalition of Sinn Fein, the Irish Republican Brotherhood, and the Irish Volunteers.

The second campaign, starting some 47 years later, was undertaken by a state whose geographical parameters had changed. It was now the United Kingdom of Great Britain and Northern Ireland. This new configuration brought with it a degree of strategic, operational, and tactical complexity that the first campaign did not have. In terms of geographical parameters, the second campaign was defined by the outcome of the first. A consequence was the creation of an internationally recognised boundary between the Irish Republic and the United Kingdom of Great Britain and Northern Ireland.⁴ This second campaign lasted from August 1969 to July 2007 and was given the official designation of Operation Banner. In July 2006, the Army produced a report titled: *'Operation Banner: An Analysis of Military Operations in Northern Ireland, Army Code 71842'*. This was an assessment of the role that the army played in conjunction with the Royal Ulster Constabulary. This report was originally classified as 'Restricted' but was then declassified against military advice. Subsequently, it was reclassified on ministerial direction.⁵ The sensitivity

---

3   The problem is that only Volumes 1 and 2 have been used by historians in their account of this campaign. These volumes were accessed using the papers of General Strickland in the Imperial War Museum. Townshend's book: *The British Campaign in Ireland 1920–1921* can now be considered less than definitive as the three other volumes were not accessible in 1975.

4   Originally an internal border inside the United Kingdom and set up by an order in council. The refusal of Sinn Fein to participate in setting up of a devolved parliament in the south of Ireland meant that by 1925 the Irish Free State, the British Government and the Northern Ireland Government confirmed the new configuration of the border now constituted an international boundary that was confirmed by all three parties in an international treaty.

5   See Storr, J., 'Irish Republican Insurgency and Terrorism', in B. Heuser, and E. Shamir, eds. *Insurgencies and Counterinsurgencies* (Cambridge: Cambridge University, 2016), 215.

pivoted around a candid institutional self-assessment, and critiques of the decision making by successive generations of British policy elites.

These two reports were separated by 84 years and have spawned a voluminous literature.[6] The two campaigns, despite the different geographical parameters, illuminate continuity in the relationship between geography strategy and politics. This has been summarised by General Sir Rupert Smith: 'Geography shapes the strategy, and politics shapes the execution of that strategy within the geography'.[7] Furthermore, both reports represent institutional attempts to assess success and failure. The narrative of defeat in the first campaign has found a number of adherents. The military historian Hew Strachan claimed that 'Britain slithered to defeat' in Ireland. The historian Charles Townshend has argued: 'The Republican guerrilla campaign is portrayed as too determined, too resilient, and too resourceful to be put down by the military forces employed against it. In the relentless pursuit of a certain type of idealism, and even more in the efficiency with which it organised itself and mobilised popular support, the Republic of 1919–1921 was outstanding in the history of Irish resistance movements.[8] David French has claimed the campaign had a particular "hallmark": which was the wide range of coercive techniques

---

6   This literature is vast and what follows is just a small selection: Mumford, A., *The Counterinsurgency Myth: The British Experience of Irregular Warfare* (London: Routledge, 2011). Strachan H., ed., *Big Wars and Small Wars in the 20th Century* (Abingdon: Routledge, 2006). Mockaitis, T. R., *British Counterinsurgency, 1919–1960* (London: MacMillian, 1990). Paget, J., *Counter Insurgency Campaigning* (London: Faber and Faber, 1967). Hart, P., *British Intelligence in Ireland 1920–1921. The Final Reports* (Cork: University of Cork Press, 2002). Townshend, C., *The British Campaign in Ireland 1919–1921*, (Oxford: Oxford University Press, 1975). Hamill, D., *Pig in the Middle The Army in Northern Ireland 1969–1984* (London: Methuen, 1985). Hew Bennett, *Un Civil War, The British Army and the Troubles 1966–1975* (Cambridge: Cambridge University Press, 2024). O'Faolean, G., *A Broad Church, The Provisional IRA in the Republic of Ireland 1969–1980* (Newbridge: Merrion Press, 2019).
7   Communication to the author from General Sir Rupert Smith dated 24 September 2012.
8   See Townshend, C., *The British Campaign in Ireland 1919–1921* (Oxford: Oxford University Press, 1975). 202.

to intimidate the civilian population into throwing their support behind the government rather than behind the insurgents'.⁹ French judged this as a major factor in the failure of the campaign. As he has phrased it: 'Southern Ireland was granted Dominion status in 1921 because Sinn Fein's resistance demonstrated the impossibility of countering violent nationalism with nothing but military repression'.¹⁰

The campaign between 1969 and 2007 has produced a huge spectrum of literature. There is a paradox identified by the academic M. L. R Smith; the military dimension of the conflict in Northern Ireland has been one of the most under-studied aspects. Yet it gave the conflict its crucial form: 'The academic study of the conflict in Northern Ireland has been, to a great degree, insulated – intellectually interned, to coin a phrase, from influences and debates at work in the wider academic world'.¹¹

The military dimension has produced a variegated literature. This ranges from a claim of a victory denied¹² to a 'draw': 'The British Army obviously became more skilled in counterinsurgency terms as the campaign in Northern Ireland went into the 1970s and the 1980s. But it was a case of locking the stable door after the horse had bolted, and later improvements were mere sticking plasters that could only hold until peace had been negotiated with the PIRA leaders in the 1990s'.¹³

M. L. R. Smith assessed the evolution of a violent Irish Republicanism from the rebellion of 1916 to the early 1990s with reference to strategic theory.¹⁴ However, this analysis does not have the British Army as its

9   See French, D., *The British Way in Warfare, 1688–2000* (London: Unwin Hyman, 2000), 247.
10 Ibid, p. 182.
11 Smith, M. L. R., 'The Intellectual Internment of a Conflict: The Forgotten War in Northern Ireland International Affairs', 75/1 (1999), 78.
12 See for example van der Bijl, N., *Operation Banner: The British Army in Northern Ireland 1969–2007*. (Barnsley: Pen and Sword Books, 2017).
13 Rod Thornton, 'Getting it Wrong: The Crucial Mistakes Made in the Early Stages of the British Army's Deployment to Northern Ireland (August 1969–March 1972)', *Journal of Strategic Studies* 30/1 (February 2007), 105.
14 Smith, M. L. R., *Fighting for Ireland* (London: Routledge, 1995).

Preface

main focus. Another interpretation was the reciprocal effect of the British Army, and the IRA on each other, which produced a unique outcome.[15]

Another pathway has been the lack of organisational learning within the British Army. The longevity of the second campaign made this a focus. Douglas Porch has claimed the British Army was not a learning institution with respect to counterinsurgency, and was incapable of differentiating between the domestic and expeditionary counter – insurgency campaigns: 'The British Army's record in Northern Ireland, or in Iraq or Afghanistan after 2003 for that matter, fails to support the assertion that the British were able through institutional learning to develop a travelling circus technique to deal with insurgent challenges to imperial authority'.[16] David Ucko has claimed the soft weapon of doctrine was missing in Northern Ireland and the British Army was not 'a doctrine-driven organisation'. Instead, it prefers extemporising on the ground. This had consequences for military effectiveness: 'The problem arises when flexibility is achieved at the cost of forgetfulness – not of the step-by-step guides and templates, but of the basic considerations and principles unearthed through past experiences'.[17]

The narrative of a military stalemate has become an article of faith for Gerry Adams: 'the IRA could not be defeated by the use of tactics which could clearly have been counter-productive for the London government. British policy instead aimed more and more towards containment, though this strategy was exposed as being inadequate. There was a military and political stalemate'.[18] The political scientist Aaron Edwards has given a more nuanced interpretation of this claim. He has argued that by the early 1990s a more effective Counter-Terrorism strategy did constrain the IRA's

---

15 See Tonge, J Shirlow, P., and McAuley, J., 'So Why Did the Guns Fall Silent? How Interplay, Not Stalemate Explains the Northern Ireland Peace Process', *Irish Political Studies* 26/1 (2011) 1–18.

16 Porch, D., *Counterinsurgency: Exposing the Myths of the New Way of War* (Cambridge: Cambridge University Press, 2013), 287.

17 Egnell R., and Ucko, D., 'True to Form? Questioning the British Counterinsurgency Tradition', in B. Heuser, and E. Shanir, eds., *Insurgencies and Counterinsurgencies*, (Cambridge: Cambridge University Press, 2016), 32.

18 Adams, G., *Selected Writings* (Dingle: Brandon Press, 1997), 278.

options with the following consequences: 'They could neither escalate their violence – and thereby risk alienating their support base-or-opt for the path of least friction, that is, negotiation and dialogue'.[19] The senior hierarchy of PIRA choose the latter pathway.[20] After the Belfast Agreement of 1998, a distinct narrative of the 1994 ceasefire emerged. It represented a: 'tautological argument that the peace process was a by-product of a military stalemate between the IRA and the state's security forces'.[21] In addition, Edwards has argued that this narrative became the dominant one in terms of republican explanations for the end of the conflict.[22]

Work on this book started 20 years ago and is a product of a research project I undertook into the geopolitics of Anglo-Irish Relations in the twentieth century. In 1994, I was appointed a Defence Fellow at St Antony's College, Oxford by the British Ministry of Defence. What struck me about the literature at that time was a narrative that endorsed two political outcomes. First had already happened, the secession in 1922 of the south of Ireland from the rest of the United Kingdom. Second, the literature suggested Northern Ireland would, at some point in the future, secede and become part of the Irish Republic. There was no acknowledgement of the complex character of the Anglo-Irish relationship. There was a geopolitical paradox that lay at its heart: it is close but tortuous.[23] Furthermore, the nature of the union is a multilayered and variegated entity, which has much in common with the kingdom of Spain. This has been largely ignored in the literature.

In terms of methodology, this book will use the following approach. At each of the three levels of warfare: the strategic, operational and tactical, there is an independent variable that enables an assessment of success

---

19 Edwards, A. 'Deterrence, Coercion and Brute Force in Asymmetric Conflict: The Role of the Military Instrument in Resolving the Northern Ireland "Troubles"', *Dynamics of Asymmetric Conflict* 4/3 (November 2011), 237.
20 This is confirmed in an interview Edwards conducted with Danny Morrison in 2010.
21 Ibid, p. 229.
22 See Adams, G., *Selected Writings* (Dingle: Brandon, 1997).
23 See Sloan, G. R., *The Geopolitics of Anglo-Irish Relations in the 20th Century* (London: Leicester University Press, 1997).

Preface

and failure in both campaigns to be made. A critical question is to what extent were these variables were recognised by successive generations of army commanders and given expression on the ground? If they were is it now necessary to revise the accepted judgements about what constitutes failure and success? If only one or two of these variables were recognised, what are the implications for judgements about failure and success?

At the strategic level, the independent variable it is the willingness and ability to engage with and counter, and if possible, erode the narrative of the insurgents. This was dependent on the support and commitment of the government of the day. It was something that an army should or could not do on its own.

At the operational level, the independent variable is the ability to subvert, divert and destroy the various networks that the insurgents need to sustain their campaign. This includes financing, bomb making, engineering, procurement of intelligence, access to weapons and ammunition, the ability to import weapons from overseas, and keeping them secure. With respect to Operation Banner, there were a number of state agencies involved, apart from the British Army. For example, the Royal Ulster Constabulary Special Branch was responsible for investigating sources of finance. Both MI5 and MI6 were involved in intercepting supplies of weapons, ammunition and explosives.

At the tactical level, there were three functions that have to be performed. First, the capabilities of the insurgents have to be reduced through intelligence-informed operations. Second, the security forces have to deter the launch of attacks. Finally, they must reassure the public that lives, and property were being protected. All three of these functions have to operate within the framework of the legal constraints of the state.[24] These independent variables encapsulate the principles of counterinsurgency[25]. Furthermore, they constitute three criteria that can be

---

24 I am grateful to General Sir Rupert Smith for this insight.
25 There are ten of these recognised principles: primacy of political purpose, unity of effort, understanding the human terrain, secure the population, neutralise the insurgent, gain and maintain popular support, operate in accordance with the law, integrate intelligence, prepare for the long term, learn and adapt.

applied to both campaigns. Attention will be paid to the extent to which success and failure can be discerned in both campaigns. In addition, did success and failure happen at the same levels in both campaigns. If this is the case, how do we explain it?

One way of explaining success and failure is the concept of 'operating codes'. They have their origins in a book, and a series of articles written by Nathan Leites between 1951 and 1955.[26] They are now regarded as landmarks in the behavioural approach to the study of political elites. The focus is on unstated rules of conduct and norms of political behaviour. Alexander George reinterpreted these separate elements into a tight set of beliefs about the issues and questions associated with political action. He viewed them as: 'a set of premises and beliefs about politics and not as a set of rules and recipes to be applied mechanically to the choice of action – that the "operational code" construct is properly understood'.[27] This will be examined in detail in the first chapter.

The three independent variables will be used as a fishing net to trawl through the history of both campaigns and illuminate the impact that these 'operating codes' had on both the military and political outcomes. Furthermore, it will be argued that these levels are connected. A tactical success can result in strategic failure if policy objectives fail to provide guidance and legitimacy for the tactical use of force.

An important qualification to make is that both reports constitute institutional accounts. Inevitably, these official reports have omissions and weaknesses. To compensate for this new archive material will be used to provide a more comprehensive understanding of the assessments made. In the case of Operation Banner, classified information is limited beyond 1995. To address this dearth of material, a number of elite semi-structured interviews have been undertaken with former members of the Royal Ulster Constabulary and British Army officers who served in Northern Ireland during Operation Banner.

---

26 See Leites, N., *A Study of Bolshevism* (Glencoe, Illinois: The Free Press, 1953).
27 George, A. L., 'The "Operational Code": A Neglected Approach to the Study of Political Leaders and Decision-Making', *International Studies Quarterly* 13/2 (1969), 196–197.

Preface

Irregular wars, despite their different character have the same logic as regular wars: the application of military force to change or modify the enemy's will and destroy his fighting power. What is different is the context in which this takes place. The insurgents do not have access to the resources of a state. By contrast they have to construct a strategic path whereby force is used to modify the enemy's will, but they have to develop a cause which has legitimacy and can access resources. Critically they have to affect the perception and will of the local population and the degree of support they give to the police and other security forces. Another important dimension is the degree of external support, both political and practical, they can attract and rely on. In both conventional and irregular wars, conventional armies face the same challenge: they are dependent on the government to develop and sustain at the strategic level the coordination of the political and military dimensions. However, this is more demanding in the counter-insurgency warfare: 'Militaries confronting insurgency must therefore seek to use force appropriately on the operational and tactical levels, in concert with an integrated political – military approach, rather than simply focussing on exit strategies. There is no shortcut to success in counterinsurgency'.[28] These variables, while central to producing an answer to the main research question, raise another key question. To what extent did British policy makers adhere to an 'integrated political-military approach'? The pivotal importance of this has been articulated by the French army officer David Galula: 'every military move has to be weighed with regard to its political effects and vice versa',[29] In both campaigns, there was a proclivity of British policymakers to pursue separate political initiatives with inconsistent results. This systematically undermined the key goal of achieving integration.

---

28 Burton B., and Nagl, J., Learning as we go: the US Army adapts to counterinsurgency in Iraq, July 2004–December 2006, Small Wars and Insurgencies, Vol. 19, No. 3, p. 323.

29 Galula, D., *Counterinsurgency Warfare* (Westport: Praeger Security International, 2006), 5.

To paraphrase Colin Gray,[30] there was a black hole where integration should have resided.

In order to provide answers to these questions, I have adopted the following construct. The first chapter identifies a number of similarities and differences in both reports. It will begin to develop an understanding of the nature and impact of the 'operating codes' of the British policy elite. It is these codes that defined behaviour, decisions and outcomes in both campaigns. To what extent did they affect the strategic level and what were the consequences, if any, at the operational and tactical levels? In particular, did it affect the manner in which a violent Irish Republicanism was dealt with?

Chapter 2 provides an assessment of the period from April 1916 to December 1919. This formed a vital backdrop to the first campaign. Three related perspectives are examined: the decisions taken by the British policy elite, the operational challenges the British Army faced, and the actions of the Irish Republican movement.

Chapters 3 and 4 will assess the British Army's response to the campaign from January 1920 to July 1921. Particular attention will be paid to the role played by Assistant Undersecretary Alfred Cope. He was the only British civil servant named in the Army's 1922 report. New archive material reveals he was sent to Ireland as a Special Representative of the British Cabinet. His official civil service post was merely a cover for this secret political mission.

Chapter 5 will assess the early years of Operation Banner from August 1969 to August 1980. This includes the events leading up to the killing of civilians in Londonderry in January 1972. The final chapter will cover the period from 1980 to the Good Friday Agreement of 1998. It will assess the effectiveness of the primacy accorded to the Royal Ulster Constabulary from 1976, and the role the army played in support. The key question to be addressed is the extent to which the IRA had been brought by the Army and the RUC to a point whereby it could no longer sustain the tempo of its operations, and therefore sought a negotiated settlement

---

30   See Gray, C. S., *Another Bloody Century: Future Warfare* (London: Routledge, 2005), 111.

out of the impasse? Are the two accepted judgements: a stalemate or an honourable draw still credible?

The conclusion provides a synthetic analysis of the two campaigns. The ground-breaking aspects of this book are twofold: it will provide comparable criteria for understanding the competence with which both campaigns were conducted at the tactical, operational and strategic levels; it will illuminate, for the first time, the impact of the 'operating codes' of successive generations of policy elites. In particular, to what extent, they represent the importing into the conduct of war the values of commerce? Do these 'operating codes' explain failure at the strategic level? Finally, to what extent did Army commanders in both campaigns achieve success at the operational and tactical level while having to confront the consequences of failure at the strategic level? What were the consequences of this for sustaining an integrated political–military approach?

Acknowledgements

Many individuals helped to make this book possible, and it would be a discourtesy on my part not to give them the thanks they deserve. This book is a product of the period from 2006 that I have spent at the University of Reading in the Department of Politics and International Relations. It has provided a stimulating environment to work in, and a number of colleagues have been generous in providing me with insights from their expertise.

The University of Reading also provided me with human resources. I have benefited from having a post-graduate student, Jacob Thomas Llewellyn who unearthed pertinent but obscure material. Jacob proved a diligent and enthusiastic researcher. These qualities, among many others, have recently enabled him to secure a post at the Rabdan Academy in the United Arab Emirates.

I would like to pay tribute to a number of retired Army officers for granting me interviews and providing me with accounts of their operational experiences in Northern Ireland. A number have requested anonymity, which I have respected. In equal measure, I would like to express my gratitude to former senior police officers of the Royal Ulster Constabulary for granting me interviews, in particular, to those officers who served in Special Branch for being patient with my questions and generous with their time. Unsurprisingly, they have all requested anonymity for their contributions. To both groups of dedicated and courageous men and women this book owes a considerable debt.

I am also grateful for an eclectic expertise I have been able to call on. My erstwhile colleague and friend Major David Hazel who commented on the early draft chapters of Operation Banner has also been pivotal in locating and designing the two maps in this book. Cheri Hunston of Wildwood Arts in Devon was instrumental in inspiring the cover design. I would also like to thank Professor Len Hochberg, formerly of Louisiana State University. He brought an analytical perspective to Operation Banner that was very insightful. The historical periods in which these two campaigns took place have produced a vast literature. I would like to thank Dr Aron Edwards from the Royal Military Academy Sandhurst and Professor Caroline Kennedy-Pipe from the University of Loughborough for providing metaphorical handrails to identify the literature pertinent to the aims of this book.

No creditable work of research can be completed and published without editorial support. I would like to acknowledge Richard Baggaley, now with London Publishing Partnership, for convincing me of the virtue of presenting material in an accessible and engaging manner. Jen McCall from Lynne Reinner was full of advice and insight about publishing. Critically, Tony Mason, my editor at Peter Lang, has been unfailing in his support and enthusiasm for the book. I cannot thank him enough.

Without sustained access to and support from a number of libraries, archives, and their staff, this book would not have been written. Inter-Library Loans at Reading University Library have been excellent at locating the books I required. The libraries at King's College London, in particular, the Basil Liddell Hart Archive, were excellent. In addition, the LSE Library were ever ready to deal with my requests. A special mention is due to the staff at the Imperial War Museum for their support. As ever the National Archives proven to be critical in their provision of primary source material. The Military History Bureau at Cathal Brugha Barracks in Dublin proved to be a unique and invaluable archive. It provided material that would have been unobtainable anywhere else. I hope the late Commandant Peter Young, former OIC of the Irish Military Archives, would think I have used his hidden treasure to good effect.

Finally, to Jill above all, my thanks for her support and encouragement. This book was much debated, an eternal excuse for trespassing on her generosity, and imminent if always tomorrow. It has finally arrived!

CHAPTER I

The Operating Codes – Echoes from Two Campaigns

Introduction

It is assumed that all states react in the same manner when presented with a violent internal challenge to their political authority. In reality, they all respond differently. However, the initial issue is always the same: 'As soon as the challenge is in the open the success of the operation depends not primarily on the development of insurgent strength, but more importantly on the degree of vigour, determination and skill that with which the incumbent regime acts to defend itself, both politically and militarily'.[31]

One way of explaining different responses by individual states is the concept of 'operating codes'. These codes are culturally specific and have unique premises and parameters. The departure point for understanding British codes in fighting both regular and irregular warfare was given by the military historian Basil Liddell Hart. He argued the First World War represented an apparition and a betrayal of Britain's approach concerning the conduct of war. He denounced the 'unbusiness-like allurements of the Continental theory'. Britain's best practice was based on economic pressure exercised through sea-power. He claimed the 'operational codes' lay hidden: 'A romantic habit had led us to hide and has even hidden from

---

31 Sonderland, W., 'An Analysis of Guerilla Insurgency and Coup d 'Etat as Techniques of Indirect Aggression', *International Studies Quarterly* (December 1970), 345, Quoted in O'Neill, B. E., *Insurgency and Terrorism* (Washington: Brassey's, 1990), 125.

us our essentially business-like tradition in the conduct of war'.[32] This tradition assumed reciprocity, and a transactional process would be accepted by an enemy, whether it was a state, or an extreme political organisation committed to the use of violence. Its key characteristic was a synthesis of mutually beneficial exchanges and interactions that would elicit a pathway to a desired political outcome satisfying both parties.

With respect to fighting an insurgency, these assumptions, embraced by successive generations of British policy elites, had a detrimental effect, they compromised and undermined the tactical and operational success the British Army and the three police forces achieved. In both campaigns, this 'business-like tradition' in conducting a counterinsurgency and fighting terrorism had a negative effect at the strategic level. Critically, they acted as a catalyst to failure and multiplied that the challenges of crafting and conducting a campaign that was both intelligence led and conducted within the confines of the law.

The two reports drew attention to the characteristics of these codes. The first was the proclivity of policymakers and their civil servants to pursue separate political initiatives with inconsistent results. It was the antithesis of what the relationship between security forces and a policy elite should have been. The strategist Colin Gray identified the 'challenge of currency conversion': 'the relationship between strategy and its enabling tactics requires, as a matter of absolute need, that policy needs, which is to say political choices, provide both legitimacy and practical guidance'.[33] Without this relationship, there is a waste of human and material resources. As Carl von Clausewitz stated, 'war should never be thought of as something autonomous, but always as an instrument of policy'.[34] Legitimacy and practical guidance were often in short supply to both the army and the police forces in both campaigns.

---

32 Liddell Hart, B., *The British Way in Warfare* (London: Penguin Books, 1932), 29.
33 Gray, C. S., *Tactical Operations for Strategic Effect: The Challenge of Currency Conversion*, JSOU Report (November 2015), 14.
34 von Clausewitz, C., *On War*. Michael Howard, and Peter Paret, ed. and translated (Princeton, New Jersey: Princeton University Press, 1976) 88.

The second characteristic was a consequence of the first one. Ministers and civil servants were unwilling to take an integrated approach to counterinsurgency and to coordinate political and military approaches. This often resulted in political choices operating independently from tactical actions by the army and thus compromising the outcomes the latter was trying to achieve. This failure was compounded by the nature of the challenge any state faces in an insurgency. The conflict between the two sides unfolds in a competitive and fast-moving environment. Neither side can monopolise control, consequently, the dynamic and reciprocal nature shapes strategy more than strategy shapes war. Hew Strachan has attributed the lack of integration in the campaign between 1919 and 1921 to the experience of the First World War: 'The most important consequence of the Great War was Lloyd George's distrust of the generals. It undermined civil-military co-ordination and hence worked against the formation of clear policy'.[35]

The third characteristic was the unwillingness of successive British governments to systematically counter, engage, and challenge the strategic narrative of Irish Republicanism. This was a product of assumptions about the need to negotiate in a 'business-like manner' with the representatives of a violent insurgent organisation. The last paragraph of the second volume of the Record of the Rebellion contains direct reference to the consequences of this in what it described as a 'highly competent' Sinn Fein Publicity Department: 'This department was energetic subtle and exceptionally skilful in mixing truth, falsehood and exaggeration and was perhaps the most powerful and least fought arm of the Sinn Fein Forces'.[36]

The exact same comments appeared in the Operation Banner report which stated that many contributors to this analysis have described the information campaign in such terms as 'woeful', 'pitiable' and 'grossly inadequate'. In simple terms, rarely would anybody in authority other than in

---

35 Strachan, H., *The Politics of the British Army* (Oxford: Clarendon Press, 1997) 168.
36 Record of the Rebellion in Ireland in 1920–1921, Vol 2 Intelligence in Ireland, 1920–1921 (secret copy No. 39), Papers of Lt Gen Sir Hugh Jeudwine IWM 72/82/2, p. 46.

the Army take a positive, proactive stance. The result was a regular series of information failures in which PIRA (and occasionally loyalist paramilitaries) held and exploited their advantage ... *The absence of a unified, proactive information strategy for most of the campaign was a major failing.*[37]

The Army had learned hard tactical lessons about media relations in the 1970s. However, it had received little support at the strategic level: 'the high-level information operations effort was, during the campaign, as a rule, weak. Information operations should be conducted at several levels: they are not just a tactical military activity'.[38] This failure of information strategy fed into a more general critique by the authors of the Banner report: 'From a military perspective for most of the campaign there was little coherence and synergy. There was little evidence of a strategic vision and no long-term plan. Below the level of Westminster White papers, there was no clearly articulated strategy, or a view of the future and how to achieve it that involved all the relevant agencies. As a result, the "wheel was often reinvented" and progress was unnecessarily slow'.[39] The impact of these 'operational codes' were clearly stated: 'Ministers and civil servants were sometimes reluctant to engage in the comprehensive, fully coordinated cross-government activity which the Army would recognise as a campaign plan ... The events of the Troubles provide no evidence for the utility of the current set of campaign planning tools, because they were not used'.[40]

The Banner report highlighted an example of the tactical consequences of the first code. Ministers pursued political initiatives regardless of the consequences they had for the security forces. In the 1970s, successive Secretaries of State for Northern Ireland ordered the release of detainees whilst the security service was rounding them up. Repeatedly, the same individuals were re-arrested, having broken the law again.[41]

37 Operation Banner, *An Analysis of Military Operations in Northern Ireland*, Army Code 71842, 2006, para 815, p. 8-4.
38 Ibid, para 854, p. 8-15.
39 Op cit, para 812 p. 8-3.
40 Op cit, para 813-814, p. 8-4.
41 See Operation Banner; *An Analysis of Military Operations in Northern Ireland*, Army Code 71842, para 406, p. 4-2.

Two Campaigns and the Operating Codes

The Record of the Rebellion stated clearly the principles of counterinsurgency; fourteen points that were factors common to all rebellions. They were juxtaposed with the claim they were revealed in the campaign, chiefly by their omission. Operating codes were not mentioned per se, but highlighted their consequences. For example, the third point stated: 'A policy once started should never be given up'.[42] The eleventh point stated: 'The Home Government must state its policy in clear and unequivocal terms as soon as possible'.[43] The final point underlined the rule of the law and the importance of avoiding separate political and military initiatives: 'The political leaders of the rebel movement should be arrested and tried for high treason or conspiracy, and should not be allowed to go free on the chance of their being willing to treat with the Government'.[44]

The Record of the Rebellion was more radical in one important aspect than the Operation Banner report. It named two members of the policy elite who embraced these codes. This candour was absent from the second report. The first person named was the Chief Secretary of Ireland: 'Sir Hamar Greenwood did his utmost to initiate a policy of conciliation'.[45] The second person named was a civil servant, who exemplified all three of these codes: 'Mr Cope replaced Sir John Taylor as Assistant Under Secretary'.[46] No other member of the new civil servant team posted into Dublin Castle between April and May 1920 was identified in this manner.[47]

---

42   Record of the Rebellion in Ireland in 1920–1921 (Vol. 1) Operations, 1920–1921 (secret copy No. 39), Papers of Lt Gen Sir Hugh Jeudwine IWM 72/82/2, p. 54.
43   Ibid, p. 55.
44   Ibid, p. 55.
45   Op cit, p. 11.
46   Op cit, p. 11.
47   Mark Sturgis was posted into Dublin Castle on the same date as Cope as the other Assistant Under Secretary and got no mention in the report. The same applied to Sir John Anderson the new Under Secretary.

Alfred Cope's appointment was a product of political patronage from Lloyd George. What was missing from the Record of the Rebellion was the fact that Alfred Cope was a special representative of the British Cabinet in Ireland.[48] Within four months of his arrival, he was passing information, much of it secret, to Sinn Fein, and gave its members unauthorised access to Dublin Castle.[49] He also enjoyed, uniquely among Crown civil servants in Ireland, immunity from attack. This was sanctioned at the behest of Michael Collins: 'it was conveyed to me that Cope ... who was well known to be one of our closest enemies, was regularly visiting the house of Martin Fitzgerald, proprietor of the Freeman's Journal. I reported the matter personally to Collins and told him I could deliver Cope into his hand at any moment he so desired. The reply I got back almost immediately was, Don't interfere with Cope'.[50] This evidence underlined a clear understanding by Collins of Cope's role.

With respect to Northern Ireland an understanding of the persistence of these codes emerged in a more tangential manner. The political scientist Richard Rose initially posed a question in a chapter of a book he published in 1982. He asked the following question: Is the United Kingdom a State? Northern Ireland as a Test Case.[51] He identified two generic qualities of any state: 'Notwithstanding many differences in the institutions and purposes of modern states, a state must insist upon the integrity of two defining attributes-territorial boundaries and effective force-or-fail in the claim to be a state'.[52] The second attribute was a claim to a nationwide monopoly of organised force.[53] An insurgency

---

48   O'Connor, J. J., BMH Witness Statement 1214.
49   See Sloan, G., 'Hide Seek and Negotiate: Alfred Cope and Counter-Intelligence in Ireland 1919–1921'. *Intelligence and National Security* 33/2 (2017) 180.
50   O'Connor, J., Bureau of Military History Witness Statement 487, Cathal Brugha Barracks, Dublin.
51   Rose, R., 'Is the United Kingdom a State? Northern Ireland as a Test Case', in P. Madgwick, and R. Rose, eds., *The Territorial Dimension In United Kingdom Politics* (London: MacMillan Press, 1982) 100–136.
52   Watkins, F. M., 'State: The Concept', *International Encyclopaedia of the Social Sciences* (Vol. 15) (New York: MacMillan, 1967) 155.
53   Op cit, p. 103.

can challenge integrity and manifest itself in the form of an alternative organisation effectively competing with the security forces of the state for the de facto control within a geographical portion of a state's territory.

In addition, any government 'must secure compliance with basic political laws, especially laws intended to secure public order'. When this is lacking, politicians have two choices. They can rely on coercion to secure these basic political laws or reduce their demands for compliance with respect to the bulk of the population. Rose suggested British Governments had a predilection for doing both simultaneously with poor outcomes: 'In Britain, the government has the technology (the apparatus) but not the political values to govern by the systematic invocation of coercion. The "on again, off again" use of conciliation and coercion in nineteenth century Ireland provides a historical example of this'.[54]

Up to the mid-1960s Rose claimed Northern Ireland was secure as an integral part of the United Kingdom. This was a consequence of two factors: 'The boundaries established by the 1921 Anglo-Irish Treaty had persisted for more than a generation; the defence forces of Stormont had demonstrated the ability to defend the state against from its most vulnerable points'.[55]

The Civil Rights Association in 1967 was the catalyst for a challenge. The slogan 'one man, one vote, one value', claimed a lack of universal suffrage for the Catholic population. It was only in local government elections, not in parliamentary elections, where the voting franchise was restricted. What was omitted, either by design or ineptitude, was that this affected Protestants as much as Catholics. In the rest of the United Kingdom, the same local election franchise existed until 1948 when the Labour Government of Clement Attlee reformed it.[56]

There were three categories for local government franchise. First, you had to reside as an owner or a tenant in a dwelling house, a spouse qualified but an occupant did not. Second, you had to occupy other land or

---

54   Op cit, p. 105.
55   Op cit, p. 110.
56   Little research has been done as to why this local government franchise persisted in Northern Ireland after 1948.

premises valued at not less than £10. Third, a commercial company could nominate up to six electors, one for every £10 of the valuation of its premises. The consequence of this was that more than a quarter of parliamentary electors had no local government vote.[57]

Rose highlighted two aspects about the Civil Rights Association: there were no legally enforceable rights that Catholics had been deprived of that could be remedied through the courts as American blacks had successfully done; the civil rights marches affirmed the refusal of thousands of Catholics to comply with the basic political laws that Stormont attempted to uphold. Eamonn McCann, one of the leaders of the NICRA,[58] was candid about the sectarian tone of the civil rights movement: 'Everyone applauds loudly when one says in a speech that we are not sectarian, we are fighting for the rights of all Irish workers, but really that's because they see it as a way of getting at the Protestants'.[59]

The suspension of devolved government in Northern Ireland in 1972 resulted in the British state taking over a variety of administrative tasks. Rose interpreted this as evidence that Northern Ireland has been treated as a place apart. He articulated three defining tests of statehood 'Westminster must assert an effective monopoly of force and protect the territorial boundaries of the United Kingdom. It must also maintain the integrity of the United Kingdom and not treat Northern Ireland as if it were an alien land or a colony, but rather as an integral part of the United Kingdom. On all three of these criteria, Westminster fails'.[60] Rose argued that a willingness to pursue separate political initiatives meant the British policy elite granted Irish Republicanism 'political recognition as a *de facto* part of the politics of Northern Ireland'.

---

57 See Lawrence, R. J., *The Government of Northern Ireland* (Oxford: Clarendon Press, 1965) 26.
58 Northern Ireland Civil Rights Association.
59 McCann, E., *New Left Review* 55/May/June (1969) 6. Quoted in Bew P., and Patterson, H., *The British State and the Ulster Crisis* (London: Verso Books, 1985) 19.
60 Op cit, p. 119.

The Operating Codes – Echoes from Two Campaigns 9

He contended the policy elite have been, at best, ambiguous about defending the territorial integrity of Northern Ireland as part of the United Kingdom. The former Ulster Unionist MP Enoch Powell gave a richer expression to this in 1980. He characterised, the then Foreign and Commonwealth Office, as being a nest of vipers and a nursery of traitors. The aim of this government department was the expulsion of Northern Ireland from the United Kingdom: 'its eyes and its affections are fixed outside the realm, on Dublin, on Brussels on the Vatican, and above all else on Washington DC, for whose favour and delectation this province is to be offered up as a sacrifice'.[61] The territorial integrity of Northern Ireland as part of the United Kingdom was undermined in a public statement ten years later when a Conservative Secretary of State for Northern Ireland, Peter Brooke stated: 'the British government has no selfish strategic or economic interest in Northern Ireland: our role is to help, enable, and encourage'.[62] What was omitted from Brooke's statement was the geostrategic fact that Northern Ireland had been an integral part of the geographical parameters of NATO since 1949.[63] This will be examined in detail in Chapter 6. It is impossible to imagine the policy elite of the French Republic making a similar statement about Corsica.

Rose sought recourse in the normative standards of international law. These required the British state treat its sovereign territory as a single integral unit, and not as a 'qualified state'. There is in international law no central mechanism of control for forcing states to behave in a manner that would give expression to these standards. Rose underlined the dysfunctional nature of the British state by a comparative analysis to European states: 'The continental tradition of politics is that "the state defends"

---

61 *The Times*, (4th January 1980) 3.
62 'The British presence', speech by Rt Hon Peter Brooke MP, Secretary of State for Northern Ireland (9 November 1990).
63 Article 6 of the treaty stated that for the purpose of Article 5, 'an armed attack on one or more of the Parties is deemed to include an armed attack: on the territory of any of the Parties in Europe or North America, on the Algerian Departments of France, on the territory of Turkey or on the Islands under the jurisdiction of any of the Parties in the North Atlantic area north of the Tropic of Cancer'. Northern Ireland was an integral part of the 'Parties in Europe'.

itself, and both the Fifth French Republic and the Republic of Italy give public evidence of doing so in the face of armed attacks. The English tradition is to attempt conciliation, to ignore protests or, in the extreme case of Northern Ireland, to distance Westminster from a challenge'.[64] With great prescience (he was writing in 1982) Rose indicated the possibility of another geographical area of the British state manifesting this 'qualified state' characteristic:[65] 'there is no certainty that challenges to authority will always be confined to one part of the United Kingdom'.[66] Rose understood there was no such thing as a natural state. There existed in all states human associations, economic wants and political opportunities that kept a state together. These same forces can pull it apart and ultimately bring about secession. An armed insurgency is one of the most toxic challenges internally a state can face.

The Literature on Counter-Insurgency and Operating Codes

In 1938, a British Army officer, Major General Simpson, published, a book titled: *British Rule and Rebellion*.[67] It had a close congruence to the behavioural approach Leites and George called 'operational codes'. One of the two case studies in the book was the insurgency of 1920–1921. His conceptual innovation was the term 'Sub-War'. This was the precursor of what became known as counterinsurgency. In some respects, it was more coherent: 'Sub-war lies half-way between a political strike on a national scale and civil war ... In sub- war, every effort is made to use force

---

64   Op cit, p. 131.
65   The demand of the Scottish National Party for a second referendum after the General Election of December 2019 underlined the prescience of his work.
66   Op cit, p. 131.
67   Simpson, H. J., *British Rule and Rebellion* (London: W. Blackwood, 1938).

under the cover of the laws of the Government which is being attacked. Organisation is secret'.[68]

He set out a typology of functions that must be co-ordinated to deal with this sub-war. They were listed as: 'the civil, the police, the legal, and the military'. The civil was critical for co-ordinating the other three functions. It should be willing to use force and quickly and decisively before responding to the need to address grievances real or imagined. The consequences of not doing this were clearly elucidated: 'If the civil power does not follow the policy that resort to force must be stopped promptly and decisively, then there can never be successful co-ordination, because there can never be unity of purpose. Neither the police part nor the military part of British rule will willingly be used as dogs in a dogfight, not to win, but to produce concessions to those who kill their friends'.[69] He identified the paradoxical challenge that both the police and soldiers faced. The police in a sub-war tend to become soldiers, yet soldiers display no inclination to become policemen. However, the soldiers require local information which only the police can provide.

In a chapter titled 'Sub-War – The Other Side', he started with the proposition that since 1918, sub-wars had been common in territories under British rule. Looking back over a 20-year period, he claimed the one most skilfully managed by the other side, was the Sinn Fein campaign in Ireland in 1920-1921. Simpson did not identify the specific operational codes that had prevented effective coordination. However, there was a close similarity to what George called 'approaches to political calculation'.[70] He argued that a British Government, for reasons he did not specify, would not allow drastic action to be taken against the political leaders of a rebellion conducted on sub-war lines. It never adopted the attitude that those who lead a movement which results in murder are themselves liable to be tried and found guilty of murder. Even when political leaders went on the run, as in Ireland, government officials chased after them, not to arrest, but to keep in touch and discuss.

---

68   Ibid, p. 36.
69   Ibid, p. 119–120.
70   Op cit, p. 220.

The French academic Sylvain Briollay, writing in 1921, identified operating codes that applied to Sinn Fein and British policy makers respectively. His typology was not as nuanced as Simpson's, hence: 'The most striking thing in the mind of Sinn Fein is the character of extremism, the clear and deliberate determination to ignore that which deserves attention and even life, only to what has the right to be. Nothing is stranger to the undying spirit of compromise and bargaining so dear to the English'.[71]

Operating codes were alluded to in the unpublished memoir of Major General Hawes, who served in Ireland during the period 1919–1921. He claimed that tactical innovation and adaptation had not been translated into strategic success as a consequence of these codes: He argued that 'Techniques for quelling the rebellion were perfected and the rebellion was being subdued, H. M. Government chose this moment to give in. All the casualties we had suffered were wasted'.[72]

Another account of the first campaign, while not mentioning the operating codes, has provided a localised account of the insurgency in Cork.[73] It is rare in providing, albeit for one local area, an account of the tactical successes of the British Army and how intelligence was acquired and used. It gave an understanding of how army tactics and doctrine were developed to counter the insurgency, and an insight was given to the intelligence structures at a local level. Its judgement about the Army represents a minority view in the existing literature: 'The British army's role has been under researched and under analysed, with some historians still portraying it as a lumbering giant around whom the pimpernels of the IRA ran rings'.[74]

---

71 Briollay, S., *L'Irlande Insurgee* (Paris: Plon-Nourrit, 1921), 21.
72 Major General Hawes, The Memories and Dreams of an Ordinary Soldier, Imperial War Museum 87/41/1.
73 See Sheehan, W., *A Hard-Local War: The British War and the Guerilla War in Cork, 1919–1921* (Stroud: The History Press, 2011).
74 Ibid, p. 11.

Continuities and Discontinuities

Before assessing the two campaigns, continuities and discontinuities need to be identified. The academic Philip Cunliffe has argued: 'undertaking historical comparisons are a complex task, there being at least as many significant points of difference as resemblances'.[75] The undertaking is nonetheless worthwhile, because it will enable an understanding of the context and the factors that persisted and those that were unique in the eighty-five years that separated these reports. The historian E. H. Carr has stated, our understanding and knowledge of the past although based on facts is not factual at all; but based on a series of accepted judgements. However, this book will argue that a number of operating codes of the policy elite persisted despite the decades separating both campaigns and challenge the accepted judgements about both campaigns.

Irish republicanism

The most important continuity in both campaigns was the protagonist – Irish Republicanism as represented by the IRA and PIRA. Both organisations can be interpreted as unconditional social constructs that demonstrated the ability to acquire material capabilities. The structure of this nationalist ideology is social rather than material.[76] It represented inter-subjective knowledge clustered around a number of unproven assumptions.

---

75   Cunliffe, P. *The New Twenty Years' Crises* (Montreal: McGill-Queens University Press, 2020), 56.
76   For an understanding of this concept in the context of international relations see Wendt, A., 'Anarchy is What States Make of It: The Social Construction of Power Politics', *International Organization* 46/2 (1992).

First there will be a redemptive future for ALL of Ireland if political, social, and economic links, with the British state were severed. Secondly, this future nirvana could only be achieved by the taking human life. Patrick Pearse a member of the IRB[77] and leader of the failed rebellion of 1916 stated: 'We must accustom ourselves to the thought of arms, to the sight of arms, to the use of arms. We may make mistakes in the beginning and shoot the wrong people; but bloodshed is a cleansing and sanctifying thing, and the nation which regards it as the final horror has lost its manhood'.[78]

This future was framed by geographical determinism: because Ireland is geographically an island, it presupposed unity in a political sense. In short, geography was and is political destiny. This was built into Sinn Fein's unilateral declaration of independence[79] on the 21st January 1919 in Dublin's Mansion House. Parallel to this declaration was a geographically deterministic message to the 'Free nations of the World': 'Her independence is demanded by the Freedom of the Seas: her harbours are empty and idle solely because English policy is determined to retain Ireland as a barren bulwark for English aggrandisement'.[80]

The phrase, the 'island of Ireland' became pivotal. It was coined by Eamon de Valera when he unilaterally repudiated the 1922 constitution of the Irish Free State and introduced a new constitution in 1937. Article two claimed: 'The national territory consists of the whole island of Ireland, its islands and seas'. Critically, it claimed ownership over Northern Ireland. This was despite the fact that in 1925 the Irish government had signed a tripartite international treaty acknowledging Northern Ireland as an integral part of the United Kingdom. It was, as the Irish historian

---

77 The Irish Republican Brotherhood was a secret organisation dedicated to achieving Irish independence by the use of violent means.
78 Pearse, P. *Political Writings and Speeches*, quoted in Y. Alexander, and A. Day, eds., *The Irish Terrorism Experience* (Aldershot: Dartmouth, 1991), 17.
79 This was an illegal declaration of independence that had no electoral mandate.
80 Declaration of Independence, 21 January 1919, *Documents on Irish Foreign Policy* 1 (1919–1921) 1.

Paul Bew has suggested: 'a rhetorical constitutional claim ... an ideological provocation to unionists'.[81]

Geography does not determine political outcomes; it merely conditions other factors that unfold within a geographical framework. The fact that Ireland is geographically an island creates no presumption that it should have one political authority any more than the Scandinavian and Iberian peninsulas determine that Norway and Portugal should not exist as independent sovereign states. In 2018, the Sinn Fein MP Paul Maskey underlined the continuity of this social construct: 'For 100 years now, Irish republicans have refused to validate British sovereignty over the island of Ireland by sitting in the parliament of Westminster'.[82] The abuse of geography in this manner is not confined to Irish nationalism.[83]

For 61 years, successive Irish governments maintained a claim on the territory of another state. This made the Irish Republic an outlier with respect to other European states. In 1998 it was replaced as a quid pro quo for endorsing the Belfast Agreement. Ironically the new Article Two still interpreted geography as destiny.[84] In the text the 'island of Ireland', was used ten times. It performed a twofold function: first it kept alive the issue of the ownership of Northern Ireland; secondly it excluded the geographically conditioned human associations that exist within the British Isles as a whole.

---

81 Bew, P. *Ireland, The Politics of Enmity, 1789–2006* (Oxford: Oxford University Press, 2007), 533.
82 <www.theguardian.com/commentisfree/2018/mar/06/sinn-fein-mp-british-parliament-irish-republicans-brexit> accessed 14/8/18.
83 See Matthes, J., 'Framing Politics: An Integrative Approach', *American Behavioural Scientist* 56/3 (2012) 247–259.
84 The revised Article Two of the Irish constitution which was part of the Good Friday Agreement of April 1998 claimed: "It is the entitlement and birth right of every person born in the island of Ireland, which includes its islands and seas, to be part of the Irish nation. That is also the entitlement of all persons otherwise qualified in accordance with law to be citizens of Ireland. Furthermore, the Irish nation cherishes its special affinity with people of Irish ancestry living abroad who share its cultural identity and heritage".

Sir John Peck, British Ambassador to the Irish Republic between 1970 and 1973 also endorsed this crude geographical determinism: 'The only assumption I make is a basic one that Ireland, being an island, forms a natural political entity'.[85] His statement illustrated the traction that this geographical determinism gained by the early 1970s. The American theologian Reinhold Niebuhr made a critical insight about the degrees of artifice required to hold a state together: 'it was tempting to forget that communities are composed of organic and contrived forms of cohesion. In civilised societies both are necessary … but the proportion between them is variable'.[86] Irish Republicanism has always been addicted to high levels of artifice.

The antithesis has been argued by the Dutch political geographer Heslinga.[87] He identified the human associations that existed throughout the British Isles. Bizarrely his work has been interpreted as being an ideological handmaiden for inarticulate Ulster Unionists.[88] He maintained the Irish Sea rather than representing a natural boundary and a rationale for political separation facilitates human interaction: 'In many respects contacts across the Irish Sea are more numerous and more intensive than those across the land boundary'.[89] He built on the work of the American Richard Hartshorne, who identified three different kinds of human associations that could exist between different geographical locations: cultural, socio-economic and historical.

Configurations of land and sea are of importance as they facilitated an east–west axis of movement. The first is the proximity of the west coast of Scotland to the northeast coast of Ireland. The North Channel

---

85   Peck, J., *Dublin from Downing Street* (Dublin: Gill and MacMillan, 1978), 214.
86   Neibhur, R., *Nations and Empires* (London: Faber and Faber, 1959), 260.
87   Heslinga, M. W. *The Irish Border as a Cultural Divide* (Assen: Van Gorcum, 1962).
88   "It is interesting that the fullest statement of the Ulster Unionist case should come from a foreigner. Some might say that this illustrates the inarticulateness which Unionists have always displayed, as compared with their nationalist counterparts", Whyte, J., *Interpreting Northern Ireland* (Oxford: Clarendon Press, 1991), 146.
89   Ibid, p. 12.

at its narrowest point between Fair Head in Co Antrim and the Mull of Kintyre in Scotland is less than 12 miles wide. The second is the east–west axis that runs across the Irish Sea from Dublin to the Cheshire Gap. In England, this location is bounded by mountains to the north and south and gives access to the Midland Plain.

Heslinga argued that the geography of Ireland offers little evidence of natural unity: 'The general physiographical plain, a central basin surrounded by groups of mountains and hills is repeated on a smaller scale in the northeast of the island'.[90] His seminal analytical insight is that the Irish border actually conforms to one of the important regional divides in the British Isles. It marks off the 'Scoticised' part of Ireland from the 'Anglicised' part.

This denial of the geopolitical reality found expression in the assumption of subordination of other political parties to Sinn Fein. This manifested itself in a bizarre ritual enacted when the first meeting of the Dail took place on the 10 April 1919. A roll call was taken of the 104 members who had been returned to Westminster in the British election of December 1918. Only 28 Sinn Fein MPs were present, but the names of Unionist MPs such as Edward Carson, James Craig and Edward Archdale were read out and declared absent along with Irish Parliamentary Party MPs such as Captain Redmond and Joseph Devlin.[91] The declaration of absence underlined an unarguable membership.

Intelligence

Intelligence runs like a golden thread in both campaigns. General Sir Frank Kitson summed up its importance: 'Clearly an adequate supply of the right sort of information is needed at the top so as to enable the

---

90   Op cit, p. 43.
91   Coogan, T. P. Michael Collins (New York: Palgrave, 1990), p. 104.

government to work out a sensible policy for countering the insurgents. Information of a slightly different kind is also necessary at every level for the successful conduct of operations. Establishing an effective intelligence organization is therefore a matter of the first importance'.[92] Its key advantage is its ability to manage the uncertainty inherent in any conflict. Although it has to be stressed that intelligence cannot eliminate this uncertainty. Intelligence can be best understood as consisting of two dimensions. It is a process and a product. However, a poor process can undermine good intelligence. An intelligence product can have relevance to all three levels of warfare and political policy. However, there is a key metaphorical bridge that has to be crossed before it has utility: 'One of the most critical phases … lies in convincing the military and political leadership to make best use of the information and analysis supplied to them'.[93] A failure to use it or to discard it can negate its force multiplier effect.

Intelligence featured prominently in both reports. The Record of the Rebellion devoted a whole volume to it, a total of fifty-five pages including appendices A and B. It was extensive in its scope and candid about the British Army's failures and successes with respect to intelligence. For example, its assessment of the reasons for the existence of IRA informers in British government service was based on two assumptions: class solidarity and the power of intimidation: 'Informers in the Civil service and the police were of considerable value to the IRA. In all known cases, these informers were Irishmen of the same social class as the average Republican, and this plus the intimidation caused them to furnish the information required'.[94] This assessment was accurate with respect to social class, but not gender.

The Operation Banner report did not give the same prominence to intelligence. There were only five paragraphs plus a paragraph in the concluding section devoted to intelligence.[95] However, specific successes

92 Kitson, F., *Bunch of Five* (London: Faber and Faber, 1977), 287.
93 Handel, M. J., *Intelligence and the Problem of Strategic Surprise* 7/3 (Sept. 1984), 252.
94 Op cit, Vol. 2, p. 43.
95 See Operation Banner Army, Code 71842 (2006), Chapter 5, paras 502–505 and 537.

were cited in detail: 'In March and April 1974 a total of 106 PIRA officers were arrested, including three successive OCs of the Belfast Brigade. This was a major factor in the defeat of the 1974 summer bombing campaign and helped destroy the remainder of the "insurgent" PIRA. At one stage, the active tour of duty of a PIRA officer from appointment to arrest was about four weeks –roughly the same as the average time that a subaltern might survive during the Battle of the Somme. The quality of intelligence became very good indeed-by the end of the 1980s, PIRA was unable to mount a bombing operation in Belfast for about two years'.[96] However, there was no assessment of the overall trajectory of the intelligence campaign that underpinned Operation Banner. The concluding section acknowledges the process of intelligence, what was produced, and its relevance and impact: 'Their importance (the intelligence aspects) is hard to understate. The insurgency could not have been broken, and the terrorist structure could not have been engaged and finally driven into politics without the intelligence organisations and processes'.[97]

A key explanation given by historians for British failure with respect to the first campaign was the lack of an effective intelligence organisation: 'Neither the Army nor the police were able to build the essential foundation for success in guerrilla warfare, a dependable intelligence service'.[98] Townshend failed to acknowledge that a new intelligence community was created by Brigadier Winter very quickly in the midst of this insurgency.[99] Despite this achievement, Peter Hart has claimed: 'British intelligence' outwitted and outspied-emerges from most accounts of the revolution as a contradiction in terms: a disastrous compound of misdirection, malice and ignorance.[100] By contrast, Michael Foy gave a realistic assessment of the intelligence system set up by Michael Collins, the

---

96 Ibid, Chapter 5, para 505.
97 Ibid, Chapter 8, para 818.
98 Townshend, C. The British Campaign in Ireland 1919–1921 (Oxford: Oxford University Press, 1975), p. 205.
99 See Sloan, G., 'Hide, Seek and Negotiate: Alfred Cope and Counter-intelligence in Ireland 1919–1921', *Intelligence and National Security* 33/2 (2017) 181–182.
100 Hart P. ed., British Intelligence in Ireland, 1920–1921: The Final Reports (Cork: Cork University Press, 2002), 1.

Director of Intelligence. It had limitations in terms of scope and effectiveness: 'He never penetrated the higher echelons of the British political, military and police system in Ireland. IRA agents like Broy, Neligan, McNamara and Mernin were junior figures in the bureaucratic hierarchy whose main value lay in their access to confidential documents and information about their colleagues and superiors'.[101]

Intelligence in counterinsurgency performs a different function from a conventional war. There is a difference of focus.[102] In conventional war the enemy formations are 'the most dangerous element in the environment'. In counter-insurgency intelligence on insurgent formations is harder to obtain and does not have the premium that population focused intelligence has.

Counter-insurgency is even more complex and unpredictable than conventional war. In particular the political identity and sympathies of the population have a fluidity that is unique: 'populations in insurgency negotiate a complex process of continuously morphing identity, where each person's or groups' status (friend, enemy, neutral, ally or opponent, bystander, sympathiser) changes moment by moment depending on the nature of the groups with which it is interacting'.[103]

The potential weakness of insurgents is a consequence of population fluidity. The efficacy of any insurgency can be challenged by the conventional security forces provided: 'insurgents can be rendered mission-irrelevant provided the population is effectively secured, governed, and won over. This makes the population the centre of gravity in an insurgency, which in turn makes the population the central focus for intelligence collection and analysis'.[104]

---

[101] Foy, M. T., *Michael Collin's Intelligence War*, (Stroud: Sutton Publishing, 2006), 240.
[102] See Kilcullen, D., T. Rid, and T. Keaney, eds., *Intelligence, from Understanding Counterinsurgency* (Abingdon: Routledge, 2016), 143.
[103] Ibid, p. 144.
[104] Ibid, p. 144.

Conclusion

What is at stake in presenting a new interpretation of these two campaigns? Previous histories and assessments have omitted to assess the extent to which failure and success were vitiated and refracted through the intervening variables these operating codes represented. The proclivity of the policy elite to pursue political initiatives with inconsistent results was a persistent intervening variable. In both campaigns, a consequence of this was that the release of detainees was not linked to any behavioural advantage for the security forces. The insurgents took advantage of this, and it was interpreted as a sign of weakness.[105]

In the first campaign, an important civil servant was Alfred Cope, Special Representative of the British Cabinet in Ireland. His naming in the Record of the Rebellion was instructive. In addition, he was protected by Michael Collins. Evidence will be provided to show he passed sensitive and comprising information to Sinn Fein. Furthermore, his activities bore little relationship with the security policy. In fact, at various times, he actively undermined both the army and the police. Lloyd George claimed: 'For dirty work, give me the dirty man'.[106] Was Alfred Cope Lloyd George's 'dirty man' in Ireland? This raises the question as to whether there was another 'dirty man' who performed a similar function in the period from 1997 onwards?

The academic writer David Ucko stressed the need to move beyond what he described as 'totalising notions' to a 'particularised understanding' and provide a pathway to learning three things from past campaigns: 'Understanding their context, their evolution and the political interests at hand'.[107] Operating codes provide an insight to all these factors.

---

105 The Operation Banner report stated that 60 per cent of released detainees rejoined PIRA and they even ran an explicit rehabilitation programme. See para 4–2.
106 Quoted in the *Sunday Times* (14 September 2019).
107 Egnell, R., and Ucko, D., 'True to Form? Questioning the British Counterinsurgency Tradition', in B. Heuser, and E. Shanir, eds., *Insurgencies and Counterinsurgencies* (Cambridge: Cambridge University Press, 2016), 33.

They explain the absence of a coherent strategy in both campaigns: 'Strategy implies that the government has a policy and that the strategy flows from the policy: it is an attempt to make concrete a set of objectives through the application of military force to a particular case'.[108]

In the next chapter the context and evolution of the Irish Republicanism will be analysed. In particular, how an alliance was forged and dominated by the Irish Republican Brotherhood and Michael Collins. A particular focus will be on the construction of networks that could sustain the insurgency once it was unleashed. By contrast the context and evolution of the challenges the British Army faced in Ireland from 1916 to the end of 1919 will also be examined.

---

108 Strachan, H., *The Direction of War* (Cambridge: Cambridge University Press, 2013), 64.

CHAPTER 2

A Slow Burning Fuse

Introduction

On the 21st January 1919, Sinn Fein made a unilateral declaration of independence at the Mansion House in Dublin. It was a direct challenge to the legitimacy and social authority of the government of the United Kingdom of Great Britain and Ireland: 'Whereas English rule in this country is, and always has been, based on force and fraud and maintained by military occupation against the declared will of the people'.[109] The Times commented: 'The whole thing is, of course, childishly illegal'.[110]

On the same day in January 1919, as this declaration, Sean Treacy[111] and eight Irish Volunteers attacked and stole a horse-drawn cart loaded with gelignite going to a quarry at Soloheadbeg near Tipperary and murdered two members of the Royal Irish Constabulary. This attack was undertaken without the sanction of the grandly named Irish Volunteer 'GHQ' in Dublin. The Irish historian Townshend has argued it represented an inflection point: 'Soloheadbeg shocked many moderate Sinn Feiners, and probably many nominal Volunteers as well'.[112] There were two components of the Irish Republican movement: one represented by the illegal assembly of Dail Eireann; the second represented by the Irish

---

109 Declaration of Independence, 21st January 1919, *Documents on Irish Foreign Policy* (Dublin: Royal Irish Academy) (Vol. 1), 1919–1921, p. 1.
110 *The Times* (21st January 1919).
111 Treacy was eventually killed in a gun fight with the British security forces in Dublin in October 1920.
112 Townshend, op cit, p. 16.

Volunteers and the IRB. This was, at times, an uneasy alliance. One of the leaders of the insurgency Michael Collins was able to achieve traction in both elements: 'Being at the same time Minister of Finance responsible to the Dail, Director of Organization and, from June 1919, Director of Intelligence on the Executive of the Irish Volunteers, and finally President of the Supreme Council of the IRB, with notional leadership of the whole movement'.[113]

This chapter will examine the events leading up to the involvement of the British Army in a counter-insurgency campaign. It was relatively short lasting eighteen months from January 1920 to July 1921. The period prior to this formed a vital backdrop. There are three questions to be addressed. Did the operational codes of the policy elite and their civil servants begin to compromise the legitimacy of the British state? Second, what functions did Ireland fulfil for the British Army between 1916 and 1919, and how successful was it in anticipating the emerging insurgency? Finally, how did the Irish Republican movement evolve in this period, and how successful was the Irish Republican Brotherhood, a secret and violent sect of Irish nationalism, succeed in manipulating the other elements of Irish Republicanism in forging a 'forward policy'?

The departure point is the intelligence capability of the two police forces in Ireland, the Royal Irish Constabulary, and the Dublin Metropolitan Police.[114] It was the attrition of the latter's capability that brought about the involvement of the British Army. At the beginning of 1919, both police forces had effective intelligence organisations with the capability to acquire accurate and timely intelligence. In addition, they both had a functioning structure of collection, analysis and dissemination.

The challenge for the Irish Volunteers was to set up operational networks, recruit members, and obtain arms. Success in these three dimensions enabled them to mount a serious challenge to the governance of

---

113 Townshend, op cit, p. 17.
114 These were the two legally constituted police forces in Ireland. The former covered the whole of Ireland apart from the Dublin metropolitan area which was the responsibility of the DMP.

Ireland. They achieved what could be described as 'radical embedding'.[115] In this initial phrase, networks were vulnerable to being detected, diverted, and subverted. The challenge for intelligence organisations was to obtain exploitable intelligence about these networks. Furthermore, there was a need for this insurgent organisation to protect their nascent networks from detection by effective counter measures.

In one sense British policy makers faced a timeless challenge. The key issue was the ability to forge a coherent response. This was and is the vital indicator that illuminates the prospects of success for any counter-insurgency. Sonderland, as previously, mentioned identified the key issue: 'the success of the operation depends not primarily on the development of insurgent strength, but more importantly on the degree of vigour, determination and skill that with which the incumbent regime acts to defend itself, both politically and militarily'.[116]

The First World War formed a critical context in two respects. The wartime demand for animals, agricultural produce and fodder for horses made the small farmer in the Irish economy increasingly prosperous. The emerging insurgency was not driven by economic want. Ireland, as an integral part of the United Kingdom, was at war with Germany. The unfolding of military operations on the Western Front had a major impact on Cabinet decisions taken with respect to Ireland. A key issue was conscription. This provided Sinn Fein with an issue that it exploited deftly and gained the sympathy of other political and theological institutions in Ireland.

---

115 This was a process whereby those who subscribed to what was then an extreme political ideology, Irish Republicanism, were able to connect together a tight knit group of activists and secretly develop networks that provided the infrastructure for a guerrilla warfare campaign.

116 Sonderland, W., 'An Analysis of Guerilla Insurgency and Coup d 'Etat as Techniques of Indirect Aggression', *International Studies Quarterly* (December 1970), 345. Quoted in O'Neill, B. E., *Insurgency and Terrorism* (Washington: Brassey's, 1990), 125.

Chapter 2

The British Army in Ireland 1916–1919

The British Army in Ireland performed a number of operational tasks. The first was the maintenance of internal security. This was no different from the rest of the United Kingdom. The most dramatic challenge occurred in April 1916 when it defeated an open rebellion. The rebellion had been assisted by Britain's wartime enemy, Imperial Germany. The last time this had occurred in Ireland was in 1797 when the French revolutionary government dispatched an expeditionary force to Bantry Bay on the southwest coast of Ireland commanded by one of Napoleon's Generals, Lazare Hoche, to facilitate an insurrection against British governance. The landing was unsuccessful due to inclement weather.

In the aftermath of the failed rebellion of 1916 the historian Charles Townshend has suggested the British Army could take a degree of satisfaction in its own performance: 'if one considers the weakness and inexperience of the troops (some of whom had never fired a rifle before) and the advantages of the defence in street fighting, it had been something of a success to root out 1,500 men in the space of a week'.[117] The internal security exercises carried out in the subsequent months were predicated on an assumption about the character of future challenges to the British state. It would manifest itself in another open rebellion, and would have the support, as the last one had, of Imperial Germany. One order promulgated for these exercises stated that: 'Any German troops south of the Liffey are to be vigourously attacked'.[118]

The signals and human intelligence assets the British state had in its possession prior to, and after the rebellion, put it in a powerful position to manage this uncertainty. In March 1916, a message from Irish

---

117　Townshend, C., *The British Army Campaign in Ireland 1919–1921* (London: Oxford University Press, 1975) 6.
118　Ibid, p. 6.

Revolutionary Headquarters had been intercepted. It requested both munitions and manpower: field guns, German gun crews and officers, machine guns, rifles and ammunition. There was also a request for the German High Seas Fleet to make a demonstration in the North Sea and a submarine to be deployed in Dublin Bay. Eventually, the Germans decided only to supply rifles, machine guns and ammunition, and ordered elements of their High Seas Fleet to bombard the town of Lowestoft in Kent. The weapons and ammunition were transported by a captured British merchant ship, the SS Castro owned by the Wilson Line in Hull. It had been captured in the Keil Canal at the beginning of the war. It was subsequently disguised as a Norwegian ship, the Aud, for the purposes of transporting arms and ammunition to Ireland.

On 12 April 1916 Sir Roger Casement, Robert Monteith and Daniel Julian Bailey, the latter two members of the German 'Irish Brigade' embarked on U-20 at Wilhelmshaven. The night before their departure, they had been given a final briefing by a Captain from the German General Staff.[119] They were given two important things: a secret code for communication; and a clear commitment of further supplies of arms and ammunition if required. This line of communication was to be maintained from 22 April to 20 May 1916. Due to a mechanical failure, they transferred to U-19 after a day and a half at sea.

The Aud set sail on 10 April disguised as a Norwegian steamer commanded by a naval reserve Lieutenant, Karl Spindler. The crew consisted of three officers, one helmsman, and 15 sailors of the Imperial German Navy. It was carrying a cargo of 20,000 Italian rifles which had been captured by the Germans from the Russian Army on the Eastern Front, plus 10 million rounds of ammunition, ten machine guns, 1 million rounds of machine-gun ammunition, explosives, landmines, bombs, and hand grenades.

---

119   Although Captain is a relatively junior rank, admission to the German General Staff was by a rigorous academic exam and this body constituted the intellectual and planning elite of the German Army.

The Royal Navy's signals intelligence unit Room 40 had broken the German Satzbuch code, which had been used to send messages to the United States via the US State Department cable. This gave the British authorities a month's notice of the planned rebellion.[120] The Prime Minister Herbert Asquith was also warned.[121] The Aud was intercepted on the 21st April 1916 by HMS Bluebell off the entrance to Tralee Bay in the west of Ireland. It was escorted to Cork where the German crew then scuttled the ship at the entrance to the harbour off Daunt's Rock. This signals intelligence was exploited too late by the civil servants and policy makers in Dublin Castle.[122]

Despite these triumphs, Britain missed an opportunity to create an intelligence organisation in Ireland. The Record of the Rebellion was candid about this: 'Even after the rebellion in 1916, the opportunity was not taken to create an intelligence branch of trained brains working together to examine the military possibilities of the Sinn Fein movement'.[123] This was partly due to the fact that there were no trained intelligence officers available for duty in Ireland. Up to the end of 1918, no attempt was made to compile anything like an IRA order of battle. In addition, a 'blacklist' that had been run by the police in Ireland had not been kept up to date.

When war was declared in 1914 Ireland provided a considerable number of volunteers. From August 1914 to February 1915 a total of 50,107 recruits enlisted in Ireland. By the end of the conflict in November 1918 a total of 140,460 Irishmen had joined the British Army.[124] Ireland also

---

120 See Larsen, D., 'British Signals Intelligence and the 1916 Easter Rising in Ireland', *Intelligence and National Security* 33/1, 60.

121 Memorandum from the Asquith Papers, Box 42, Folder 5–9, Bodleian Library, Oxford.

122 See Sloan, G. R., 'The British State and the Irish Rebellion of 1916, An intelligence Failure or a Failure of Response?' *Intelligence and National Security* 28/4 (August 2013), 453–494.

123 Record of the Rebellion in Ireland in 1920–1921 (Vol. 2), Intelligence, p. 5. Papers of Lt General Sir Hugh Jeudwine IWM 72/82/2.

124 For a more detailed account see P. Callan, Recruiting for the British Army in Ireland during the First World War, *Irish Sword* 17 (1990), 43–45.

played a full part in raising Kitchener's New Army. Less than a month after the start of the war in August 1914 the main elements of the 10th (Irish) Division began to assemble at the Curragh Camp. The General Officer Commanding was Lieutenant General Sir Bryan T. Mahon from County Galway.[125]

Despite these recruitment successes manpower levels in the British Army had become critical by 1918. The event which crystallised this shortage and turned it into a crisis occurred on the 21st March 1918. Imperial Germany launched its last great offensive on the Western Front. The German General Staff named it 'Kaiserschlacht' (Kaiser's battle).[126] In reality it was a series of five offensives (Somme, 21 March–4 April; Lys, Flanders, 9–29 April; Aisne 27 May–4 June; Noyon–Mondidier, 8–12; Champagne–Marne, 15–17 June). In the first offensive the Germans did break through the British lines. It was the British Third and Fifth Armies who endured the worst of this onslaught. The German army advanced 40 miles and got close to the vital rail junction at Amiens. They wheeled north–west in an attempt to cut the lines of communication behind the Artois front. By the time the offensive lost momentum on the 5th April the British Army had suffered 177,739 casualties killed, wounded or missing.

Although there were twenty-five United States Army divisions in France by spring 1918, they were not, at American insistence, integrated into the Allied command structure and played little part in blunting this offensive.[127] The manpower crisis the German offensive caused can be further illuminated by a breakdown of the British casualty figures. Two of the Irish divisions heavily engaged in the fighting were the 36th (Ulster) Division and the 16th (Irish) Division suffered 7,310 and 7,149 casualties,

125 For a detailed account of the British Army in Ireland during the First World War see Costello, C., *A Most Delightful Station* (Cork: The Collins Press, 1996), 274–301.
126 This was General Ludendorff's gamble to decisively win the war by transferring from the now defunct Eastern Front hundreds of thousands of German troops to the Western Front.
127 See Trask, D. F., *The AEF & Coalition Warmaking, 1917–1918* (Lawrence, Kansas: University Press of Kansas, 1993).

respectively. Both these divisions were effectively destroyed and had to be taken out of the order of battle to be rebuilt.

This military offensive had political implications for Ireland. It brought into sharp focus the need for more manpower. There was a long-standing tradition in Ireland of service in the British Army.[128] A comprehensive network of regimental recruitment and service challenged the narrative that Ireland was a subjugated colony in the western fringe of the British Isles. In reality Ireland was the recruiting ground for eight infantry regiments. Their depots extended throughout the whole of Ireland: Royal Irish Regiment (Clonmel), The Connaught Rangers (Galway), The Prince of Wales Leinster Regiment (Birr), The Royal Munster Fusiliers (Tralee), The Royal Dublin Fusiliers (Naas), The Royal Inniskilling Fusiliers (Omagh), The Royal Irish Fusiliers (Armagh), The Royal Irish Rifles (Belfast).

In addition, there were four Irish cavalry regiments: 4th Royal Irish Dragoon Guards, 6th Inniskilling Dragoons, 5th Royal Irish Lancers, 8th King's Royal Irish Hussars. All these regiments had their depots in Dublin. There were also two Yeomanry Regiments consisting of Special Reserve volunteers: The North Irish Horse (HQ Belfast) and the South Irish Horse (HQ Dublin).

In August 1918, the balance between soldiers training for overseas deployments and convalescents was in favour of the former. There was a total of 111,222 soldiers in Ireland. Of this total, 52,572 were being trained for deployments overseas, and 48,731 were recovering from their wounds. This left only 9,919 soldiers available for internal security duties.

The British Army, already short of manpower, had reached a tipping point and led the Government to announce on the 9th April 1918 that conscription would be applied to Ireland. An estimate of the manpower

---

128 This included both officers and men. By 1832, 42 per cent of the soldiers in the British Army were Irish. In addition, by 1878 one-fifth of its officer corps were from Ireland.

A Slow Burning Fuse 31

reserve the army hoped to tap into was given by the Chief of the Imperial General Staff, Field Marshal Sir Henry Wilson (himself an Irishman), who believed there were 150,000 'recalcitrant Irishmen' who could be conscripted. The Military Service Bill was passed through the House of Commons on the 16th April 1918.

The figure has come from the Army Museum not a book or article.

Figure 2.1 Image Courtesy of the National Army Museum, London.

The German High Command, as they had done in 1916, added a political warfare dimension to run in parallel to the 'Kaiser's Battle'. They landed from a German U-boat, Joseph Dowling, a Corporal in the Connaught Rangers, and now a member of the German 'Irish Brigade', on Crab Island off Galway on the 12th April 1918. Dowling had been sent to Ireland with the express purpose of setting up a communication channel for the Germans to land arms on the west coast of Ireland. A communications system had been set up whereby messages could be sent to Germany via POW parcels to fictitious British soldiers. These messages would be hidden in the contents, and there was a scheme for confirming that the message had received. These messages would give the Germans the location for delivery of arms and ammunition within a three-week window. Dowling's job was to ensure that the personnel and transport would be available to distribute and hide the shipments.[129]

This need for manpower was quickly turned into a political issue by Sinn Fein. They used the Military Service Bill to do two things: first to build their influence with other political parties and key institutions to campaign against conscription in Ireland; second to challenge the legitimacy of the British state. At a meeting held in the Mansion House in Dublin the leaders of Sinn Fein, the Irish Parliamentary Party and the Irish Labour Party passed a resolution against the Military Service Bill. The Catholic Church in Ireland also endorsed this stand. The resolution drafted by de Valera stated: 'The passage of the Conscription Bill by the British House of Commons must be regarded as a declaration of war on the Irish nation'. In the end, conscription was not enforced and was replaced by a voluntary recruiting campaign. The British army recruitment in Ireland

---

129 When he was arrested, he lied and claimed that his name was James O'Brien, and he had been washed ashore from the torpedoed ship Mississippi the previous night. He was also found in possession of £70 sterling. At his subsequent Court Martial he was found guilty of the following charge 'When a prisoner of war, voluntarily aiding the enemy by going to Ireland in a German submarine with the object of aiding the King's enemies in prosecuting the War against His Majesty'. His sentence was penal servitude for life which was annulled by the King George V for political reasons in February 1924.

continued to have a different tempo from the rest of the United Kingdom for the last seven months of the war.

The British authorities did have access to timely and accurate intelligence. The Royal Irish Constabulary had been active and diligent in compiling a full analysis of the organisational structure of the Irish Volunteers by March 1918.[130] In addition, they acquired highly exploitable intelligence from the Irish Volunteers with respect their plan to disrupt conscription if it was introduced. This was confirmed by Eamonn Broy:[131] 'One of the successes of the RIC was acquiring, before the ink was well dry on it, the secret Volunteer plan for combating conscription in 1918 ... I send a copy back to the Volunteers as soon as G. Division received it from the R.I.C., to the utter consternation of the Volunteers'.[132]

The issue of conscription formed the context for new appointments made by London to the Irish Executive. The new Lord Lieutenant was Field Marshal Viscount French. On the 8th of May 1918 the Cabinet told him to focus on suppressing seditious speeches and assessing the Sinn Fein relationship with Imperial Germany[133] and the application

130 Inspector General of the RIC to Under Secretary, Dublin Castle WO35 69/8 quoted in Townshend, C., *The British Army Campaign in Ireland 1919–1921* (London: Oxford University Press, 1975) 7.
131 Eamonn Broy joined the DMP in January 1911. In March 1915, he was appointed to the political section of G. Division of the DMP. From March 1917 to February 1921, he passed intelligence material to Collins from both the DMP and more importantly the RIC. He also provided tactical advice to Collins. His was arrested as a consequence of documents retrieved in an organised search, based on a tip off from a member of the public, carried out by the Auxiliary Division of the RIC on the flat of Eileen McGrane (Collin's secretary) on the 31st December 1920. He was charged and found guilty of passing documents to Sinn Fein and given a custodial sentence in Arbour Hill Military Prison.
132 Eamonn Broy, Witness Statement, 1280, Bureau of Military History, Cathal Brugha Barracks, Dublin.
133 By the 22nd April Corporal Dowling had been taken to New Scotland Yard where he was interrogated by Sir Basil Thomson and Captain William Hall RN, Director of Naval Intelligence.

of conscription.[134] Edward Shortt seen as an able administrator of conscription, replaced Henry Duke as Chief Secretary. Finally, Lieutenant-General Sir Frederick Shaw was appointed GOC-in-C, Irish Command.

The consequences of German attempts to wage political warfare in Ireland again, underlined by Dowling's arrest and subsequent interrogation, were not long in making themselves felt. Field Marshal French obtained Cabinet approval to arrest the leaders of Sinn Fein. Under the provisions of the Defence of the Realm Act, a trial could take place act if 'association with the enemy' could be proven. On the 17th May, the leadership of Sinn Fein was arrested[135] and imprisoned. In May and June, other measures were put in place, such as a system of controls on entry into Ireland from Britain.

As the fighting on the Western Front continued the British Army was simultaneously being drawn into providing manpower for internal security duties in Ireland on 28 September 1918 West Cork was made a Special Military Area: troop strength was increased to two battalions, centred on Bantry and Macroom, with companies at Dunmanway, Skibbereen, Bandon, and Millstreet. Fairs and markets were prohibited without a military permit; public houses were closed at 7 pm.

The end of the conflict brought qualitative and organisational changes in Ireland as far as the British Army was concerned: 'At the beginning of 1919 the garrison in Ireland (composed mainly of Young Soldiers and Reserve units, Cyclists and Yeomanry) was grouped in three divisions – the Northern, the Midland & Connaught, and the Southern ... On 1st November 1919 the 5th and 6th Divisions were reconstituted; the 5th Division taking over the Midland (less Connaught Sub-District), Dublin and Northern Districts; the 6th Division taking over the Southern District and the Connaught Sub-District of the

---

134 War Cabinet, 8th May 1918, Cab 23/5. Quoted in Townshend, C., *The British Army Campaign in Ireland 1919–1921* (London: Oxford University Press, 1975), 9.
135 This included: de Valera, Arthur Griffith Darrell Figgis, Count Plunkett, William Cosgrave, Mrs Tom Clarke, Countess Markievicz, and Sean MacGarry, General Secretary of the Irish Volunteers.

Midland District'.[136] One month after the armistice General Shaw put his requirements at 12,000 infantry (15 battalions) and 10,800 cyclist soldiers. This was an internal security commitment of 22,800 troops that the British government was not able to fulfil until the summer of 1921.[137]

The year after the armistice was important both tactically and operationally for the British Army in Ireland. There was a recognition in the 'Special Military Areas' where the army had been committed to help maintain law and order that there was a need for an intelligence gathering capability. By the end of January 1919, in the area which included the South Riding of Tipperary, steps were being taken to collect information about the local order of battle of the Irish Volunteers, and to work independently of the police.

Operationally the changing nature of the threat presented by the Irish Volunteers was recognised along with the implications for intelligence: 'It was realised guerrilla warfare was the only military action to be expected on the part of the IRA and that a general rebellion was unlikely, and that the necessity for a military intelligence organisation working on independent lines became apparent'.[138] The British Army had correctly answered what Carl von Clausewitz called the 'supreme act of judgement' that statesmen and the commanders have to make. To identify the kind of war in which they could be embarking. This was the premier strategic question and the most comprehensive.[139]

In contrast policy makers refused to recognise the threat posed by guerrilla warfare. Responses when they did come can be characterised as a fusion of paralysis and appeasement in the forlorn hope of a reciprocal response. The army's judgement was simply ignored. This bifurcation was to have real consequences from January 1920 onwards. It was to impede the integration of political and military efforts. The Army was unable to

---

136   History of the fifth Division in Ireland, Papers of Lieutenant General Sir Hugh Jeudwine 72/82/2 IWM.
137   Op cit, p. 13.
138   Ibid, p. 8.
139   von Clausewitz, C., *On War*, ed. and trans, Michael Howard and Peter Parret (Princeton, NJ: Princeton University Press, pp. 88–89).

conduct a campaign in a holistic manner. Critically it deprived them of what the strategist Colin Gray has described as: 'the pattern of multiple reciprocal dependencies that interconnect, indeed bind, strategy's many dimensions. It was always so'.[140]

The Record of the Rebellion[141] acknowledged the initial lack of success of the army's attempts in early 1919 to gain intelligence pertinent to the operational networks of the Irish Volunteers: 'The Irish Volunteers were studied as a hostile force, intended to take part in a rebellion, and efforts were made to discover details about their: organisation, armament and strength. No information was obtained about individuals other than about 30 to 40 well-known leaders'.[142] The report also made it clear that the army would not approve an increase in military intelligence staff in Ireland at this stage. There was an assumption that these matters were in the remit of the two police forces.

This impasse was partly resolved by a rebellion of human intelligence assets. The Record of the Rebellion does not reveal what prompted this dramatic action: 'In May 1919, the services of a group of agents, who refused to work under the police, were placed at the disposal of the intelligence of officers at GHQ. From this group a considerable amount of information about Sinn Fein and the Irish Volunteers was obtained'.[143] The historian Michael Foy identified them as being army officers who had come under the command of Major Hill Dillon, a GHQ staff officer.[144] Foy doesn't comment on the improved intelligence produced. There appeared to be considerable latitude for individual initiative.

The Record of the Rebellion stated in late summer 1919 that an army officer began to work in Dublin individually and independently with a view to finding out about Sinn Fein. He was joined by others and

140 Gray, C. S., *Modern Strategy* (Oxford: University of Oxford Press, 1999), p. 357.
141 This was a secret two-volume report that was compiled by the British Army in 1922. The first volume was on operations and the second on Intelligence.
142 Op cit, p. 8.
143 Op cit, p. 8.
144 Foy, M. T., *Michael Collins's Intelligence War* (Stroud: Sutton Publishing 2006) 68–69.

eventually 'they obtained touch[145] with a certain section of the IRA'. No details were given about the quality of intelligence obtained. This 'touch' did provide exploitable intelligence: 'In this way information was collected which proved invaluable in the early months of 1920 and formed the first of the records collected subsequently in the Dublin area'.[146] The institutional structure under which these officers worked evolved as the campaign unfolded. In a relatively short period of time, they went from reporting to GHQ, to forming a Special Branch of the Dublin Military District. Eventually they were organised as the 'D' Branch of the Auxiliary Division of the RIC.[147] All these developments have to be seen in the context of changing circumstances, and the need for the Government to call upon the army to play a much larger role than before in providing intelligence.

Radical Embedding: The Road to Salvation

Between the 1st May and 16th June 1916 the British deported at total of 2,519 men arrested for their part in the Easter rebellion. Initially they were imprisoned in a number of jails across Britain, from Glasgow to Reading. By 7th of June a partial process of centralisation had begun to take place. With the exception of jails such as Lewes the first contingent of prisoners arrived in Frongoch, a German prisoner of war camp in North Wales.

As British citizens their greatest fear was being conscripted into the army. Consequently, they gave false names to the camp authorities. The culmination of this defiance was a three-day hunger strike by two hundred prisoners. The propaganda generated by this event impacted in the

---

145 This phrase can be interpreted as working on experience and intuition – without formal systems of written records.
146 Op cit, p. 7.
147 These changes in bureaucratic responsibility will be examined in detail in Chapter 3.

United States. Westminster chose to distance itself from the challenge. The Chief Secretary for Ireland, Henry Duke responded by declaring an amnesty for the prisoners in Frongoch on the 21st December 1916. There were no conditions placed on their future behaviour. Their release was a strategic error from which there would be no redemption.

For the committed members of the Irish Republican Brotherhood[148] it was back to business. A good example was Paddy O'Daly, a member of the Fintan Lalor Circle of the IRB since 1907, and would later ran Collin's 'squad': 'I was released from Frongoch and arrived home on the morning of Christmas Eve 1916. In January 1917, we started to re-organise "B" Company, 2nd Battalion'.[149] Joseph O'Connor a member of the Dublin Brigade of the IRA had been released earlier than the prisoners from Frongoch and started to organise: 'Coming back to my release from prison in August 1916, I immediately summoned representatives from the companies who had been released previous to me'.[150] Vincent Byrne another member of the 'squad' was too young to be deported. He gave an insight to the tactical and operational effect the deportation had on the Irish Volunteers, and the disastrous consequences of Duke's amnesty: 'The majority of the Company had been deported and, as a result, the company became disorganised for the time being ... After the general release of the prisoners in England-the week after they had come home – the company was called together, on the orders of Lieutenant Shields'.[151]

Michael Collins had been in both Stafford jail and Frongoch. While he was in the POW camp he came to a judgement about the rebellion. (He had been in the GPO.) In a letter to Kevin O'Brien in October 1916 he wrote: 'I think the Rising was bungled terribly costing many a good life. It seemed at first to be well organised but afterwards became subjected

---

148 The IRB was a secret Irish Republican organisation formed in 1867 and had as its core aim the use of violence to end British rule in the whole of Ireland.
149 O'Daly, P., Witness Statement No. 387, Bureau of Military History, Cathal Bruga Barracks, Dublin.
150 O'Connor, J., Witness Statement No. 487, Bureau of Military History, Cathal Bruga Barracks, Dublin.
151 Byrne, V., Witness Statement No. 423, Bureau of Military History, Cathal Bruga Barracks, Dublin.

to panic decisions and a great lack of very essential organisation and co-operation'.[152] Collins arrived back in Dublin on the 25th December 1916. After three weeks at home at Woodfield near Clonakility he returned to Dublin in January 1917.

By the 17th January 1917, an intelligence report had been submitted by G Division of the DMP with the subject title: 'Michael Collins-interned prisoner-released'. The report identified him as having a sister who lived in Sunday's Well, Cork. They had also identified the address he resided in prior to the rebellion: 16, Rathdown Rd, and his place of employment in the months of March and April 1916. He had been a temporary clerk in Messrs Craig, Gardner & Co. The G Division detectives also knew he had been employed as a clerk in the Post Office in London.[153] By the 4th May a report written on a 'suspect John Milroy' had Collins living at 44 Mountjoy Street Dublin since the end of January 1917.[154]

Around the same time Collins, in a letter to Sean Deasey, gave his interpretation of the political landscape, and the opportunities he believed now existed: 'Consider the situation. It is ripe for whatever one may wish. Both British Authority and the Irish Parliamentary Party (IPP), are in a corner, driven there by what they have done and by the will of the people. There now exists a wilderness – ripe for any advancement along the road to salvation'.[155]

The Irish Republican movement from 1917 was increasingly influenced by a 'forward policy' driven by the IRB and Michael Collins. At its core was a policy of violence and murder. Collins started to develop an insurgent organisation and co-operate with other elements of the Republican movement who were proselytising in public. A good example of this was his involvement in the North Roscommon by-election campaign. Count Plunkett defeated the Irish Parliamentary Party candidate by 1,708 votes although; he announced his intention to form his own

---

152 Quoted in Taylor, R., *Michael Collins* (London: Hutchinson, 1958), 78.
153 See Stewart, A. T.Q., ed., *Michael Collins the Secret File* (Belfast: Black Staff Press, 1997), p. 44.
154 Ibid, p. 53.
155 Quoted in Ibid, p. 82.

party. Another victory occurred on the 1st May 1917 in Longford County where Joseph McGuiness, a prisoner in Lewes Jail was elected, against his wishes, by just 37 votes. Collins was involved in this campaign as well. These by-election victories were followed by two further victories in East Clare where de Valera was elected in June 1917 and in Kilkenny which saw W. T. Cosgrave being elected as Sinn Fein MPs.

His involvement in the first two campaigns should be understood in context of Collin's new job. On the 19th February 1917 he became the Secretary of the Irish National Aid Fund. This had been set up by the widow of Tom Clarke, executed for his part in the Easter rebellion, to provide financial aid to the dependents of those killed in the fighting and those who had been deported. The funding came from public subscription; the most important element was from Clan na Gael in the United States. This charity post provided cover for the construction of new operational networks: 'it was very widely understood that it was an IRB appointment, particularly in view of the fact that the major portion of the work of the Society, that is, looking after the widows and orphans had been accomplished. Mick was able to give a great amount of attention to the re-organising of the Volunteers in general'.[156]

Collins's new job and his position in Sinn Fein's organisation was subject of another intelligence report submitted by G Division of the 13th August 1917: 'I beg to state that Michael Collins was appointed paid Secretary to Irish National Aid in January, 1917 and last June he became a member of the Executive Council of Sinn Fein'.[157] This report and previous ones underlined the extent of the actionable intelligence the DMP obtained through human intelligence sources. This report also contained an accurate description of Collins.[158]

---

156 O'Connor, J., Witness Statement 487, Bureau of Military History, Cathal Bruga Barracks, Dublin.
157 Op cit, p. 58.
158 He was described as '28 years, 5ft 10 in high, well built, square shoulders, dark brown hair, round face, clean shaven, pale complexion, wears tweed suit and brown trilby hat'.

The policy developed by the British Government at this time was to announce the convening of an Irish Convention on 11th June 1917 designed to 'recommend a settlement of the Irish problem', As a precursor to this Bonar Law announced on the 15th June an amnesty for 120 prisoners from Lewes Jail deported after at the 1916 rebellion. This decision was taken 'in order that the convention may meet in an atmosphere of harmony and good will'. As with the releases from Frongoch there were no conditions set for the future behaviour of these prisoners. Their arrival in Dublin in September 1917 presented the DMP with a security problem. There was a demonstration in O'Connell Street. Some of these former prisoners went up on the building of the G.P.O. to put the tricolour over it again and the police fired on them. These men were arrested and prosecuted.

The seminal event of 1917 for the Irish Republican movement was the Sinn Fein Convention on the 25th October. It was at this meeting a number of disparate organisations: Irish National League, the IRB, Count Plunkett's followers and the 1916 Revolutionary wing were able to forge a common platform that satisfied both moderate and extreme opinion: 'It was highly successful in uniting these hitherto diverse national forces which were opposed to the Irish Parliamentary Party, in agreeing the question of leadership, and in presenting a constructive policy'.[159] The agreed objectives were economic nationalism, a programme of absenteeism and a programme put forward by de Valera to establish the legitimacy of an independent Irish Republic, through international recognition. In addition, de Valera was elected President of Sinn Fein. Two days later on the 27th October 1917 at a Convention of the Volunteers de Valera was elected President. The continuous search for issues which it could be fashioned into political weapons was underlined by a resolution passed at the meeting that the Executive would 'declare war' should the British Government introduce conscription in Ireland. This was a full five months before the launch of the German offensive.

The next year 1918 was one of continued agitation by Sinn Fein. This was tempered by three successive defeats at by-elections in South Armagh,

---

159   Op cit, p. 91.

Waterford, and East Tyrone. An intelligence report by the RIC Crimes Special Branch, dated 17th February 1918, gives a flavour this agitation from a meeting held in Ballinamuck in County Longford. Written from 'mental notes', one of those who addressed the meeting, held after Mass, was a 'Captain' Collins: 'he advised all over 18 years to join the Irish volunteers and get to work in earnest to be ready for self-independence, he told them to drill and be prepared to assert their rights when the time came, the convention had failed and it was now up to the Irish people to decide whether they were going to demand independence or remain a vassal state of John Bull'.[160] At this meeting, Collins peddled a hubristic narrative. He claimed Ireland was being crushed by taxation. Furthermore, after three years of independence Ireland would have the revenue to 'build 10 submarines'.[161] They could then make England keep her Dreadnoughts and Super Dreadnoughts in their own ports. These statements underlined the inherent advantage an insurgent has. As French army officer David Galula stated: 'he can lie, cheat, exaggerate. He is not obliged to prove; he is judged by what he promises, not what he does'.[162]

A British Army report written as part of a history of the 5th Division gave a very accurate account of the economic reality: 'the large majority of the agricultural population was contented and prosperous; never had the bank balance of the small farmer been so large; the economic effects of the war had not disturbed rural Ireland, and high prices had been obtained for food products sold to England'.[163]

Collins was actively involved in insurgent activities. By 20th March 1919, a Bench Warrant at Assizes was issued as a result of a Bill of Indictment against Michael Collins in the City of Londonderry. It listed a number of charges dated from the 14th July 1918. What they had in common was unlawful incitement. They included incitement to riot, raid

---

160 Op cit, p. 92.
161 The Irish Republic did not have a naval service until September 1946.
162 Galula, D., *Counterinsurgency Warfare* (Westport, Praeger Security, 1968), 9.
163 The History of the 5th Division in Ireland Papers of Lt General Sir Hugh Jeudwine IMW 72/82/2, p. 1.

A Slow Burning Fuse

for arms, forcible entry, and assault on persons, and stealing arms. He had failed to 'abide his trial' and as a result he was to be apprehended on sight. Between these dates, two events took place that were to be of pivotal importance. The external one was the announcement of an Armistice on the 11th November 1918. At one stroke, the issue of conscription in Ireland was removed. Internally, a General Election was called for the 14th December 1918. Sinn Fein shaped its approach to the election in two ways. Michael Collins and Harry Boland[164] structured the candidate selection process to endorse only those candidates that represented a particular part of the Irish Republican coalition established at the Sinn Fein convention in 1917: 'They went over with a fine tooth comb the list of candidates chosen to represent Sinn Fein at the General Election ... to ensure that only those who favoured a "forward policy" were selected'.[165] Second, the Irish Volunteers successfully embedded themselves in the election campaign: 'Sinn Fein was contesting the election on behalf of Republicans. Their organisation was scant and it became necessary to utilise the volunteer machinery for the purpose of the election, organising, canvassing, arranging meetings, arranging speakers'.[166] On the day of the poll the Irish Volunteers were able to exercise control over the ballot boxes in a manner inconceivable today: 'From the day of the poll until the counting of the votes all ballot boxes were under constant guard day and night. This was done in the full military manner and was again useful for training'.[167]

This General Election has been judged a triumph for Sinn Fein. It won 73 seats out of a total of 106. Sinn Fein's political target, the Irish Parliamentary Party, had been emasculated and reduced to six seats. There are some important qualifications to this result. In 25 seats, Sinn Fein candidates were returned unopposed. For example, Michael Collins in Cork County East, Eamon de Valera in Clare East and Arthur Griffith

---

164 They were both members of the IRB.
165 Coogan, T. P., *Michael Collins* (New York: Palgrave, 1990), 92.
166 O'Connor, J., Witness Statement 487, Bureau of Military History, Cathal Bruga Barracks, Dublin.
167 Ibid.

in Cavan East had no electoral opponents. Maurice Headlam, a civil servant who served in Ireland from 1906 to 1920, claimed this result involved intimidation: 'I was told that corps of "whisperers" had been organised, who knocked up the cottages at night and whispered that the man of the house must vote Sinn Fein, or his hay would be burnt and his cattle driven off. There was no means of protecting him, he knew it, and did as he was told'.[168] Despite this behaviour, Sinn Fein won less than half of the popular vote at just 46.9 per cent. It was also the first General Election in Ireland where women had the vote. In the north of Ireland, the Unionists, in the nine Ulster counties, won more than twice as many votes as Sinn Fein (234,376–110,032). This election identified the personalities and parties that would wield political power in the future, in the two parts of Ireland.

Collins continued to build his operational networks. He had learnt from the 1916 rebellion how important intelligence was. In particular, how detectives of 'G' division were able to walk through a group of two thousand prisoners sitting on the floor of the gymnasium of Richmond Barracks in Dublin and identify those prisoners who, from their intelligence files, could be charged under the Defence of the Realm Act. Collins was initially selected to join this group.[169]

Every insurgency needs an enemy,[170] the first target selected by Collins was G division of the Dublin Metropolitan Police responsible for the detection of political crime. It had a total 18 detectives. The Irish Volunteers had already recruited three junior members of 'G' division, who were acting as inside agents.[171] The period from April to September 1919 saw an increase in the tempo of violence and intimidation. In April Sinn Fein designated the RIC as a military target and initiated a boycott as the first stage of this strategy. Eamonn Broy a serving member of the DMP had been supplying intelligence to Collins since March 1917, gave

---

168 Headlam, M., *Irish Reminiscences* (London: Robert Hale, 1947), 208.
169 See Coogan, T. P., *Michael Collins* (New York: Palgrave, 1990), 45–46.
170 I am grateful to my colleague Dr Andreas Behnke for this insight.
171 This phrase comes from Sun Tzu's typology of human intelligence. See *The Art of War*, Chapter 13.

Collins an assessment of the tactical and operational benefits that would accrue from attacking RIC stations. These attacks began in January 1920: 'I mentioned to Mick [Collins] the danger of the village with a small number of police ... We agreed that ruthless war should be made on the small stations, attacking the barracks if the police were in them, and burning them down where they had been evacuated. The RIC would then be compelled to concentrate on the larger towns and attempt to patrol the vacated areas from these distant centres. Such concentration would cause the police to lose their grip psychologically and otherwise, on the inhabitants of the vacated areas because the police, who returned from a distance to patrol the area, would be in no better position than the British military'.[172]

Broy acknowledged the high regard the RIC were held in: 'The mere fact that these men were rather decent men in peaceful times made them all the more a menace when the national resurgence burst forth, and it took some time and some exhortation to convince local people that the RIC were really enemies'.[173] In addition to loosening its psychological grip these attacks were motivated by a desire to eliminate a specific intelligence capability. Outside Dublin the RIC performed a unique function: 'A particular menace to the Volunteers was the small area, policed by one sergeant and five constables. The police in this case knew almost everything about every native of the area, and when a prominent Volunteer officer from Dublin came to the area, although previously unknown to the police in Dublin, was soon noted by the RIC as a stranger'.[174]

The Record of the Rebellion recognised the capability of the RIC Crimes Special Branch, and the threat that they represented to the Irish Volunteers: 'Sinn Fein were not long in recognising that these men (Crimes Special Branch) and the best and most energetic of the RIC ... were the most dangerous of their opponents. From 1919 onwards, they

---

172 Witness Statement by Eamon Broy No. 1280 Bureau of Military Affairs, Military Archives Cathal Brugha Barracks, Dublin, 1955.
173 Witness Statement by Eamon Broy No. 1280 Bureau of Military Affairs, Military Archives Cathal Brugha Barracks, Dublin, 1955.
174 Ibid.

carried out a systematic murder campaign. Consequently, the police source of information dried up and the intelligence service paralysed. This was exactly what Sinn Fein desired and intended and was their first distinct success'.[175]

Between July and September 1919, Collins calibrated the reaction of the general public to a series of murders. Specifically, two of 'G' division's most effective and experienced detective sergeants: Patrick Smyth and Daniel Hoey. However, it was a murder of a soldier by the Irish Volunteers on the 7th September in Fermoy, the first since the failed rebellion of 1916, which invoked the intervention of King George V, and belatedly caused the British Government to declare Dail Eireann illegal on the 12th September, 8 months after the declaration of UDI.

Constructing Operational Networks

One effect of declaring the Dail Eireann illegal was that it forced the Irish Republican movement underground. The initial lack of vigour, determination and skill displayed by the British state in countering this threat had major implications. The initiative passed to Collins. The existing intelligence organisations were unable to detect or impede the construction of a series of operational networks. The British Army, in terms of exploitable intelligence, was not yet organised to detect, divert, subvert or contain these networks. In terms of locating Collins, the RIC Crimes Special Branch had submitted a report in February 1920 that confirmed Collins now permanently resided in Dublin and was a 'constant visitor to the residence of John P. Twohig, who is employed in the Education Office'.[176] There is no evidence of any attempt being made to arrest him.

---

175 Op cit, Vol. 2, p. 4.
176 Op cit, p. 182.

Irish Republicanism recognised the narrative of propaganda as vital. A 'Department of Publicity' operated during the entire campaign. Its key publication was the *Irish Bulletin*. Townshend described it as: 'a cyclostyled newssheet which first appeared on 11th November 1919, and which was later issued every few days, and widely circulated to political and public figures, the press and so on'.[177] The first issue had a print run of a mere 30 copies. The last issue was printed on 11th July 1921, and it was compiled and printed in secret at 6 Harcourt Street in Dublin. The stated aim was to break the 'paper wall' that Britain had allegedly constructed around Ireland with respect to the outside world.[178] The strategic narrative projected was that the whole of Ireland already enjoyed the status of an independent state, and the attacks on the police and army represented the defence of this imaginary state against a foreign invader.[179] The first editor was Desmond Fitzgerald. He was succeeded by Erskine Childers, when the former was arrested by British security forces.[180]

Intelligence was another key network. Collins used the history of failed Irish insurgencies to educate selected members of the Irish Volunteers; specifically, those who would become known as the 'squad'. There was an analysis of the importance of counter-intelligence: 'He gave us a short talk, the gist of which was that any of us who had read Irish history would know that no organisation in the past had an intelligence system through which spies and informers could be dealt with, but that now the position was going to be rectified by the formation of an Intelligence Branch, an Active Service Unit or whatever else it is called'.[181] This intelli-

---

177 Op cit, p. 67.
178 See Kennelly, I., *The Paper Wall: Newspapers and Propaganda in Ireland 1919–1921* (Cork: The Collins Press, 2008).
179 For a detailed insight to the pivotal use of propaganda see Rust, M., *Tactics, Politics, and Propaganda in the Irish War of Independence, 1917–1921* (MA: Georgia State University, 2011).
180 Dáil Éireann Department of Publicity: History and Progress (August 1921), National Archives of Ireland NAI DE 4/4/2. Available online: <https://www.difp.ie/docs/1921/Publicity-Department-His-tory/102.html accessed 6/9/20>.
181 Witness Statement by Patrick Daly, No. 387 Bureau of Military Affairs, Military Archives Cathal Brugha Barracks, Dublin.

gence network was established on the 19th September 1919.[182] The key personnel, apart from Collins himself, were: Liam Tobin as Deputy Director of Intelligence. Tom Cullen was Assistant Director of Intelligence, and Frank Thornton Deputy Assistant Director of Intelligence. These 'titles' should be seen in the context of a small organisation whereby men performed a number of functions. For example, Tobin: 'functioned as office manager, field agent, and triggerman'.[183] The group lacked any professional training or experience in intelligence, and all had manual jobs.[184] Collins himself was untutored as far as the process and products of intelligence was concerned. He was to learn by studying his first designated enemy, the DMP. He gained access to the G division intelligence reports. He came to understand that exploitable intelligence was a consequence of a particular process: acquisition, analysis, and counterintelligence. Once this process was understood it was exploited by the squad to murder both policemen and soldiers. This intelligence network was to be an expanding network. By July 1920, eleven new full-time intelligence officers were active.[185]

The murder of Assistant Commissioner Redmond underlined the threat that the DMP now faced. G Division had been penetrated by Collins. One of his agents, Detective McNamara was appointed principal aide detective to Redmond. This enabled him to report to Collins the temporary address Redmond was using. The Record of the Rebellion accurately identified that Sinn Fein had been informed of his movements by his own detectives. More importantly, this murder ended the ability of police in Dublin to produce exploitable intelligence: 'After the death of Mr Redmond, the work of "G" division ceased to affect the situation, and the force did little more than point duty during the years 1920–1921'.[186]

182   Ibid.
183   Foy, M. T., *Michael Collin's Intelligence War* (Stroud: Sutton Publishing, 2006), 41.
184   Tobin had worked in a hardware firm. Cullen had been a shop assistant. Thornton had been a shipyard painter. All were unmarried, and they had all taken part in the failed rebellion of 1916.
185   For details of their names, see op cit, p. 43–44.
186   Record of the Rebellion in Ireland 1920–1921 (Vol. 2), Intelligence, War Office, 1922, p. 5.

This was a major setback for the British authorities. The ability of the DMP to provide intelligence had broken down by December 1919, and the Record of the Rebellion acknowledged there was now an imperative for a military intelligence organisation working on independent lines.

The success that the 'squad'[187] enjoyed in murdering the key detectives from G division of the DMP produced a response from the British intelligence community. It brought a re-configuration of the intelligence organisation in Ireland. The Record of the Rebellion gave an insight to this: 'Towards the end of 1919 it was decided by the Irish Government that the Secret Service in Ireland should be controlled from London and directed from the office of Sir B Thomson, in Scotland House ... The military authorities in Ireland agreed that with the exception of any agents already employed by the Intelligence Branch at GHQ, all agents should be controlled from Scotland House, and an officer from Scotland House was attached to GHQ for liaison duties. The G Branch of the DMP was not linked up with this scheme as their best detectives have already been murdered, and the Crimes Special Branch of the RIC continued to work independently. A small amount of general and political information was collected through this source but none on which any action was possible'.[188]

This re-organisation enjoyed initial success. By early December Scotland House had infiltrated one of their agents, a former British Army Warrant Officer, called Jack Byrnes into Ireland.[189] He arrived in Dublin on the 6th December 1919. Two days later he had his first face to face meeting with Michael Collins.[190] His legend was a proposal to supply arms and ammunition to the IRA. His subsequent report was a breakthrough for this London-based intelligence agency as it accurately

---

187 The initial members of the squad were Paddy Daly, Joe Leonard, Sean Doyle, Ben Barrett. By the first half of 1921 its numbers had gone up to 21.
188 Record of the Rebellion in Ireland 1920–1921 (Vol. 2), Intelligence, War Office, 1922, p. 7.
189 He had initially worked for an Army domestic intelligence organisation called A2, which had as its focus combating subversion in the British armed forces after the First World War.
190 The alias he used in this meeting was John Jameson.

identified the role that Michal Collins was playing in the organisation: 'No. 8 is convinced that this man Michael Collins is the Chief Director of all active movement amongst the Sinn Feiners and that he now takes the place of de Valera owing to the long absence of the latter.[191] Although Collins does not take any active part in the shooting affairs there seems to be no doubt that he is the organiser'.[192] There was also a desire to understand the social profile of the various elements of the Irish Republican movement. Jack Byrnes interpretation is conveyed in the same report: 'No. 8 is of the opinion that the Sinn Fein movement is limited to the middle classes and that the bulk of working class are becoming Socialist Republicans'.[193] By contrast Lieutenant General Sir Hugh Jeudwine, commander of 5th division had a view of the social composition of the Irish Volunteers: 'This ill trained, ill armed and badly disciplined force was largely recruited from the youth of the country, the corner boys, shop assistants and sons of small farmers, whose numbers had grown considerably owing to the stoppage of emigration during and after the war'.[194] Jack Byrnes was murdered by Collins's squad on his third visit to Dublin on the 28th February 1920.[195] There is evidence to suggest that Collins had initially been taken in by Byrnes: 'Cope twitted Mick [Collins] that clever as he was the British agent, Jameson (his cover name), had been able to get in contact with him without Mick knowing that Jameson was an intelligence officer'.[196]

The Record of the Rebellion recognised that Collins had put in place a 'Contre-Espionage System'. It was not structurally separate from Front Line Intelligence and Secret Intelligence, as the same personnel and

---

191   De Valera had left for the United States in June 1919.
192   Putkowski, J., The Best Secret Service Man We had –Jack Byrnes, A2 and the IRA. Lobster No. 28 28/2/95, p. 20.
193   Ibid, p. 22.
194   History of 5th division in Ireland, Papers of Lt General Sir Hugh Jeudwine, IWM 72/82/2.
195   For a detailed account of the three trips that he made to Dublin. See Foy, M. T., *Michael Collin's Intelligence War* (Stroud: Sutton Publishing, 2006), 70–76.
196   Witness Statement by Eamonn Broy, No. 1280 Bureau of Military Affairs, Military Archives Cathal Brugha Barracks, Dublin.

A Slow Burning Fuse 51

organisation were used for these three functions. There was an oblique reference to the method used to uncover Jack Byrnes: 'The chief method of detecting our agents was simple but effective. When an agent became suspect, false information was given to him and if any action ensued by the Crown Forces he was immediately murdered. The murder of an agent employed by Scotland House ... were examples of this form of counter espionage'.[197]

Another pivotal network was the acquisition of arms and ammunition. As the campaign developed from 1919 to 1921 supplies would be sourced both domestically and internationally. In terms of overseas supplies, there were both successes and failures. The willingness of Sinn Fein to co-operate with other revolutionary organisations, such as the Bolsheviks, led to a well-organised attempt to smuggle arms into Ireland. It was foiled by the American authorities: 'A Treaty was made with Russia, and the Irish Republic was the first of all the nations to recognise the Soviet Republic. Running parallel with the Treaty, there was an arrangement made to import from Russia 50,000 rifles that the Russians were putting at our disposal. All the arrangements were in the hands of Dr McCarten, Joe McGarrity and Harry Boland. The function of my company was to handle these guns when they would arrive, but unfortunately, the American authorities got information of them, which they handed over to Great Britain'.[198] The Ballina businessman Moylett was responsible for smuggling 104 cases of Thompson sub-machine guns into Ireland. They arrived from the United States and were landed in Kerry in August 1921, three weeks after Sinn Fein signed an armed truce with the British Government.[199]

The Irish Volunteers identified British Army personnel who were willing to sell their weapons. The first instance occurred in August 1919. It was organised by Brian Holohan, who was employed as a civilian by the War Office as the superintendent of all Officers' Messes in Dublin.

---

197 Op cit, p. 44.
198 Patrick Moylett, Witness Statement, No. 767 of Military History, Cathal Bruga Barracks, Dublin.
199 Ibid.

He was also a member of the IRB, and the first Intelligence Officer that the Irish Volunteers had. Holohan also supplied the Irish Volunteers with the latest copies of British Army instructional manuals, and copies of the King's rules and regulations.

The contact for the arms was a British Army Quartermaster based in Dublin. The first sale was substantial. The weapons and ammunition were sold for a modest price: 'Altogether we got 100 guns and approximately 5,000 rounds of ammunition, and I think it was £90[200] we paid. The result of the deal was that we got more ammunition than we expected and we paid approximately £10 less than was originally bargained for'.[201] These weapons stayed in circulation for the entire length of the rebellion, and one was used for a high-profile murder: 'Sometime after the Squad was formed we presented Michael Collins with one of the guns, and it was one of those guns that shot Redmond.[202] Most of these guns eventually drifted to the country, at the request of Dick McKee or Michael Collins or some of the Headquarters staff'.[203] Brian Holohan continued to procure and supply arms and ammunition to the Irish Volunteers. He also supplied intelligence up to July 1921.

Earlier in 1919, on the 20th March, the Irish Volunteers used another method that would become common in the campaign, they raided for arms.[204] The first instance of this was an attack on the military arsenal at RAF Collinstown, four miles north of Dublin. Five of the twelve republicans involved were working as contractors at the facility before the raid, and their knowledge of the facility and inside preparations enabled

---

200   That is £4,682.05 in today's money. Source: Bank of England website.
201   O'Daly, P., Witness Statement No. 387, Bureau of Military History, Cathal Bruga Barracks, Dublin.
202   Assistant Commissioner William Redmond from Belfast was appointed on the 1st January 1920 to revitalise G division. He was murdered by O'Daly on 21st January 1920 outside the Standard Hotel in Dublin.
203   O'Daly, P., Witness Statement No. 387, Bureau of Military History, Cathal Bruga Barracks, Dublin.
204   By the beginning of the truce in July 1921 there had been a total of 3,218 raids for arms. See Townshend, C., *The British Campaign in Ireland* (Oxford: Oxford University Press, 1975), 214.

it to take place. 'GHQ' approved the raid and supplied khaki uniforms and masks to disguise the Irish Volunteers. The raid netted the IRA an enormous haul, consisting of seventy-five rifles with bayonets and 5,000 rounds of ammunition. Patrick Houlihan, who planned the raid, admitted the military authorities suspected some of the contractors had been involved. As a consequence, they all lost their jobs shortly after.

Another critical network set up during this period were premises from where the illegal Dail and the Irish Volunteers could operate from. All the leases were obtained by Michael Noyk, a Jewish solicitor and a law graduate of Trinity College Dublin. He was able to obtain offices at several different locations in Dublin.[205] In the St Andrew Street premises, there was a secret room built into the wall where papers could be kept. Premises in Crow Street, Dublin were the home of the 'Intelligence Department' of the Irish Volunteers and functioned under the cover name of the 'Irish Products Company'. It was located a mere 200 yards from the entrance of Dublin Castle. Noyk used deception and greed as his weapons: 'I had to resort to all kinds of ruses and, in particular, to appeal to the greed of the various owners, by stating that I would be prepared to pay 6-, or 12-months' rent, in advance. 'I always had to give the names of certain people in the Movement who were prepared to lend their names as tenants, and in other cases, to invent names'.[206] The ability to invent appropriate names helped embed this network. A good example was securing an agreement for rooms tenanted by 'Unionist solicitors' James Henry & Son. The ruse that was used for this agreement was to invent a respectable but false double-barrelled name of Llewelyn-Davis. It had the desired effect of securing the premises.

The final network was finance. Three months after the Unilateral Declaration of Independence, Michael Collins was appointed 'Minister of Finance' on 2nd April 1919, and he was authorised to use money that had been raised initially to fight an anti-conscription campaign. These funds

---

205 They were at: 22 and 29 Mary Street, 3 St. Andrew Street, Henry Street, 29 Wicklow Street, Molesworth Street, and 3 Crow Street.
206 Noyk, M., Witness Statement No. 707, Bureau of Military History, Cathal Bruga Barracks, Dublin.

were known as 'Republican Bonds'. On the 19th June 1919, a decision was made to raise what became known as the First Dail Loan. It was divided into two parts. There was what was known as the Internal Loan which was raised in Ireland. The target was for a sum of £500,000. The actual amount raised was £375,000.[207] The second was called the External Loan and was raised in the United States and Argentina. The initial target was for $1.25 million. However, the external limit was subsequently increased in August to $25 million. The money raised was held in bank accounts in Ireland and the United States and was controlled by four trustees: Eamon de Valera, Michael Fogarty, the Roman Catholic Bishop of Killaloe and James O'Mara.[208] By the time of the succession of the south of Ireland from the United Kingdom on the 6th December 1921 a total of $2,500,000[209] had reached the accounts of the Irish Republican movement out of a total of $5,800,000 that had been raised[210] in the United States.

The reimbursement of these funds was complex. It was not until 1925 that the Irish Free State Courts released the Dail funds in Irish bank accounts to the Free State Executive Council. This institution undertook the task to redeem the bonds. The Dail funds remaining in the United States became the subject of a court ruling in the Supreme Court of New York in 1927. The ruling was that the remaining money $3,300,000, should be returned to subscribers, 'as the purpose for which the moneys were subscribed by the so-called bondholders, that is, the establishment of a Republic of Ireland free and independent of any allegiance to Great Britain, was never accomplished'. It was not until 1936 that repayment was completed by the Irish government.

---

207 Today that would be worth £19,508,561 million pounds. Bank of England website.
208 James O'Mara was a businessman and MP for the Irish Parliamentary Party between 1900–1907. In 1918 he was Sinn Fein Director of Finance and a Sinn Fein MP for Kilkenny South. He resigned from both posts in 1921 after a disagreement with de Valera.
209 Today that would be worth $32,489,750 dollars. Bank of England website.
210 For a detailed account of how the Irish Republican Movement raised money for their insurgency see: Adams, R. J. C., Shadow of a taxman; how, and by whom, was the Republican government financed in the Irish War of Independence, PhD thesis (University of Oxford, 2018).

de Valera abused his position as a trustee of these funds to cross-finance the Russian Bolsheviks. In 1958 an American diplomat with the help of Sean MacEoin a former Irish Minister of Defence[211] was able to confirm what had happened: 'While Mr De Valera was in the United States in 1920, a fugitive from the British and raising funds to prosecute the war of independence, he was approached by members of a Bolshevik delegation, apparently a purchasing commission of some kind ... De Valera loaned the Soviet delegation 50,000 American dollars and received in trust a quantity of the "bloodstained Tsar's jewels". MacEoin said there could be no doubt that this transaction took place since he personally examined and handled the Russian jewels when he was a member of the Inter-party government in 1948. He stated that the jewels were returned to the Soviet Embassy in London in 1950 or 1951 and that the equivalent amount of American dollars was deposited into the account of the Irish government'.[212]

Conclusions

In answer to the first question posed at the beginning of this chapter: there is evidence, of a set of premises and beliefs about politics being applied to the choices of action with respect to the emerging insurgency by the British policy elite. The need for what Sonderland identified[213] as the degree of vigour, determination and skill which the incumbent regime acts to defend itself, both politically and militarily was completely absent. The reluctant manner in which the British state defended its legitimacy and social authority in Ireland despite a declaration of UDI was

---

211   He was Irish Minister of Defence from 1954 to 1957.
212   Despatch from the US Embassy, Dublin, to the Department of State, Washington, 31 December 1958, 740 A 00/12-3158, National Archives, Washington, DC.
213   See Chapter 1, p. 1.

underlined by the fact that it took the intervention of King George V to force a British government to declare the Dail an illegal organisation.

Second, the decision of British policy makers to sanction the release of prisoners who had taken part in an armed rebellion with no conditions placed on their future behaviour was, it can be argued, evidence of these operational codes. In particular, the decision to declare an amnesty for those men held in Frongoch on the 21st December 1916.

Finally, the release of 120 prisoners prior to the Irish Convention failed to facilitate its success. This error was compounded a decision by the British Cabinet on 19th February 1919 to the 'gradual and unostentatious' release of the imprisoned Sinn Fein MPs.[214] In addition, a decision was made by the Attorney General of Ireland to drop the case against Michael Collins in July 1919. All these choices underline the proclivity of policymakers to pursue separate political initiatives with inconsistent results.

The British Army in this period 1916–1919 regarded Ireland as a vital recruiting and training ground. It also recognised the changing character of the threat posed by Sinn Fein, evolving from one of open rebellion to guerrilla warfare. The Record of the Rebellion was candid about the failures of judgement, and resource problems that afflicted the army during this period. Regret was expressed of the missed opportunity to create an intelligence branch after the 1916 rebellion, and to evaluate the military possibilities of the Sinn Fein movement. These failures had consequences. It explains the relative slowness of the army in building up an intelligence organisation that was independent of both the DMP and the RIC.

For two years, the demands of Western Front restricted the intelligence resources that could be allocated to Ireland. This was combined with an institutional assumption about the provision of intelligence being a matter for the police. There were some inroads to the networks of the Irish Volunteers, but not enough to subvert or divert their ability to launch attacks on the police and to a lesser extent, the army. From January 1919 to June 1920, 55 members of the police were murdered. This was in addition to five soldiers and fifteen civilians.[215]

---

214 See CAB 23/9, Quoted in Townshend, C., The British Campaign in Ireland (Oxford: Oxford University Press, 1975), 15.
215 Op cit, p. 214.

A Slow Burning Fuse 57

The Irish Republican movement evolved during this period. It registered a number of successes. It was able to forge a political and military alliance at the Sinn Fein Convention of 1917. The new political objective was the succession of the whole of Ireland from the rest of the United Kingdom. British policymakers regarded the Irish Republic as a fever dream endorsed by a small minority, and it did not constitute the beliefs of the Irish population as a whole. The key to this new alliance was the language in which it couched its objectives: 'its romantic vagueness which detached it sufficiently from practical detail to allow it to secure the adherence of many groups whose real aims and approaches were significantly different'.[216] Tucked in behind this was the willingness to commit murder against the police and any civilians, catholic or protestant, who got in the way. The objective of an independent Ireland may have been conveniently vague, but it was unconditional and had no democratic consent.

Second, what was underestimated, or not known to British intelligence in sufficient detail, was the character and extent of the operational networks Collins had succeeded in setting up by the end of 1919. A lack of an army intelligence branch in Ireland and a calculated onslaught on the RIC and G division of the DMP, meant that Collins was able to build operational networks with relative impunity.

Despite these failings, the DMP and the RIC obtained and submitted detailed intelligence on Irish Republican leaders like Michael Collins. Furthermore, there was initial success in breaching the counter-intelligence structure of the Irish Volunteers. Sir Basil Thompson's agent Jack Byrnes correctly identified Michael Collins as the leader of the Irish Volunteers and accurately assessed his role in the organisation. In particular, his role of ordering murders as opposed to participating in them.

Two issues will be the focus of the next chapter. The persistence of the operating codes in precluding an integrated political–military approach to the insurgency. Second, how quickly did the army and the police construct a functioning intelligence community that encapsulated both a process and product, and could in turn produce actionable intelligence useable at the tactical and operational levels?

216   Op cit, p. 60.

CHAPTER 3

Fire and Water: Fighting an Insurgency

Introduction

The ability of British policy makers to respond to the challenge the Irish Volunteers presented was dependent on two things: understanding the nature of the conflict they were engaged in; and making a conscious choice to confront the challenge. The requirement for this normative behaviour has been set out by the strategist Colin Gray: 'No government is willingly going to concede combatant status to its domestic enemies, thereby gratuitously according them political legitimacy. It has been a cardinal principle of the international political system since the middle of the seventeenth century that the state should have a monopoly on the legitimate use of force ... So, for political reasons, the state must treat the domestic exponents of irregular violence as criminals'.[217]

Countering an insurgency is no great mystery. The generic principles are widely known. There are eight in number: legitimacy, unity of effort, political primacy, understanding the environment, intelligence as the driver of operations, isolating insurgents from their support, security under the rule of the law, and finally, long-term commitment.[218] An important question this chapter will address is the extent to which the British Army fought a campaign whereby these principles were continually compromised by a set of operational codes adhered to by the policy elite concerning choices of action?

---

217 Gray, C. S., *War, Peace and International Relations* (Abingdon: Routledge, 2012), 287.
218 Cohen, E., Crane, C., Horvath, J., Nagl, J., *Principles, Imperatives, and Paradoxes of Counterinsurgency*, Military Affairs, March–April 2006, p. 49–53.

Any insurgency is a struggle for legitimacy, and maintenance of the belief that the existing political institutions are the most suitable for a particular society. Why was Lloyd George's government unwilling to systematically engage, counter, and challenge the insurgents' narrative at the strategic level? An answer to this question starts with the role and activities of Alfred Cope. Officially he was an Assistant Under Secretary at Dublin Castle. As stated in the preface of this book[219] he was the undeclared special representative of the British Cabinet.[220] This title needs qualification; he did not act on behalf of that collective body, although he reported to it a number of times. The patronage of Lloyd George sent Cope to Ireland and kept him there. The key question about Cope is the one that was posed earlier[221]: was he Lloyd George's 'dirty man' in Ireland?

Did he purposely undermine the counter-insurgency efforts of both the Army and the two police forces? Major General Simpson highlighted the consequences of awarding insurgents' political legitimacy, and the failure to achieve unity of effort: 'if the civic power does not follow the policy that resort to force must be stopped promptly and decisively, then there can never be successful coordination, because there never can be unity of purpose. Neither the police nor the military part of British rule will willingly be used as dogs in a dog-fight, not to win, but to produce concessions to those who kill their friends'.[222] Did Cope's actions result in the British Army and the RIC being used as dogs in a dog fight?

In the five volumes of the Record of the Rebellion it is impossible to find any acknowledgement a unity of effort was achieved. In volume one there was recognition of the extent to which political choices impacted the campaign: 'It may be claimed that in a record of military activities reference to political aspects and actions are out of place. It is

---

219 See p. 8.
220 The evidence that confirms this secret role can be found in James J. O'Connor, Witness Statement 1214, Bureau of Military History, Cathal Brugha Barracks, Dublin.
221 See Chapter 1, p. 14.
222 Simpson, H. J., *British Rule and Rebellion* (London: W. Blackwood, 1938), 36.

Fire and Water: Fighting an Insurgency

however, pointed out that in the case of Ireland under review political and military activities were so closely interwoven that it is impossible to disentangle them'.[223]

The Record of the Rebellion was clear about the tactics Sinn Fein used to challenge British legitimacy and social authority. First they attacked the two police forces, the Royal Irish Constabulary and the Dublin Metropolitan Police. Secondly, they intimidated the civilian population. This is done by murdering policemen and the systematic terrorising of people into silence. This led the government to conclude that the two police forces could no longer cope, and it was necessary for the Army to be called upon to assist. The Irish journalist Kevin Myers has captured the scale of the onslaught against the RIC: 'The RIC had a strength of 9,400 in 1919, in the following 3 years prompted by a twin campaign of terror and boycott, nearly 7,500 men – about 80 per cent resigned. Proper policing ceased throughout much of Ireland'.[224] From the 1st of January 1919 to 11th July 1921, 405 were killed and 682 wounded.[225]

Success and Appeasement – January To May 1920

The historian Peter Hart summarised the first five months of the campaign: 'The army's first offensive in the winter and spring of 1920 was a clear and clean success'.[226] This raises two questions. Why was it a success? What were the reasons for it not being followed up? The answers to these questions were only partly addressed in the Record of the Rebellion.

---

223 Record of the Rebellion, (Vol. 1), A3. Papers of lt Gen Sir Hugh Jeudwine IWM 72/82/2.
224 K. Myers, An Irishman's Diary, Irish Times, 16th September 2003.
225 Record of the Rebellion (Vol. I), p. 56.
226 Hart, P., *British Intelligence in Ireland 1920–1921* (Cork: Cork University Press, 2002), 10.

The legal basis for the army being called upon to support the two beleaguered police forces was initially framed to avoid the use of Martial Law: 'Law officers of the Crown asserted that the powers existing under the Defence of the Realm Act provided all that was necessary and that such powers could be administered by the Competent Military Authority'.[227] Volume three of the Record of the Rebellion provided an answer to the first puzzle: 'The amendment to Regulation 14B had placed a powerful weapon in the hands of the Irish Executive. At the beginning of the year 1920, it was determined to make use of it, and preparations were begun for an offensive on a very comprehensive scale. The country was to be searched for arms and ammunition. For these purposes the police forces were placed under the orders of the GOC – in C'.[228] There was to be a transfer of the powers previously vested in the police and magistrates. It entailed instituting and organising actions against perpetrators of 'outrage and the lawlessness'. In addition, the competent military authority was empowered to search individuals and buildings for arms, explosives and seditious literature. Clearly at this point there was the beginning of a coherent response to this challenge of legitimacy and social authority.

However, the application of this new legal framework was erratic. On the 8th January 1920 authority was given to Divisional GOCs to carry out the arrest of individuals as soon as the warrants were received. The date on which the initial arrests were to be made was the night of the 23rd of January and the morning of the 24th January. However, on the 21st January the Government decided the proposed actions based on this procedure were to be suspended. It was then decided that no warrants would be issued prior to arrest, but the people suspected of complicity in outrages were to be arrested under Defence of the Realm Regulations and detained under a 'Detention Order'. Furthermore, if evidence was forthcoming against those people who were arrested then they would be

---

227 Op cit, p. 5.
228 Record of the Rebellion (Vol. 3), p. 12.

Fire and Water: Fighting an Insurgency 63

dealt with by the civil powers. The night of the 30th/31st January 1920 was fixed for the start of this new procedure.

These arrests were a product of exploitable intelligence. The Record of the Rebellion was clear about the impact: 'considerable alarm was caused amongst leading rebels who had imagined that they were working for Sinn Fein under impenetrable camouflage'.[229]

Even more important was the positive effect these arrests had on the civilian population. The centre of gravity in any counter-insurgency campaign is the reassurance and continued security of civilians: 'The immediate result of the arrests was a decrease in the number of outrages for a short period, and loyal people, thinking that a strong line was to be taken with rebellion and outrage, began to take heart, and information concerning outrages began to come in rather more freely'.[230] This centre of gravity had the potential to erode the ability of the Irish Volunteers to maintain the tempo of their insurgency.

Intelligence collected was a result of planned searches by the Army and police. For example, a Sinn Fein Office in Dublin was targeted at the end of February 1920. The papers seized contained the receipts for *An T Oglac*, the in-house journal of the IRA, it contained the names of a number of IRA brigade and battalion commandants and their staffs in each county of Ireland.[231] The scale of this success is set out in the Record of the Rebellion. It represented the highest number ever arrested, in terms of senior rank, for the whole campaign. The numbers up to the 14th April 1920 were:

> Brigade commandants 27.
> Brigade staff 13.
> Battalion commandants 16.
> Battalion officers 116.
> Others prominent officers 145.

229 Op cit, Vol. 1, p. 7.
230 Op cit, Vol. 1, p. 8.
231 Op cit, Vol. 2, p. 8.

The command network of the Irish Volunteers was seriously disrupted. The Record of the Rebellion cited evidence from a captured copy of An T Oglac: 'In some area's things are in a decidedly unsatisfactory condition. It is only fair to remember that many districts have been hard hit through capture of their best officers by the enemy .....'.[232]

The army's initial approach to intelligence was a product of its recent experience of large-scale conventional war. The assumption was 'one's opponents' order of battle must be the principal objective of intelligence'. This reflected an insufficiently correct understanding of the intelligence requirements of an insurgency. Brigadier Winter[233] demonstrated a more nuanced understanding: 'one fact is clear and that is, a war-time Intelligence system cannot be employed in dealing with the class of political crime now under consideration. The information required by the War Office Intelligence Service is, to a great extent, of a different nature to that required under the circumstances under discussion ... the plans and intentions of an underground organisation, information as to acts of violence committed by individual assassins, and even the order of battle of improvised guerrillas dressed in the garb of peasantry cannot be obtained by onlookers or by the ordinary commercial traveller'.[234] One response was a reorganisation of the Army's intelligence staff in early 1920 to enhance the process of intelligence: 'An officer was appointed to deal with the records of each divisional area and ensure that the now greatly enlarged registry and card index at GHQ contained all available information about IRA personal and organisation'.[235] The development and adjustment of the army's intelligence organisation was a continual process throughout the campaign. This was a sign of strength not weakness.[236]

---

232 Op cit, Vol. 1, p. 11.
233 Brigadier Ormonde Winter served as Head of the Combined Intelligence Service in Ireland from May 1920 to July 1921.
234 A Report on the Intelligence of the Chief of Police from May 1920 to July 1921, National Archives, CO904/156B, p. 3–4.
235 Op cit, Vol. 2, p. 9.
236 In Vol. II of the Record of the Rebellion there are detailed accounts of these changes. They are given on pages 16–22.

Fire and Water: Fighting an Insurgency 65

By the end of April, 241 known and suspected members of the Irish Volunteers had been interned in English prisons. The response from the insurgents was not long in coming. It took the form of a general hunger strike amongst untried Sinn Fein prisoners. It started in Cork and spread to Mountjoy prison in Dublin, and Wormwoods Scrubs and Brixton prisons in London. Prisoners in Galway and Belfast joined in as well.

A number of prisoners had been convicted under the Defence of the Realm Act, others were awaiting trial. They demanded 'political treatment'. This was supported by street demonstrations that took place in Dublin on the 12th April and was followed by a 1-day strike in Dublin on the 13th April. The Record of the Rebellion was clear about where responsibility lay for the subsequent turn of events: 'The claim of the prisoners that they were imprisoned without any charge being brought against them created a situation of which newspapers took the fullest advantage. The Government gave in'.[237] Between the 14th and 17th April, 224 prisoners were released on parole from Irish prisons, including 16 sentenced for illegal possession of arms.[238] The Viceroy, Field Marshal Lord French ordered these releases. General Macready, the new GOC for Ireland and Thomas Jones[239] were also involved in this decision.

The Record of the Rebellion described it as: 'a severe blow to Intelligence in Ireland. It decreased still further the *moral* of the R.I.C. and correspondingly raised that of the IRA, whose organisation was expanded and improved'.[240] The outgoing Commander-in-Chief, Lieutenant General Sir Frederick Shaw, recognised the need of a counter-narrative to Irish Republicanism: 'it is interesting to note that the last document signed by the retiring Commander-In-Chief was an appeal to the Lord Lieutenant for greater publicity'.[241] This shortcoming was never

---

237 Record of the Rebellion, Vol. III, p. 13.
238 Ibid, p. 13.
239 Thomas Jones was Deputy Secretary to the Cabinet under Lloyd George. See Thomas Jones, Whitehall Diary, Vol. 3, Ireland 1918–1925, K. Middlemas ed. (Oxford: Oxford University Press, 1971), 16.
240 Op cit, Vol. 2, p. 8.
241 Op cit, Vol. 1, p. 11.

systematically addressed. Brigadier Winter credited this inaction to the choices of action made from 1916 onwards: 'it must be remembered; a process of arrest and release had been continuous since 1916 – struck a deep note of discouragement and despondency in all concerned'.[242]

This capitulation was compounded by a second decision taken on the 3rd May 1920, to cancel the powers that had been granted to the army in January 1920. The Competent Military Authority enabled the army search individuals and homes for arms and arrest people committing offences. The security forces were now thrown back on the defensive. In particular, the army reverted to its previous role of carrying out duties in aid of the civil power. The historian Charles Townshend has commented: 'The whole policy of the first quarter of 1920 was more or less reversed'.[243] No explanation for this reversal is offered. The Record of the Rebellion recognised the consequences on the public: 'Law-abiding people recognised that the Government had receded from the strong position which it appeared to be taking up, and that, as the combined activities of troops and police had been curtailed, the domination of Sinn Fein backed by an ever increasing membership of the IRA, would be able to intimidate them into acquiescence in a political demand for which they have no particular wish, and even into open and armed hostility to the forces of law and order'.[244]

The Crown forces were thrown back on the defensive. This was combined with the capability of the Irish Volunteers, despite the arrest of a number of their senior commanders, to pace the insurgency. Central to this was the strategy of attacking small police stations. As previously stated, this had been conceived by Eamon Broy.[245] The scale of these attacks was revealed in the statistics collected and published by the Irish Office from the 1st of January 1919 to end of June 1920:[246]

---

242 Op cit, p. 9.
243 Townshend, C., *The British Campaign in Ireland 1919–1921* (Oxford: Oxford University Press, 1975), p. 77.
244 Record of the Rebellion, Vol. 1, p. 12.
245 See Chapter 2, p. 18.
246 Quoted in Townshend, C., *The British Campaign in Ireland 1919–1921* (Oxford: Oxford University Press, 1975), 214.

Vacated RIC barracks destroyed 343
Occupied RIC barracks destroyed 12
Occupied RIC barracks damaged 24

During this period fifty-five policemen and five members of the Army were murdered.

The reversal of policy can only be understood by a focus on the engine room of government – the civil service. London based civil servants began to take an active role in setting a new policy. This sense of change was described by George Chester Duggan.[247] He discerned a 'policy of conciliation was gathering strength'. Sir John Taylor, Assistant Under Secretary was over-ruled on the issue of the hunger-striking prisoners. The Prime Minister Lloyd George, despite being preoccupied with the negotiations at Versailles, moved to bring the Irish Executive under London's control. The justification for this change was the timeless excuse of the need for institutional reform. This was quickly given expression by new military and political appointments.

The new GOC for Ireland General Sir Nevil Macready replaced Lieutenant General Sir Frederick Shaw in March 1920. Macready's appointment was a personal choice by Lloyd George.[248] The Prime Minister made it clear what his strategic objective should be: 'bring about a better feeling between the authorities at the Castle and De Valera's followers'.[249] On his arrival in Ireland, Macready submitted a series of reports that made an issue of the existing bureaucracy: 'administrative chaos seems to reign here, where the machine was hopelessly out of

---

247 He was Assistant Under Secretary from 1919 to 1922.
248 Macready was favoured over other candidates for the post because he was liked by Lloyd George and was deemed to have a right experience. He: had made his mark as Adjutant General in the last two years of the war, and as Commissioner of the London Metropolitan Police, where had had dealt with the police strike of 1919. His career had embraced the command of troops in South Wales at the time of Tonypandy, as well as in Belfast during the crisis of 1914 Townshend, C., *The British Campaign in Ireland 1919–1921* (Oxford: Oxford University Press, 1975), 74.
249 General Sir Neville Macready, *Annals of an Active Life*, London: 1923, p. 426.

gear'.[250] Macready identified the perilous state of the two police forces. He concluded the effectiveness of 'G' division had been blunted by what he described as systematic murder, and the RIC was in a state of disintegration.[251] Two months later, Macready had offered little by way of a concrete plan apart from a vague demand for the need to increase the army's mobility. The Chief of the Imperial General Staff, Field Marshal Sir Henry Wilson was less than impressed: 'A vain ass like Macready goes over to Ireland and in a week thinks he can solve the Irish problem'.[252]

At the end of March, Sir Hamar Greenwood was appointed Chief Secretary for Ireland. He had been a junior minister in Lloyd George's Coalition Government. Managing the reform was the responsibility of Sir Warren Fisher, the Head of the Civil Service, and Permanent Secretary at HM Treasury. On the 18th April he commissioned a report examining the functioning of Dublin Castle. Fisher arrived in Dublin on the 4th May with a two-man team: R. E. Harwood from the Treasury and Alfred Cope listed as being with the Ministry of Pensions. The main focus was the Chief Secretary's office. Fisher's report was completed on 12th May. In addition, Cope and Harwood submitted their own reports on the same date.[253]

An additional memorandum was submitted by Fisher on the 15th May and circulated to both the Chancellor of the Exchequer and the Prime Minister. The activities of the army were framed in a negative light. It was a harbinger of things to come. Underpinning all this was an assumption that ran like a golden thread: there existed a moderate faction of the Irish Republican movement susceptible to a transactional negotiation. There was no appreciation that Michael Collins's IRB forward policy was firmly in control. There had been committed what Fisher

---

250 Quoted in O'Halpin, E., *Head of the Civil Service, A Study of Sir Warren Fisher* (London: Routledge, 1989), 85.
251 Macready, op cit, p. 435.
252 Wilson's diary, 10 May 1920, quoted in Townshend, C., *The British Campaign in Ireland 1919–1921* (Oxford: Oxford University Press, 1975), 84.
253 See, M. Hopkinson, ed., *The Last Days of Dublin Castle* (Dublin: Irish Academic Press, 1999), 237.

described as: 'Acts of "stupid violence" by government forces under the Defence of the Realm Act were calculated to drive to extremism the moderate elements of Sinn Fein; and the indescribable folly of proscribing Sinn Fein as a political creed'.[254]

These reports provided the rationale for at least a dozen new civil service appointments. The Under Secretary Sir Ian Macpherson was replaced by Sir John Anderson then Chairman of the Board of Inland Revenue. Alfred Cope was appointed Assistant Under Secretary along with Mark Sturgis from the Treasury.[255] Anderson arrived in Dublin on 22nd of May 1920 according to Charles Townshend. By contrast Tim Pat Coogan claimed that many of these new appointments were in place by April 1920.[256] George Chester Duggan described the process of change: 'In the month of May the Controlling Civil Service personnel at the Castle underwent a complete change. Some avant couriers of the new regime appeared for a few days to spy out the land and then vanished'.[257] These newly appointed civil servants shaped and drove policy between 1920 and 1922. The British Cabinet only sketched in the barest outline the policy in Ireland. As a consequence, there emerged 'almost autocratic power in the hands of civil servants'. Critically they eschewed any commitment to unity of effort. They 'carried matters to the appointed end which was to extricate England from Ireland'. Political stage management was their critical function: 'it was they who filled the picture, who decided what was to its foreground and background, what figures sinister, commonplace or mystical were to fill the canvas'.[258]

---

[254] Further memorandum by Sir Warren Fisher to the Chancellor of the Exchequer, Lord Privy Seal and Prime Minister, 15th May 1920, HLRO Lloyd George papers F31/1/33. Quoted in Mc Colgan, J., *British Policy and Irish Administration* (London: George Allen and Unwin, 1983), 9.

[255] Sturgis was not gazetted for two years for fear of wounding Cope's sensibilities. See Townshend, C., *The British Campaign in Ireland, 1919–1921*. (Oxford: Oxford University Press, 1975), 80.

[256] Coogan, T. P., *Michael Collins* (New York: Palgrave, 1990), 125.

[257] George Chester Duggan WS 1099, Bureau of Military History, Cathal Brugha Barracks, Dublin.

[258] Ibid.

Alfred Cope's willingness to undermine the existing legal procedures can be discerned from a rare public address given in 1927. He was reported as stating: 'One of the first things he (Sir Alfred) noticed on his arrival in Ireland was the very large number of men awaiting trial, so he proceeded to expedite matters which he thought were improper. He made a move to get them treated on the same lines as those in his own country'.[259] If Coogan's assertion of Cope's April arrival date is correct, then it points to his direct involvement in the decision to parole prisoners. The unfolding of events can only be fully understood by examining his personality and the objectives he pursued on behalf of Lloyd George.

Alfred Cope – 'A Dirty Man in Ireland'

Uncovering evidence about Cope's secret activities and understanding the effect he had presents an empirical and analytical challenge. The current accepted judgements are partial. The historian Michael Foot, in the Dictionary of National Biography,[260] alluded to Cope's relationship with the leaders of the insurgency, yet failed to identify Cope's appointment was as a special representative of the British Cabinet: 'After several false starts, he secured the confidence of the principal Irish revolutionary leaders, Michael Collins, Arthur Griffith and Eamon de Valera, in his own good faith, while remaining perfectly loyal to the crown…and

---

259 Lessons of the Irish Rebellion, an address given by Alfred Cope to the Tabernacle Chapel, Cwmgorse. Reported in The Amman Valley Chronicle and East Carmarthen News, 10th March 1927.
260 Alfred William Cope was born in 1877 and entered government service as a boy clerk. He joined the detective branch of the department of customs and excise in 1896; and was made a preventative inspector in 1908. His energy and intelligence soon made him head of the branch in London and he spent ten adventurous years pursuing smugglers and illicit distillers, especially in the docklands. Foot, M. R. D., *Dictionary of National Biography 1951–1960* (Oxford: Oxford University Press, 1971), 251.

Fire and Water: Fighting an Insurgency

he played a major part in securing the truce of 11 July 1921'.[261] Foot does acknowledge the patronage of Lloyd George: 'Ostensibly his task was to preserve civil order through the Royal Irish Constabulary; in fact he had already been charged by Lloyd George with the task of sounding out Sinn Fein opinion about the possibilities of a truce in the Anglo-Irish war'.[262] Hopkinson endorsed Foot's judgement[263] but underlined the challenge of achieving a comprehensive understanding of Cope's activities: 'The secretive character of Cope's work and the absence of personal papers make him a tantalisingly enigmatic figure'.[264] The diaries of Mark Sturgis[265] provide only a partial understanding.

Macready's pen portrait of Cope was instructive: 'a tireless worker, highly strung, a firm believer in self-government for Ireland ... and feverishly anxious to do all in his power, even at the risk of his life, to ensure the success of Mr Lloyd George's policy'.[266] Hopkinson has argued Macready differed little from the policy of conciliation the newly appointed civil servants were aiming to enact. However, General Macready relations with these new appointments were not fluent: 'he did not have easy relations with them due it seems to his self-importance and resentment of political interference with the military. In particular he had little rapport with Cope'.[267] Macready's understanding of Cope's relationship with

261   Ibid, p. 252.
262   Ibid, p. 252.
263   'He became, probably at Lloyd George's wish, the main British contact with Sinn Fein and the IRA and set up a host of peace initiatives, nervy and highly strung by temperament, Cope was intensely hard working but seemed unable to delegate'. See Hopkinson, M., ed., *The Last Days of Dublin Castle, The Diaries of Mark Sturgis* (Dublin: Irish Academic Press, 1998), 5–6.
264   Ibid, p. 6.
265   Mark Sturgis was a British civil servant from the Treasury who was appointed joint Assistant Secretary along with Cope in May 1920. Interestingly he was not gazetted in that position until after the truce in July 1921. His diaries which he kept of this period were published in 1998. However, they omitted any specific references to Cope's contacts to the leaders of Sinn Fein.
266   Macready, N., *Annals of an Active Life* (Vol. 2) (London: Hutchinson & Co, 1926) 492–493.
267   Op cit, p. 4.

Sinn Fein was insightful: 'He was *persona grata* with the leaders of the rebellion, in whom he had a belief that was pathetic as, in my opinion, it was misplaced'.[268]

George Chester Duggan provided a granular picture of Cope, and his attitudes towards the army: 'A detective by his training in the Customs and by instinct, he seemed at first sight a curious choice for the post. But he was a man who revelled in work, who was never happier than when he held a dozen threads in his hand, and in the tangled web of Irish politics there were threads enough and to spare … His career in Ireland was a long struggle against militarism, which sought to impose itself more and more on the life of the country. He endeavoured by every means to keep that spirit out of the police'.[269] This antipathy was fused with a personality that was both dysfunctional and arrogant: 'Obstructive tactics galvanised him into a veritable rage of activity. He had no respect for age or experience as such, if their views ran counter to his own. On occasions such as these his tone would become overbearing, his choice of language something not often heard in the passionless calm of Government offices'.[270]

In terms of British society in the 1920s, Cope was an outsider. W. E. Wylie,[271] the legal adviser in Dublin Castle, asked Sturgis how he Anderson and Cope had arrived together in such high positions. Sturgis responded with the following analogy: 'Anderson came in through the front door, Cope via the back door, and himself through the drawing-room window'.[272] Sturgis described him as, 'a most interesting unique creature and was at one time an Excise Detective'. Cope's background was an advantage given his remit. He was able to mix with the predominantly working-class and lower-middle-class leaders of Sinn Fein. Sturgis,

---

268 Macready, N., *Annals of an Active Life* (Vol. 2) (London: Hutchinson, 1924) 493.
269 George Chester Duggan W. S. 1099, Bureau of Military History, Cathal Brugha Barracks, Dublin.
270 Ibid.
271 See O'Broin, L., *W. E. Wylie and the Irish Revolution 1916–1923* (Dublin: Gill & Macmillan, 1989).
272 Quoted in Hopkinson, M., *The Last Days of Dublin Castle* (Cork: Irish Academic Press, 1999), 6.

with his Eton and Oxford background, would have been either unable or unwilling to do so.

He ignored the restrictions that applied to other senior civil servants. This came to a head one month after the armed truce in August 1921. At the Royal Dublin Horseshow Cope avoided the Royal Box where most of the senior Castle officials gathered. Instead, he flaunted relationships that had until very recently been kept secret. Strugis commented: 'he goes "down the drain" not only for business but for pleasure, spends most of his evenings with Shinns of various sorts, and seems to dislike all other society. *They* remember, if he seems to forget sometimes, that he is a highly placed British official with much of the dignity of England in his hands, and I worry sometimes that his sympathy will encourage them to think they can get through him all they ask'.[273]

Cope terminated the appointments of civil servants he deemed too Unionist: 'On his appointment at Dublin Castle, Cope dismissed a number of civil servants known to be prejudiced against Sinn Fein'.[274] Two of the civil servants can be identified as Samuel Watt and Maurice Headlam.[275] The latter published an account of how Cope engineered his removal. Initially his post of Treasury Remembrancer was to be taken over by the new Under Secretary, Sir John Anderson. He then found out that a former junior of the Treasury was to be brought back to the civil service to do his job at Dublin Castle. While being 'much annoyed', he correctly anticipated the consequences: 'I was thankful not to be associated in any way with the policy of surrender to Sinn Fein which I clearly foresaw, though not the extent of that surrender'.[276]

---

273 Sturgis, op cit, p. 213.
274 Jones, T., in K. Middlemas, ed., *Whitehall Diary* (Vol. 3), (London: Oxford University Press, 1971), 25.
275 See McColgan, J., *British Policy and the Irish Administration 1920–1922* (London: George Allen and Unwin, 1983) 11.
276 Headlam, M., *Irish Reminiscences* (London: Robert Hales, 1947), 216–217.

Alfred Cope and the Intelligence Machine

The Record of the Rebellion could make no reference to Cope's relationship with the leaders of Sinn Fein. As stated in the previous chapter,[277] there was merely an acknowledgement of his appointment as an Assistant Under Secretary. This dearth of official information has been balanced by using primary material from three sources: a British army officer who served in the Special Branch, Dublin Military District; the witness statements from the Bureau of Military History and finally, the memoirs and diaries of participants on both sides. Despite this triangulation, a comprehensive account of Cope's relationship with Sinn Fein is probably not possible. However, these sources will enable the questions about Cope to be addressed. It presents a more complete picture than has hitherto been achieved.

On the 16th June 1920, Cope wrote a letter to Sir Warren Fisher stressing the need for a 'conciliatory government policy'. It was rationalised by using exaggerated language about the bureaucracy in Dublin Castle that had already been reported upon: 'The Chief Secretary's office is 1000 times worse than I imagined'.[278] There was a further attempt to drive policy at a conference held in London with Cabinet ministers on the 23rd July. Sir John Anderson, Alfred Cope, Wylie[279] and MacMahon were presented as 'experts' and proposed two policies: an end to coercion and the introduction of Dominion Home Rule.

The Commander in Chief, General Macready, displayed little inclination to question these policy proposals or engage in a debate: 'General Macready said that he was not concerned with the political situation, but he might state that he had been in touch with all sorts of opinion

---

277 See Chapter 2.
278 Extract from a letter dated 16 June 1920, enclosed in Warren Fisher to Lloyd George, 17 June 1920, HLRO, Lloyd George papers, F/17/1/2. From McColgan, J., *British Policy and the Irish Administration 1920–1922* (London: George Allen and Unwin, 1983). 15.
279 Wylie, J. O., *Lord Justice in the Government of Ireland 1909–1919*.

throughout Ireland, and that his conclusions coincided substantially with those of Mr Wylie and Mr Cope'.[280] He did read out a report from General Strickland on conditions in the south and west of Ireland. This confirmed the consequences of the policy abandoned two months ago. Sinn Fein had increased its capability, and the effectiveness of the RIC had deteriorated. Furthermore, due to the need to disperse troops and their subsequent command arrangements were becoming problematic. Most worryingly Strickland referred to a good many deserters from the British Army.

The outcome of this Cabinet conference was defined by the politics of the Coalition government Lloyd George led: 'It was clear that they would consider no settlement beyond the terms of the Government of Ireland Bill while armed opposition in Ireland remained at large'.[281] Warren Fisher advocated a policy that was the antithesis of a unity of effort, and provided a rationale for Cope's activities: 'We ought to keep in unofficial contact with them and let them know that the present Bill was not the last word and that the door was not closed'.[282]

Keeping the door open, irrespective of the human cost, was exactly what Cope had been sent to Ireland to do. The period from May to August 1920 was a regressive one for the army and police. The Record of the Rebellion showed it was a period of comparative immunity for the leaders of the insurgency, which they exploited, although a large number of them were known to the security forces. They were secure from arrest so long as they did not take part in the actual outrages.

The RIC and the Army were helped by the passing into law on the 13th August 1920 of the Restoration of Order in Ireland Act. Having been reduced to providing aid to the civil power, by early August, the Army now had the legal power to declare illegal a number of Irish Republican organisations: 'at that date the following associations had been declared

---

280 Jones, T., in K. Middlemas, ed., *Whitehall Diary* (Vol. III) (London: Oxford University Press, 1971) 25.
281 Op cit, p. 17.
282 Jones, T., in K. Middlemas, ed., *Whitehall Diary* (Vol. III) (London: Oxford University Press, 1971), 30.

unlawful and had been, in the technical language of the proclamation "suppressed": The Sinn Fein organisation and clubs; the Irish Volunteers; the Cuman-na-Ban; the Gaelic League; the Dail Eireann'.[283] This started to have results in terms of increasing the tempo[284] of counter insurgency operations. The additional power granted by ROIR soon began to have effect. The number of convictions steadily increased, running into 50–60 per week. The result of this was that the number of men 'on the run' grew week by week.

During this period, General Macready attempted and failed to get the police to be responsible for re-organising the 'Intelligence system'. The problem was that the Army had now become a target for attacks. Consequently, it took the initiative in gathering intelligence. Winter commented in his final report that during this period: 'Dublin District was busy organising an Intelligence system by recruiting ex-officers, and this organisation was of great value in collecting Intelligence in Dublin, which always remained the headquarters of the rebel organisation'.[285] This was a plain-clothes organisation called Special Branch, Dublin District. It complemented the Dublin Military District's intelligence branch. Two strands of activity can be identified. The Record of the Rebellion indicated how they infiltrated the Dublin population. They 'made friends with Dublin citizens of every class and both sexes, they mixed with crowds, and they were arrested with officers and men of the IRA'. The second was the attrition of the operational networks of the insurgents. Intelligence was collected on IRA personnel, and they located the secret addresses of the Dail, Volunteer GHQ, and the Dublin Brigade offices. They pursued the leaders of the insurgency, like Collins and Mulcahy.

This new organisation has been approved by the War Office on the 4th June 1920. In a letter to Sir John Anderson of the same date, Major General Boyd, the GOC Dublin District, indicated the extensive nature of the military intelligence organisation being set up. It was commanded

---

283 Record of the Rebellion, Vol. III.
284 What is meant by this is activity relative to the insurgents.
285 Op cit, CO 904/156B, p. 10.

by Lt Col Walter Wilson[286], a decorated war hero. It contained a total complement of 99 army officers. It was structured in the following way:

1 District Agent
5 Chief Agents
3 Departmental Agents
15 Sub-Agents
75 Agents[287]

The total cost was £19,664[288] In addition, £1,000 was given to Lt Col Wilson for 'special purposes'. The aim was to compensate for the intelligence deficit caused by the disintegration of 'G' Division of the DMP. The geographical scope of Special Branch extended beyond Dublin: 'By September 1920, the system extended from Drogheda to Arklow, and much useful information was obtained not only about this area, but about Sinn Fein in England and about Irish secret societies in the USA'.[289]

It was the officers of this new intelligence organisation who carried out a counter-intelligence operation that inadvertently identified Cope's relationship with Sinn Fein. It was one that went far beyond providing channels for communication. He was unmasked because of the paradox that lies at the heart of counter-intelligence: 'Although the purpose of counterespionage is defensive, its methods are essentially offensive. It's ideal goal is to discover hostile intelligence plans in their earliest stages'.[290] Lieutenant Robert Jeune was a member of Special Branch. He described the tactics used to counter the intelligence deficit during first half of 1920: 'the work consisted of getting to know the town thoroughly, tailing the 'Shinners', and carrying out the small raids, with a view to collecting all possible information which lead us eventually to stamping out

---

286 Wilson divided the Dublin district into six areas under head agents. These areas contained cells of Special Branch officers and civilian informers. See Foy, M., *Michael Collin's Intelligence War* (Stroud: Sutton Publishing 2006), 105.
287 See <www.Bloodysunday.co.suk> accessed 12/2/22.
288 Today this would be equivalent to £761,500, Bank of England website.
289 Record of the Rebellion (Vol. 2) 18.
290 Dulles, A., *The Craft of Intelligence* (London: Weidenfeld and Nicolson, 1963) 124.

the revolt'.[291] It was one of these raids that revealed the nature of Cope's relationship with the insurgents:

> "In September 1920, a raid took place which had a significant result. It was decided to raid several houses in the Drumcondra area. Particular attention was paid to the house of a man called O'Connor, known to us as an active Sinn Feiner... There was no hostile reception, however, and the search went on. While this was happening, I was standing talking to Boddington, who was in charge of the raid, when a letter was brought to him which he read and handed to me saying: 'Money for Jam'. It was on official Dublin Castle paper and was in these words:
>
> Dear Mr O'Connor, I am having the papers you require
>
> sent up to you.
>
> Yours sincerely
>
> A. W. Cope

This was distinctly interesting. Here was the Assistant Under Secretary writing to a notorious Sinn Feiner, with whom he had obviously already been in contact. After this I made a point of trying to find out more about this individual's doings and found that he had done some rather strange things, such as arranging for some electricians of known Sinn Fein views to come into the Castle at unusual times. Also, he was one of the very few castle officials who could safely walk about the streets of Dublin. But it was decided that no drastic action could be taken against him, as it turned out he was a protégé of Lloyd George, who picked him out of Fisheries (Pensions) and sent him over to Ireland under Sir John Anderson in order to get a foot in the Sinn Fein Camp.[292]

Within 5 months of his appointment, Cope was secretly passing government papers to Sinn Fein and giving unauthorised access to Dublin Castle. He also occupied a sensitive post in Dublin Castle. 'He (Cope) has now taken over the RIC transport and correspondence branch en bloc! I'm not sure he has not done his reorganisation Castle job

---

291 Papers of Captain Robert Jeune 76/172/1 IWM.
292 Ibid.

Fire and Water: Fighting an Insurgency 79

(as nobody else could)'.²⁹³ This gave him access to sensitive information such as police ciphers.

Building a New Intelligence Community

One of the accepted judgements, which this book challenges, is the proposition British intelligence in Ireland failed to construct institutions that could process information which resulted in an intelligence product. Townshend has claimed: 'Neither the Army nor the police were able to build the essential foundation for success in guerrilla warfare, a dependable intelligence service'.²⁹⁴ A key achievement was the creation of a new intelligence community in the midst of an ongoing insurgency. Irish historians like Hart have been equally dismissive: 'British intelligence' outwitted and out-spied – emerges from most accounts of the revolution as a contradiction in terms: a disastrous compound of misdirection, malice and ignorance.²⁹⁵

These two historians failed to identify the criteria for assessing the effectiveness of an intelligence organisation. Sherman Kent a distinguished CIA officer²⁹⁶ argued that intelligence activity consists of two sorts of operations: '... the *surveillance operation*, by which I mean the many ways by which the contemporary world is put under close and systematic observation, and the *research operation*. By the latter I mean the attempts to establish meaningful patterns out of what was observed in

---

293 Sturgis Diary, op cit, p. 43.
294 Townshend, C., *The British Campaign in Ireland 1919–1921* (Oxford: Oxford University Press, 1975), 205.
295 Hart P. ed., *British Intelligence in Ireland, 1920–1921: The Final Reports* (Cork: Cork University Press, 2002), 1.
296 Sherman Kent served in both the OSS during the Second World War and the CIA after 1947. He can be credited with the developing the concept of the intelligence cycle. He wrote one of the seminal books on intelligence titled: Strategic Intelligence for American World Policy.

the past and attempts to get meaning out of what appears to be going on now'.²⁹⁷ These two criteria provide a means to evaluate the effectiveness of the intelligence organisations set up in the midst of this insurgency.

The person appointed to build this new organisation was Brigadier-General Ormonde Winter. His official title was Deputy Chief of Police. His real role was Chief of a new Combined Intelligence Service. Townshend has provided a brief pen picture: 'Winter himself was a figure to grace any spy thriller: a monocle sat in his eye and a cigarette hung from his lips; he was universally called by his adopted code-name "O"'.²⁹⁸ Sturgis's revealed his back story: 'O' is a marvel – he looks like a wicked little white snake and can do everything! He is an Artillery Colonel and commanded a Division of artillery in France; in India, they say, he was tried for murder for a little escapade when doing secret service work. He started a racecourse near Calcutta and made a pot o' money … When a soldier who knew him in India heard he was coming to Ireland, he said 'God Help Sinn Fein, they don't know what they are up against'.²⁹⁹

Within four months of his arrival Winter had produced exploitable intelligence on Michael Collins. On the 3rd September 1920 Sturgis wrote: '"O" is on the track of Michael (Collins) – he was amusing about a report he wanted to send to the Under Secretary (Sir John Anderson) but couldn't as it would have said that Michael slept with a girl, address known, once a week, and this he shrank from dictating to his chaste female shorthand writer. So, he had to give his news by word of mouth'.³⁰⁰ No evidence has been found that this intelligence was exploited.

Winter set up two new organisations: The Central Office of Intelligence and the Central Raid Bureau. The former had a number of local intelligence hubs. It covered the whole of Ireland and was divided

---

297 Kent, S., Strategic Intelligence for American World Policy, 1965, p. 4 (finish details).
298 Op cit, p. 126.
299 Hopkinson M., ed., *The Last Days of Dublin Castle, The Diaries of Mark Sturgis* (Dublin: Irish Academic Press, 1999), 32.
300 Ibid, p. 35.

Fire and Water: Fighting an Insurgency

into a number of sub organisations. Winter in his report[301] gave a description of it:

> A Central Office was formed, through which all information should pass, be tabulated[302] and disseminated. Outside Police Centres were linked up to the Central Office by the formation of Local Intelligence Centres, which were responsible for collecting and passing on information between the Army and the Police, and formed the necessary branches of the main trunk. For convenience of control, these were situated at the Headquarters of Divisional Commissioners of the RIC. Police information was augmented, as far as possible, by the employment of chosen agents, and a Bureau was established in London, under special cover, to deal with all sources of information other than those obtained through ordinary channels, to collect information and pass it to the Central Bureau.[303]

What was notable is the relative speed with which these intelligence organisations were set up – in just six months. The first Local Intelligence Centre was functioning in Belfast by January 1921. Between March and April, LICs were operational in Limerick, Kildare, Athlone, Galway and Dundalk. The last one in Clonmel was functioning by July 1921.

The greatest challenge was recruitment: 'The difficulty of obtaining and training suitable personnel somewhat retarded the formation of Local Centres, and the last one to be formed was only established at Clonmel a week before the Truce'.[304] There was also a security challenge linked to recruitment: 'The selection of suitable members for the Central Intelligence Bureau presented many serious obstacles. As a precautionary measure the personnel for the clerical services were all selected from individuals of English extraction, whose antecedents and activities were carefully screened by Scotland Yard. Nearly all the stenographers employed were women, and the male staff were all ex-officers of the Army or Navy'.[305]

---

301 It covered the period from May 1920 to July 1921.
302 A more modern understanding of this process would be the recording, collating, analysing and assessing information for necessary action.
303 A Report on the Intelligence Branch of the Chief of Police from May 1920 to July 1921. CO 904/156b, National Archives, Kew.
304 Ibid.
305 Winter, op cit, p. 302–303.

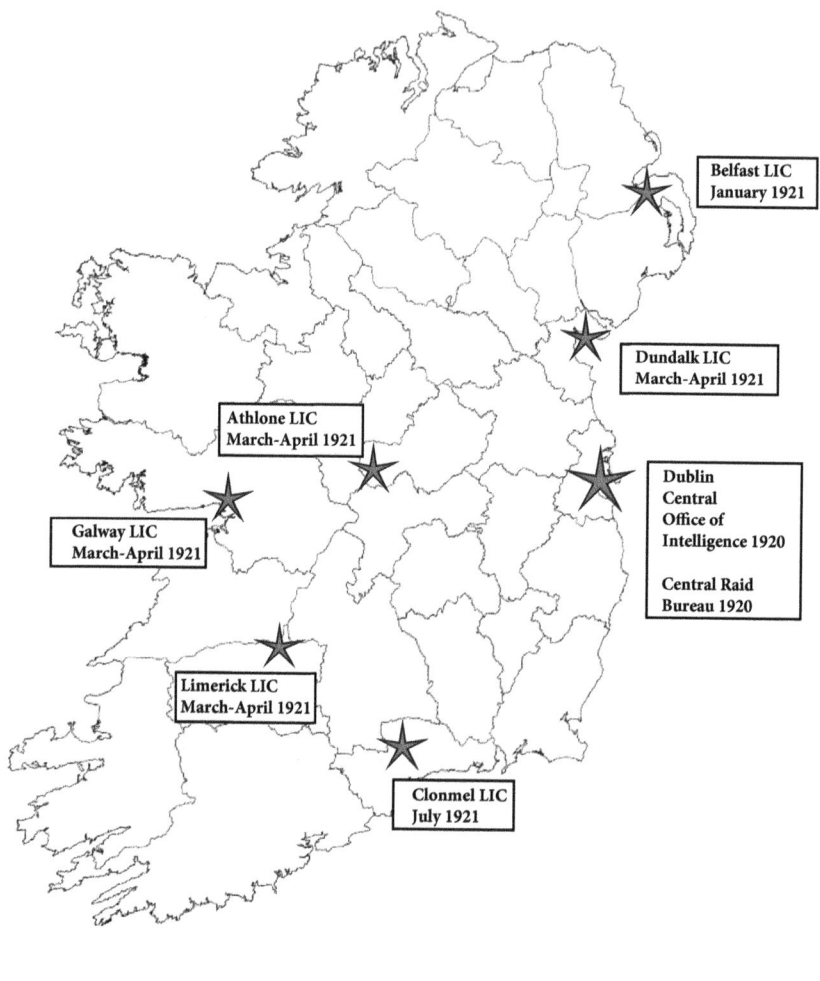

Figure 3.1 Image Courtesy of Major David Hazel.

Fire and Water: Fighting an Insurgency 83

The second intelligence organisation was the Central Raid Bureau. This was functioning by October 1920. It enabled Courts Martial officers to gather evidence to prosecute members of the IRA. The first trial took place on the 17th September 1920.[306] For a short period it overlapped with trials held under the Defence of the Realm Regulations.[307] The British Army was now able to apply a key principle of counter-insurgency: security under the rule of the law. Organised searches provided exploitable intelligence: 'The word of an informer is, very frequently, unreliable, but the evidence deduced from a captured document is tangible and can generally be regarded as conclusive. It was mainly documentary evidence that enabled the authorities to obtain and hold, in the face of appeals, the vast number of internees, and led to the successful prosecution of many agitators. Endeavours were made to inculcate into all concerned the value of forwarding to the Central Bureau all documents captured in raids'.[308]

The importance of captured documents was recognised by General Macready: 'It must be remembered also that most of our Intelligence comes from raids or from the result of captures made when actively engaged with the rebels. Some of my people put the proportion of Intelligence so obtained as high as eighty per cent of the total information received'.[309] Critical to this success was the establishment of a process to record, collate, and analyse all the documents that had been seized. The product was called an epitome.[310] They consisted of a summary of captured documents, or a quote that was judged to be of particular pertinence. If needed the army unit or police unit could call for the original document. Winter gave a sense of the scope of the operation: 'Some idea of the amount of work involved may be gathered from the fact that in

---

306 Volume III of the Record of the Rebellion gives an extensive description of the Court Martial and Military Court system and how it was organised throughout Ireland. See p. 14–18.
307 The last trail was held on the 26th October 1920. See Vol. III, p. 15.
308 Winter, op cit, p. 16.
309 General Macready to Chief Secretary (Green wood) 27th April 1921, Lloyd George Papers, F/19/4/7 House of Lords Library.
310 Each epitome consisted of a short summary or abridgement of captured documents.

the Dublin District area from October 1920 to July 1921, 6,311 raids and searches were carried out, and over 1200 epitomes of captured documents, some consisting of over 200 pages of foolscap were circulated'.[311] In this ten month period this averaged over 631 raids per month! A former member of RUC Special Branch has argued these figures directly challenge the accepted judgement of intelligence activity being a compound of misdirection, malice and ignorance:

> An average of over twenty raids per day every single day for ten months is an exceptional tempo of operations. It would have been impossible to maintain unless the raids were producing results, and I suspect that the more intelligence gleaned the more opportunities for further productive raids and searches presented themselves-a virtuous cycle of intelligence.
>
> Based on the experience of a later IRA campaign I would say that in addition to documentary intelligence recovered on suspects that a certain number of arms and munitions would have been recovered and numerous opportunities presented for information gathering from IRA members and their families and associates. Agent recruitment opportunities would also have been obvious.
>
> The physical and psychological effects upon the IRA in Dublin would have been considerable keeping them off balance, unable to mount attacks, suspicious of one another, ['who told them about me?'] stressed, paranoid, and reluctant to assemble, dreading what tomorrow might bring. Family members would also have asserted pressure to avoid activity which might invite a raid.
>
> Although intelligence officers are always working on low percentage returns on effort expended, a figure of in excess of 140 raids per week over 43 weeks must have accompanied a high level of success. If one combines the positive intelligence opportunities and results from the raids together with product from other parts of the country, postal intercepts, agent and casual contact information, local knowledge, prisoner debriefs, sighting reports with disciplined recording, collation and analysis then one could reasonably presume that they were producing sound exploitable intelligence.[312]

The IRA could not avoid committing information to paper in the absence of other types of communications technology. Verbal communication, except for messages containing no more than a few words,

---

311 Winter, op cit, p. 304.
312 Interview with a former RUC Special Branch Officer 15th March 2021.

Fire and Water: Fighting an Insurgency

was liable to corruption. Captured documents could be processed and a product quickly assembled. Winter believed ethnic proclivities were at play as well: 'It was fortunate that the Irish had an irresistible habit of keeping records'.[313]

Despite these achievements Winter's organisation was subject to extensive criticism. Sturgis stated that Cope had been called upon to assess the effectiveness of the organisation on the 19th November 1920: 'poor "O" has been struggling against a rising tide of overwork and insufficient (or inefficient, perhaps both) staff. The Great Andy is to thoroughly overhaul, advise, and get the organisation going'.[314]

Less than a month later Winter's intelligence organisation produced evidence, from a search on the 16th December 1920, linking Cope to two leaders of the insurgency. The epitome stated: '21(6) Slighting reference to Cope by J. E. Duggan[315] to Michael Collins'.[316] The granular detail of this relationship was further revealed from a document uncovered in a search on the 19th February 1921. The location was IRA Headquarters in South Frederick Street, Dublin. In epitome document no. 53/3649 on page two there was the following reference: 'Michael Collins to C/S (Mulcahy) 19/2 /21. Cope – Asking for instructions as to treatment of high RIC officials'.[317] As members of the RIC and the British Army were being murdered, the special representative of the British Cabinet was 'asking for instructions' from the leader of the insurgency as to how senior officials of the legitimately constituted police force would be treated.

By the end of 1920, other institutional changes had taken place. The detection of political crime had been transferred from the DMP to Dublin Castle as the supply of intelligence from G Division had dried up.

---

313 Winter, op cit, p. 303–304.
314 M. Hopkinson, ed., *The Last Days of Dublin Castle, The Diaries of Mark Sturgis* (Dublin: Irish Academic Press, 1999), 75–76.
315 Duggan J. E., was Director of Intelligence, Irish Volunteers in 1918 and a member of the Sinn Fein delegation to the Anglo-Irish conference in 1921.
316 Epitome of Documents seized at 5 Mespil Rd No. 53/4435, 16th December 1920. Foulkes Papers, Basil Liddell Hart Archives.
317 Foulkes papers 7/24. Basil Liddell Hart Archives, King's College London.

Collins's sources of intelligence inside 'G' division were also disrupted. Detective Kavanagh had died after an appendix operation.

During a raid by the Auxiliary Division of the RIC on New Year's Eve 1920 on a flat in Dawson Street, documents were found that linked Eamon Broy as an intelligence source for Collins.[318] The documents recovered included: 'Broy's copies of G Division reports which were well over a year old and should have been destroyed'.[319] More importantly, the Auxiliaries uncovered an important operational network. The flat was the home of Eileen McGrane, private secretary to Collins. There was a mass of intelligence documents in this flat. The importance of this organised search can be gauged from the fact that it was one of the few mentioned in Winter's autobiography: 'accompanying her (to Dublin Castle) was a van load of captured documents, together with three automatics and a quantity of ammunition. The fact that the epitome of these documents occupied 356 pages of closely typed foolscap, was indicative of the number of her activities, whilst the nature of the contents added considerably to our volume of intelligence'.[320]

The most egregious examples of Cope's behaviour concerned his relationship with Eamon de Valera and Erskine Childers, two prominent leaders of the rebellion. Cope facilitated de facto legal immunity for de Valera. Macready claimed that as soon as de Valera arrived back in Ireland from the United States, in the first week of January 1921, the GOC Ireland received instructions from Dublin Castle that he was not to be interfered with or arrested.[321]

Macready was mistaken about the source of this immunity. It came from the British cabinet. Sir John Anderson, the Under Secretary in Dublin Castle confirmed this in a letter to the Irish Situation Committee: 'The fact that de Valera had been in or near Dublin for many months; the

---

318   A member of the DMP Broy was finally arrested on 17th February 1921 detained in Arbour Hill prison in Dublin and charged with high treason in April 1921.
319   Foy, M., *Michael Collin's Intelligence War* (Stroud: Sutton Publishing, 2006), 189.
320   Op cit, Winter, p. 328–329.
321   See Macready, N. *Annals of an Active Life* (Vol. II) (London: Hutchinson, 1924), 537.

Fire and Water: Fighting an Insurgency

Irish Authorities had continually received information regarding meetings which De Valera attended personally in company of other rebels who were badly wanted. It had been impossible to raid these meetings in view of the Cabinet instructions ... These restrictions had a hampering effect far beyond the immediate inhibitions imposed'.[322] Anderson's statement underscored the accuracy of the intelligence Winter's organisation was producing. The historian Edward Holt provided a further insight of the extent Cope was fully appraised of de Valera's movements: 'When de Valera was using a doctor's house in Merrion Square as his supposedly a secret hide-out and he was there summoned to the telephone by a voice which coolly asked: "May I speak to Mr de Valera?" This is Alfred Cope, speaking from Dublin Castle'.[323]

Cope was directly responsible for the release of Erskine Childers from Winter's custody in Dublin Castle on the 9th May 1921. He was being held in an oubliette close to the Lower Castle Gate. In an edited account, Childers described Cope's behaviour: 'To my immense astonishment I was called for in an hour, taken to an officers' sitting room and given a cup of tea. After a long wait in another room Alfred Cope came and told me I was to be released ... The disgust of the officers at the whole business was amusing, but Cope was adamant ... I left the Castle myself, Cope in his effusive manner and actually carrying my valise out of the gate for me!'[324] Cope used this opportunity to leak official documents to the Sinn Fein leadership.[325]

The competence of Winter's intelligence organisation was further underlined when another search took place at 22 Mary Street in Dublin on 26th May 1921. They captured the original official papers that Cope had given Childers when he was released 13 days earlier. In addition, they captured the covering correspondence from Childers to Collins on the

---

322 Minutes of Irish Situation Committee, 15th June 1921, Lloyd George Papers F 25/1/42 House of Lords Library.
323 Holt, E., *Protest in Arms: The Irish Troubles 1916–1923* (London: Putnam, 1960), 247.
324 Ring, J., *Erskine Childers* (London: John Murray, 1996).
325 Foy, op cit, p. 224.

same subject! Epitome No. 5469 stated: 'Erskine Childers to Minister of Finance (Collins) 16/5/21. Settlement outlined to me by Cope in the Castle a week ago. He is probably a good actor, but his ostensible attitude was one of almost feverish anxiety to get something done and the business over'.[326] This epitome was described by Sturgis as 'a nasty little breeze'. The problem for Cope was the wide circulation of captured documents received, far beyond the closed circle of senior civil servants in Dublin Castle: 'all such seized documents are it seems roneoed and seen broadcast in the police office, GHQ etc.'.[327]

Cope's response was shameless. Winter was asked to assign one of his officers to intercept any captured documents that could implicate him in the future. Winter's response was to draft a letter of resignation to the Head of the police, General Tudor. He was eventually talked out of sending it by Cope.[328]

The Combined Intelligence Service provided intelligence that illuminated Cope's relationship to the leaders of the insurgency. More importantly it demonstrated the ability of the organisation to execute a *surveillance operation*, the operational networks of the Irish Volunteers were successfully targeted. The epitomes created from these captured documents constituted a *research operation*. Cope's dysfunctional impact on the security forces counter-insurgency efforts runs like the lettering through a stick of rock.

Winter's intelligence organisation was innovative in another way. It developed a counter-insurgency tactic that fused captured documents, human targets, and generated a self-sustaining tempo: 'After the first important capture, (of documents) which, to a great extent was fortuitous, other searches were made from the addresses noted and the names obtained, and the snowball process continued, leading to fresh searches, new arrests and the obtaining of more intimate knowledge of the plans,

---

326 Foulkes Papers, op cit.
327 Sturgis Diary, p. 184.
328 Foy, op cit, p. 224.

resources and methods of the rebel organisation, besides providing material for valuable propaganda'.³²⁹

This approach had the hallmarks of modernity: 'It appears that Winter and his people adopted an integrated approach of fusing together all information, both overtly and covertly obtained, secret and non-secret, from both RIC and Army sources and after recording, collating, analysing and assessing were able to produce speedy, accurate, assessed and actionable intelligence for dissemination to those who needed it. The reality of the IRA campaign of murder and destruction appears to have induced them to adopt and enact this process with commendable alacrity. It was certainly very advanced for its time. Had Winter seen similar cooperation between the Army and the Police in India? It was exactly the approach the RUC and the Army adopted fifty years later during the Troubles in Northern Ireland'.³³⁰

The ability to collate intelligence was clearly demonstrated: 'Letters seized in one part of Ireland were often meaningless, but, when compared with documents, in a similar handwriting, captured in another locality, either afforded valuable clues or led to the prosecution of the writer'.³³¹ Winter's intelligence organisation diverged from the structure of the army's military intelligence organisation. The latter was divided into three broad categories: Ia, the service of information; Ib, counter-intelligence; Ix, organisation and administration. This was a cause of tension between the army and Winter. Volume Two of the Record of the Rebellion provides ample testimony to this. In summary, the activity of the Army's Special Branch and Winter's new intelligence organisation strongly suggest more than a degree of professional competence. There is one event, the legacy of which hovers over both organisations. Why were they unable to detect and prevent the co-ordinated attack launched by Michael Collins in November 1920? This will be examined in the next chapter.

329 Op cit, p. 15.
330 Interview with a former RUC Special Branch officer, 15th March 2021.
331 Op cit, p. 16.

CHAPTER 4

Tactics, Operations, and Lost Victories

A Wilderness of Mirrors[332] and Bloody Sunday

Bloody Sunday has been interpreted by Irish historians as burnishing the image of Michael Collins as the infallible intelligence godfather. Furthermore, the murders that took place on the morning of 21st November 1920 inflicted a substantial blow against the British Army's intelligence capability. Within 15 minutes, the butcher's bill was nineteen men shot; five were wounded and fourteen dead. Of those killed, only six were from the Special Branch, Dublin Military District, out of around 160 intelligence officers believed to have been in the field at the time.[333] Mark Sturgis commented: 'It has been a day of black murder. What they hope to gain by it God alone knows – the reasons must be the forlorn hope of striking at the Military ring that is closing on them'.[334] The reference to the 'Military ring' provides a departure point to understand the military and political consequences of these attacks, and the extent to which they impeded the counter-insurgency effort of the British army at strategic, operational and tactical levels.

Insufficient attention has been paid to the fact that these murders were preceded and followed by secret negotiations involving the Prime

---

332 This phrase was first coined by T. S. Eliot in his poem Gerontion (Greek for little old man) written in 1920. It has been used by the US intelligence officer James Jesus Angleton as a metaphor for the playing out of the intelligence and counter-intelligence dynamic. It has particular pertinence for the events that preceded and followed Bloody Sunday.
333 See <www.bloodysunday.co.uk>, accessed 23 April 2022.
334 The Diaries of Mark Strugis, p. 76.

Minister, Lloyd George, two cabinet ministers: Lord Curzon, the Foreign Secretary, and H.A.L. Fisher the Minister for Education, and chair of the Cabinet committee dealing with Ireland. These negotiations illuminated the ongoing absence of an integrated approach. A senior civil servant was also involved in these meetings. His name was C. J. Phillips, Chief Assistant to the Foreign Secretary, Lord Curzon. The Sinn Fein contact who reported both to Arthur Griffith and Michael Collins was Patrick Moylett,[335] a businessman from Ballina in Co. Galway.[336]

There were two remarkable aspects about these negotiations. First, they were undertaken without the knowledge of senior civil servants in Dublin Castle such as Anderson, Cope, and Sturgis. On the 29th November eight days after Bloody Sunday, Sturgis confided to his diary: 'There is some justification for the belief that L. G. has been in touch with A. G. behind all our backs'.[337] Secondly, it showed that Lloyd George was willing to do two things simultaneously: undermine the British counter-insurgency effort, and trade the core values any state has to maintain: its legitimacy and social authority. The effect was to accelerate the distancing London from the defence of Ireland as an integral part of the United Kingdom.

Why did Collins act and what was the immediate impact of these attacks? The Record of the Rebellion was candid about the effect it had on the Army's intelligence operations: 'The murders of the 21st November 1920, temporarily paralysed the special branch. Several of its most efficient members were murdered and the majority of the other residents in the city were brought into the Castle and Central Hotel for safety'.[338] In the late 1950s they were given the name the 'Cairo Gang' in Irish nationalist mythology due to the fact it was imputed that they had intelligence

---

335   Patrick Moylett's Witness Statement to the Bureau of Military History provides the most comprehensive account and insight to the secret negotiations with Lloyd George and his associates.
336   He was also involved in the illegal importation of arms into Ireland. See Witness Statement 0767, Bureau of Military History. Dublin.
337   The Diaries of Mark Sturgis, p. 83.
338   Record of the Rebellion, Vol. 2, p. 20.

Tactics, Operations, and Lost Victories 93

experience in the Middle East, or had frequented a particular cafe in Dublin.[339] This was pure invention.[340]

Lieutenant Robert Jeune, a member of Special Branch, survived due to the fact that he spent the night sleeping in an empty railway carriage. In the period before the murders, he received unspecified warnings: 'In November (1920), information was coming in well and we were beginning to get on top of the IRA, who was becoming desperate. I happened to receive information from three different sources to the effect that something was going to happen, but there was nothing definite'.[341]

Collins's motive was survival. A 'military ring' was closing in around his networks. This is confirmed from both British and Irish sources. Sturgis's diary for 16th November 1920 gave an insight to this: 'A raid last night (15th November) on the house of the IRA "Chief of Staff" called Mulcahy has been productive of some amazing stuff. The gent himself succeeded in getting away in his nightshirt, which is a pity but the papers seized give evidence of the most thorough and complete plots to murder individuals, poison troops, horses etc. – to blow up the Manchester Ship Canal, etc.'.[342] There were also documents that led to the IRA's financial networks: 'Wilson (Head of the Special Branch, Dublin Military District) came in hot after Mulcahy's money – he also it seems has an account or accounts in the Bank at our gates in different names. Wilson and Wynne had their heads together for an hour and I hope settled satisfactorily the least illegal way of bagging the stuff'.[343] This intelligence success enabled the tempo to be maintained in terms of targeting other networks. On the 19th November, three days after the raid on Mulcahy's house, a follow-up search was launched using captured documents from the previous operation: 'Among the Mulcahy's papers is a list of 200 gunmen, names and addresses and classified as very good shots, good shots, etc. We are out

---

339 See Coogan, T. P., *Michael Collins* (New York: Palgrave, 2002), 157–160.
340 <www.bloodysunday.co.uk>, accessed 23 April 2022.
341 Papers of Captain Robert Jeune 76/172/1 IWM.
342 Sturgis Diary, op cit, p. 73.
343 Sturgis Diary, op cit, p. 74.

raiding tonight for these beauties and will have them on the run anyway if they've taken fright and bolted'.[344]

Special Branch Dublin District had identified Collins's key operational network – intelligence: 'October (1920) saw all three of Collins' top intelligence personnel were picked up and released after questioning, Thornton being held for ten days before being released, Tobin and Cullen also got away with a grilling after being detained in Vaughan's'.[345] Frank Thornton, deputy head of Collin's intelligence ASU acknowledged that Special Branch had: 'built up quite a formidable organisation and were without doubt securing quite a lot of very valuable information'.[346]

Pressure was also being exerted on Collins's networks by a freshly invigorated legal system – under the Restoration of Order in Ireland Act. The court martial system could now try people for treason, treasonable felony, and felony. Courts Martial officers began building cases against members of the Irish Volunteers and prominent Republicans. This renewed effectiveness was cited by Lieutenant Jeune as a key motivating factor for Collins planning and instigating these murders: 'The object of this exercise (the murders of the 21st November) on the part of the IRA, was to eliminate Intelligence and Courts Martial officers, because the gunmen felt that the net was closing round them. So, men were brought up to Dublin from other parts of the country, particularly Tipperary, in order to catch as many as possible of us unawares on a Sunday morning, when most people slept late'.[347]

Irish historians have constructed a narrative that presented the Irish Volunteer intelligence network as being granular in its depth and extensive in its scope: 'Snatches of information from maids and porters and wastepaper baskets, times of coming and goings, places with lights on after curfew; all manner of whispers and over hearings turned themselves into dossiers and reports. The simplest of things were noted: who wore

---

344 Sturgis Dairy, op cit, p. 76.
345 Coogan, T. P., *Michael Collins* (New York: Palgrave, 2002), 158.
346 Thornton, F. Bureau of Military History, Witness Statement 0621, Cathal Bruga Barracks, Dublin.
347 Jeune Papers, op cit.

Tactics, Operations, and Lost Victories

a signet ring on one of his left fingers, who wore a grey or a black or a navy suit'.³⁴⁸ The foundation stone of this narrative was the witness statements made by the men involved in these murders. What emerged was a uniformity of narrative to both justify these killings and the competence with which they were carried out: 'it needed to be done, that they had to be stopped, that they were all spies, that there were no mistakes, comes again and again with dreary repetition'.³⁴⁹ The IRA was never going to talk about their failures, whether it was the wrong army officers being shot or the incomplete nature of the intelligence on which the attacks were based. This is underlined by the changes in and the uncertainty of the addresses to be attacked right up to the start of the operation.

What were the lapses on the British side? The key failure was a lack of security vetting. An important source of intelligence for Collins was Lily Mernin, a War Office typist in Dublin Castle. She worked for Major Stratford Burton, the Dublin Garrison Adjutant. She started providing information to Collins in November or December 1919.³⁵⁰ She was not dismissed from her post until February 1922. The information she supplied was critical in facilitating the murders: 'Before the 21st November 1920 it was part of my normal duty to type the names and addresses of British agents who were accommodated at private addresses and living as ordinary citizens in the city. These lists were typed weekly and amended whenever an address was changed. I passed them on each week'.³⁵¹ The full extent of her activities was revealed by Frank Saurin a member of Collins's intelligence unit: 'In addition to Lily Mernin being one of our agents at Dublin Castle, she was also attached to me for visiting hotel lounges and the like for spotting and identification work of enemy personnel who

---

348 Dolan, A., 'Killing and Bloody Sunday', *The Historical Journal* 49/3 (Sept, 2006) 792–793.
349 Ibid, p. 793.
350 Michael Collins gave her the cryptic title of 'LT. G' (Little Gentleman). See Putkowski, J., The Best Secret Service Man We Had – Jack Byrnes, A2 and the IRA, Lobster, No. 28, 28/2/95, p. 37.
351 Lily Mernin Witness Statement No. 441 Bureau of Military History, Cathal Bruga Barracks, Dublin.

used to frequent such places'.³⁵² Mernin's statement needs careful qualifying; these lists did not include the addresses of 'British agents' as she claimed. They were administrative accommodation lists which included army officers who were both members of Special Branch, and officers appointed to regimental and staff duties in the Dublin Garrison. The former were not explicitly identified by these lists.

There was also a failure of vetting concerning two serving policemen in the DMP. Patrick Mannix was the most important. He provided the names of a number of army officers who were murdered: 'I secured some of the names and addresses of those who were shot on Bloody Sunday'. Keating, who was stationed in Irishtown, gave me the names of Secret Service Agents residing in Shelbourne Road and Upper Mount Street. I also learned of a Secret Service Agent named Captain McClean living in Morehampton Road.³⁵³

Armed with this incomplete intelligence Collins, on the 17th November, informed Dick McKee head of the Dublin Brigade of the Irish Volunteers that he had established the addresses of the officers he wanted to kill. Mernin even suggested the 21st November as the optimal date. She argued that on a Sunday, most of the officers would be at their addresses.³⁵⁴ The pivotal issue of who exactly was a member of the Special Branch was unresolved by Collins before the attacks were launched.

These murders have been folded into the larger Irish Republican narrative of the insurgency. Peter Hart claimed they were part of a cross – channel 'spectacular'.³⁵⁵ This originally planned to co-ordinate attacks on Special Branch, with the simultaneous sabotage of Liverpool docks and warehouses, Manchester power plants and London timber yards. The raid on Mulcahy's house meant that only the arson attacks on warehouses in Liverpool and Bootle went ahead on the 28th and 29th of November.

352 Frank Saurin Witness Statement No 715 Bureau of Military History, Cathal Bruga Barracks, Dublin.
353 Mannix, P., Witness Statement No. 502, Bureau of Military History, Cathal Bruga Barracks, Dublin.
354 See Gleeson, J., *Bloody Sunday* (London: Peter Davies, 1962), 124.
355 See Hart, P., *Mick, The Real Michael Collins* (London: Pan Books, 2006), 241.

They were not simultaneous acts as has Hart claimed.[356] Collins faced a severe logistical challenge: 'The scale of the operation was too large for Collin's intelligence officers and his "squad", his band of young and devoted gunmen, his 'twelve apostles', to do it alone. Chosen and reliable men from various battalions of the Dublin brigade were informed throughout the previous week'.[357] They were then assigned to an intelligence operative and a member of the squad who had been allocated a specific officer to murder. Furthermore, for the reasons previously given, the locations to be attacked fluctuated alarmingly even up to the night before.[358]

In the end, a total of eight houses were entered, and fourteen Army officers were killed, and a number were wounded. Inexperience of the gunmen meant that many of the wounded survived. Even the dead had been shot in unusual places: 'The shootings were by nature often hurried and frenetic'.[359] Some of these murders took place in front of the wives of these officers. A key British witness was Caroline Woodcock, the wife of Lt Col Woodcock. In their residence of 28 Upper Pembroke St, a total of seven officers were billeted. Three of these officers were murdered, and three were wounded including her husband. Lieutenant Jeune, a member of Special Branch, who as previously stated, did not return to his lodgings at this address: 'Never to my dying day shall I forget the scene in the hall and on the stairs, four officers had been shot. There were great splashes of blood on the walls, floor, and stairs, bits of plaster were lying about, and on the walls were the marks of innumerable bullets ... the murders had been so panic-stricken themselves and their hands so shaky that their firing had been wild in the extreme, and to this fact my husband and Captain Keenlyside, who was shot in the jaw and both arms, owed their lives'.[360] She also gave an insight to the response of the army wives: 'Except for the hysterical shrieks of one or two of the maids, I never

---

356 Ibid, p. 241.
357 Dolan, op cit, p. 796.
358 See Saurin, F., Witness Statement, No. 715 Bureau of Military History, Cathal Bruga Barracks, Dublin.
359 Dolan, op cit, p. 805.
360 *An Officer's Wife in Ireland* (London: Parkgate Publications, 1984), 66.

heard a cry or saw signs of fear. Everyone was perfectly quiet and self-controlled'.[361] The Irish Republican writer James Glesson drew a grim analogy concerning the events that unfolded at this address: 'The house was like an abattoir'.[362]

Caroline Woodcock confirmed there were four members of Special Branch at her address.[363] There were also two officers, including her husband, who were posted to Dublin on regimental or staff duties. These officers had been warned not to carry revolvers. Her account gives lie to the dominant narrative that all those murdered were 'English spies'. Two of those known to her were Irish Roman Catholics who had taken up 'special service work' out of a sense of duty: 'The hospital matron told me that the dead bodies of fourteen officers, many of them born in Ireland, lay in the mortuary. Nine of these were in pyjamas. That little sentence shows in what circumstances the majority of them lost their lives'.[364]

These attacks had a catalytic effect on the counter-insurgency campaign. At the highest level it: 'enabled military authorities to obtain sanction for a change of policy'.[365] There was also pressure from the military for the introduction of martial law. At the operational level, the command networks of the Irish Volunteers were attacked: 'Within a few hours of the crimes having been committed, the Irish Government had given sanction for the arrest of all known "officers" of the IRA and their internment at Ballykinlar Camp Co. Down. This was facilitated by the fact that a short time previously, an office of the IRA had been raided in Dublin and papers found which confirmed the order of Battle which had been compiled from intelligence already received'.[366]

The Record of the Rebellion detailed how the Irish Executive gave its consent to arrest known members of the Irish Volunteers, even if they were not known to be 'officers'. In Dublin alone 87 arrests were made

361 Ibid, p. 69.
362 Gleeson, J. *Bloody Sunday* (London: Peter Davies, 1962), 131.
363 Ibid, p. 60.
364 Ibid, p. 70.
365 Record of the Rebellion, pp. 54–55.
366 Ibid, p. 26.

within 48 hours, and during the week the number of arrests throughout Ireland reached 500. This resulted in a dramatic change in the tactical tempo: 'From this time the initiative may said to have passed to the Crown Forces for the first time since May 1920'.[367] However, the command structure of Special Branch was irrevocably changed: 'As a result of all this, those of us who had survived were shut up under guard in a hotel, from where it was impractical to do any work. In fact, our job had to all intents and purposes been done, and the organisation was breaking up'.[368]

What Jeune omitted to explain was the subsequent integration of Special Branch into 'D' branch, part of Winter's intelligence organisation. This brought together Secret Agents reports, Military Intelligence reports, informer's reports and documents captured by members of 'D' branch and by military and police on raids. The Record of the Rebellion claimed a diminution of its effectiveness as a consequence of this change: 'The transfer of what was in fact the military intelligence system was a grave mistake ... The organisation continued to work for the army but was responsible to a new master, the Chief of Police, consequently the driving power behind the agents gradually diminished'.[369]

The official statement issued by Dublin Castle with respect to this attack laid emphasis on the role these officers had in enforcing through the law: 'In one way or another ten officers who were killed were connected with the administration of justice, the collection of evidence and the prosecution of persons before courts martial'.[370] Eunan O'Halpin has claimed: 'Bloody Sunday was not the destruction but the intensification of the British intelligence effort'.[371] Peter Hart has argued the 'Bloody Sunday' killings were not the 'Napoleonic masterstroke' of Irish Republican legend: 'Rather than bringing relief, the shootings actually precipitated the worst setback yet for the rebels at the hands of British intelligence. Military and police intelligence officers had by now

367 Ibid, p. 26.
368 Jeune Papers, op cit.
369 Record of the Rebellion (Vol. II), p. 19.
370 J. Gleeson, J., *Bloody Sunday*, (London: Peter Davies, 1962), p. 179.
371 E O'Halpin.

identified most of their opponents. Raiding parties were unleashed all over Ireland to round up known IRA officers and activists and detention camps were hurriedly established to receive the large numbers of men caught in the net. Informers sprang up once again and arms were found in unprecedented numbers'.[372]

This intensification of security measures forced Collins to make organisational changes to his network. In a circular dated the 4th October 1920, and captured in a raid on New Year's Day 1921, Mulcahy, Chief of Staff of the Irish Volunteers described the 'Republican Army' as: 'in a great measure only a part-time Service militia'.[373] The losses in manpower meant he was forced to concentrate his gunmen into one centrally controlled force. He created a new Active Service Unit based on full time service. All of those chosen had to relinquish their day jobs. The unit would be limited to fifty men, it was the only way he could maintain tactical tempo. A former member James Cahill has given account of this process of consolidation: 'About mid-December (1920) the Company Adjutant informed me that Headquarters had ordered each company in the Dublin Brigade to pick two or three of their best men for transfer to a special unit that was about to be organised. The men of this unit would be full time soldiers, and the unit would be available at all times for immediate action ... I told them I would be very pleased to serve in such a unit'.[374] He reported to this unit on the 1st January 1921.

In the same month Lieutenant Jeune met Lieutenant General Boyd, GOC Dublin District, on the boat train to Holyhead. Their judgement was that another six months would see the IRA unable to sustain their campaign.[375] Jeune claimed that the changes made by Collins were not enough to parry the intensified efforts of the army and police: 'by the

---

372 P. Hart P., ed., *British Intelligence in Ireland: The Final Reports 1920–1921* (Cork: Cork University Press, 2002), p. 12.
373 McGrane, E., 21 Dawson Street, arrested 1/1/21 Epitome No. 53/2567, Foulkes Papers 7/24/, Basil Liddell Archive Centre, King's College London.
374 See Cahill, J., Witness Statement, No. 503 Bureau of Military History, Cathal Bruga Barracks, Dublin.
375 Op cit, Jeune Papers.

early summer (1921) the IRA, were driven into the southwest corner of Ireland, and would have been quickly finished. But certain influences were to save them'.[376]

What were these influences? Most toxic were the secret negotiations instigated by the British policy elite. They straddled the murders of the 21st November. The day after Bloody Sunday Patrick Moylett was invited by C. J. Phillips to call at Downing Street and was asked to convey the following message to Arthur Griffith: 'For God's sake to keep his head and not to break off the slender link that had been established', adding that the British soldiers who were killed in Dublin on the previous day took a soldiers risk: 'but I (Moylett) later heard from another source that Lloyd George, in discussing the question with my informant, said that it served them right to allow themselves to be beaten by a crowd of "Dublin counter-jumpers"'.[377]

Although he knew nothing of these talks, Field Marshal Sir Henry Wilson, the CIGS, demonstrated an uncanny prescience. He was suspicious of the government's attitude to Bloody Sunday. In a letter written two days after the event he stated: 'There was no Cabinet yesterday about Ireland, nor is there going to be one today, the fact being of course, that as nothing has happened in Ireland necessitating a meeting of the Cabinet, the Cabinet does not meet! The murder of 10, or 12, or 14 officers is a matter of small moment'.[378]

He did not know Lloyd George offered to call a truce for one week so he could sell the idea of a negotiated settlement to the House of Commons. For Collins and Griffith, the prize was legitimacy. Dail Eireann would be recognised by the British government despite the fact that the government had declared it 'suppressed'. The week after the 21st November, Moylett spent every day in Downing Street and met with Phillips: 'We discussed the question of a settlement in detail from every

---

376 Op cit, Jeune Papers.
377 Moylett, P., Witness Statement, No. 767 Bureau of Military History, Cathal Bruga Barracks, Dublin.
378 Letter from Field Marshal Sir Henry Wilson to Lieutenant General Jeudwine dated 23rd November 1920. Papers of Lieutenant General Jeudwine IMW.

angle. Phillips informed me that we could have a settlement by the end of the week'.[379]

There was a lack of realism, and a febrile quality to these negotiations. Moylett suggested Chester (the halfway meeting place in Tudor Anglo-Irish relations) as the venue. Lloyd George thought this was a good idea. He was afraid of the ability of the 'London political clubs' to get secret information on each day's discussion. Interestingly he stated: 'if the conference was not held while the Coalition Government existed a settlement could never be affected, as one of the English parties would not allow the other to make a settlement'.[380] The Irish Office in London tried to establish Moylett's identity. Furthermore, Phillips informed him that the Irish Executive had threatened to resign if the agreement negotiated by Moylett was enacted. On the 6th December, he met with Michael Collins at Shanahan's public house in Dublin. The key proposal at this meeting was whether a truce was to be called for that week. After an hour's discussion, Collins concluded: 'To hell with it, let's get on with the work'.[381]

Collins did not have the whole of his organisation behind him. An offer of peace emerged from inside the Irish Volunteers. The recipient was Lieutenant General Boyd, the GOC Dublin District, and a very small number of senior army officers. In a letter dated the 7th December, one day after Moylett's meeting with Collins, Lieutenant General Jeudwine,[382] deputising for Macready who was on leave, sent him a sensational letter: 'I have asked Boyd[383] to go over tonight taking this and report to you (Macready) an incident of considerable importance in which he was concerned yesterday, viz an offer on behalf of the IRA to confer with the British military authority with a view to arranging terms for a cessation of hostilities'.[384] Jeudwine added that with the exception of himself and

---

379 Ibid.
380 Ibid.
381 Ibid.
382 Jeudwine was the GOC of 5th Division based at the Curragh.
383 Lieutenant General Boyd was the GOC of Dublin District.
384 Papers of Field Marshal Sir Henry Wilson (Vol. 8), HHW 2/2F Imperial War Museum.

General Boyd and Colonel Brind no one on 'our side' knew anything of the offer that had been made, and the reaction to it was contingent on Macready's or the CIGS (Wilson's) instructions.

The identity of the interlocutor was not revealed. Jeudwine described him as a 'semi-deviant agent' who disclaimed the authority of Dail Eireann over the IRA and professed a profound distrust of politicians on both sides. This underlined the success of the intensified efforts of the police and the army. This agent sought an end to the insurgency and a cessation of operations on both sides. It led Jeudwine to conclude: 'There is therefore a situation amounting to a something like a rebellion within a rebellion'.[385] He identified the opportunity for the Army: 'Organised rebellion cannot continue without the co-operation of the IRA ... Therefore, if we can render the IRA impotent, we have won'.[386]

The weakness of Lloyd George's negotiations was the exclusion of the Irish Executive. Moylett would require the help of Cope and other senior civil servants in Dublin Castle to establish the legitimacy of Sinn Fein. The approach to Boyd from within the IRA also dissipated. There is no evidence that Macready took action to exploit this 'rebellion within a rebellion'. Both episodes illuminate the wilderness of mirrors and the choices of action taken as the insurgency unfolded.

In summary, the British Army since the beginning of 1920 had been subject to four changes of policy. During the first period from January to early May they had been granted powers as the Competent Military Authority. The second period saw these powers removed, and evidence had to be collected to bring the insurgents to trial in the civil courts. The third change came in August with the Restoration of Order in Ireland Act which replaced the civil courts with Courts Martial. This was effective, and its success prompted Collins to counter its effect by undertaking the murders of 21st November. The fourth period from November to the end of the year shifted the policy yet again with an intensified counter-insurgency operation against the IRA. A key element in this fourth stage was detention. It was a policy Macready wanted to introduce

385 Ibid.
386 Ibid.

weeks previously, but as Sturgis remarked in his diary 'but HMG were not ready to sanction the step'. What led to the policy change was intelligence obtained by Special Branch: 'The Mulcahy evidence of the direct responsibility of IRA officers generally for the policy of Murder more than justifies this – without the Mulcahy papers this would have been less defensible'.[387]

The Record of the Rebellion while not referring to these policy changes produced an assessment of the consequences. Specifically, what the IRA had been able to achieve in 1920. There were four in total: first, the unique efficiency of the Royal Irish Constabulary had been destroyed; second, they had pinned down in Ireland 'very serious forces of troops and war material'; third, it had militarised the young men of the country and formulated a system of guerrilla war that was capable of being continued practically indefinitely; finally, it has inflicted on English prestige very serious blows.[388] Despite these tactical and operational achievements the 'eventual ends' of the leaders of the rebellion: the withdrawal of Crown forces from Ireland and the realisation of an Independent Republic had not in any sense been achieved. What was left unstated was the continuing ability of the Irish Volunteers to benefit from the choices by the policy elite that bridged the gap between the declining capability of the insurgents and their political objectives.

The Sinews of Victory and Defeat

The period from January 1921 to the truce in July 1921 was full of paradoxes. Three broad trends can be discerned, and they unfolded simultaneously. First the army and the police continued to have success in attacking the operational networks of the Irish Volunteers. In addition, in May 1921

---

387 Hopkinson, ed., *The Last Days of Dublin Castle: The Diaries of Mark Sturgis* (Dublin: Irish Academic Press, 1999), 78.
388 *Record of the Rebellion* (Vol. I), p. 41.

Irish Command had appointed an officer, to be based at GHQ in Dublin, to develop a propaganda campaign to challenge the strategic narrative of Irish Republicanism.[389] Secondly Wilson and Macready planned and gained cabinet endorsement for major offensive against the IRA. Finally, Cope continued to shift the assumptions of Lloyd George and his coalition government to accepting an armed truce with Sinn Fein. This had always been something that the Coalition Government had balked at. The ambivalence in Lloyd George's attitude to the insurgency was clear in December 1920 when he stated: 'The whole point is do we want peace or not? Are we to stamp out the very embers of rebellion or is the policy a double one to crush murder and to make peace with the moderates'.[390]

In the end, he did not negotiate with moderates, but with the extreme elements of Irish republicanism led by de Valera and Collins. This intervening variable adversely affected the conditions of peace. Colin Gray identified the generic relationship between policy and military activity: 'the relationship between strategy and its enabling tactics requires, as a matter of absolute need, that policy needs, which is to say political choices, provide both legitimacy and practical guidance'.[391] The political choices made by Lloyd George and the Dublin Castle civil servants provided neither of these vital qualities. This lack of guidance was compounded by the reality that the political determinants of war rarely exhibit homogeneity or constancy; political uncertainty can carry over into military strategy and operations.

The absence of legitimacy and guidance impacted differently on Macready's senior commanders. Lieutenant General Strickland, the GOC 6th division, an area that covered Cork and Kerry, one of the crucibles of the insurgency, confided in his diary the difficulty he found in coming to terms with the reduction in personal freedoms: 'last year was bad enough but <u>nothing</u> to this. We could move about, hunt etc.

---

389 His name was Colonel Foulkes of the Royal Engineers.
390 T. Jones, T. *Whitehall Diary* (Vol. III), (London: Oxford University Press, 1971), 46.
391 Gray, C. S., *Tactical Operations for Strategic Effect: The Challenge of Currency Conversion*, JSOU Report, November 2015, p. 14.

then and personally. I can do neither ... What will be the end I can't say. Murder and crime seem so deeply rooted that one wonders how it can be stamped out'.[392]

By contrast Lieutenant General Jeudwine the GOC of 5th Division based at the Curragh Camp submitted a secret report in February 1921 which gave a more optimistic perspective: 'There is no doubt that the internment of officers of the IRA has favourably affected the situation, in that it has disorganised Sinn Fein command and communication, rendered Sinn Fein courts inoperative, forced many rebels into hiding, and discouraged some who might have otherwise have been active'.[393] This report reflected a grasp of the importance of political primacy and unity of effort. He stressed the importance the government having a clear 'conception of the political conditions which it intended to introduce'. Furthermore, he claimed that: 'it is impossible to separate military measures from political, since military measures alone can have no lasting effect, and their employment can only be effective when they are directed as the expression of a determined policy towards the foundation of a sound and practical political structure'.[394]

Jeudwine made a strong argument for the need to proclaim Martial Law. He appreciated that apart from affecting the Irish Volunteers ability to pace the war, it would have another important effect on the civilian population: 'convince the wavering that the government is determined to repress lawlessness and encourage them and the loyalists to give their assistance to the cause of order'.[395]

This lack of guidance did not prevent the British Army from becoming a learning organisation. It formulated and disseminated a tactical counter-insurgency doctrine. *Notes on Guerrilla Warfare in Ireland*[396]

---

392 Pocket diary Lieutenant General Strickland, Strickland Papers P363 IWM.
393 Lieutenant General H. Jeudwine, 5th Division Area (secret) Situation Report – February 1921. Jeudwine Papers 72/82/2 IWM.
394 Ibid.
395 Ibid.
396 See WO 35/182A Notes Etc. (5974-G).

was a product of practical experience in the field and the tactical exercises and classes on counter-insurgency held at the Curragh Camp.

Down the 'Main Drain' With Cope

Senior Army officers serving in Ireland had an intermittent understanding of how Cope's secret negotiations drove a wedge between political choices and strategy. His actions made it impossible for strategy to have a dialogue with policy.[397] Cope himself faced challenges on two fronts. First, the Conservative members in Lloyd George's coalition cabinet were aware of his activities in Dublin, and the Irish Committee of the cabinet issued a protocol that stated bluntly: 'No person serving in the Irish Government should in any circumstances be permitted to hold communications with Sinn Fein'.[398] Needless to say Cope systematically ignored these instructions. The second challenge was establishing his bona fides with the people he was not allowed to communicate with and bridging the huge gaps that existed in the British and Sinn Fein positions. An early British position was that there could be no truce unless arms were surrendered. An insight to the reaction to these demands was given by Frank Gallagher.[399] He cited a communication written by Collins on 14th December 1920 to Arthur Griffith and a number of Republican prisoners:[400] 'We have clearly demonstrated our willingness to have peace on honourable terms. Lloyd George insists on capitulation. Between these there is no mean'.[401]

---

397 See Strachan, H. *The Direction of War* (Cambridge: Cambridge University Press, 2013), 19, for a more detailed discussion of this relationship.
398 CO 704/100 National Archives, Quoted in Coogan, T. P., *Michael Collins* (Palgrave: New York, 2002), 187.
399 Frank Gallagher was a leading figure in the Irish Republican propaganda organisation.
400 They were Michael Staines, Eamonn Duggan and Eoin MacNeill.
401 Cited in F. Gallagher, F., *The Anglo-Irish Treaty*, (London: Hutchinson. 1965), p. 23.

One channel of communication Cope exploited was Irishmen holding Crown legal appointments: 'Irishmen in the Crown service were used as contacts by Cope in his secret efforts to bring about peace. Cope was in his element in these undercover activities but lacked the stability and perception to bring them to a successful conclusion'.[402] In January 1921, Father O'Flanagan, the Vice President of Sinn Fein had been contacted by Cope, although this sparked paranoia amongst Irish Republicans. In a letter to Art O'Brien[403] dated 5th January, Collins revealed his suspicions: 'To be plain about it Cope is lying. He must know that the Castle authorities made the approach to Fr O'F'.[404] Cope's expectation was that Father O'Flanagan would propose a settlement to Lloyd George on the lines of Dominion Home Rule. These 'peace plots' as Sturgis referred to them continued in the midst of the insurgency. On 9th January 1921: a 'very secret interview was arranged for that morning between the PM, O'Connor[405] and Father O'Flanagan and that the two Irishmen would have a preliminary rendezvous in the Treasury with Andy [Cope] and myself [Sturgis] and that probably the Chief Secretary would come in'.[406] The outcome of these talks was recorded by Sturgis: 'Father O'Flanagan is ready to stump Ireland *against* the Republic, in favour of working the Home Rule Act if he can have to offer to the Irish electors the Act plus "fiscal autonomy"'.[407]

Sturgis's diary revealed a paucity of understanding of the unconditional and violent organisation these civil servants were dealing with: 'there is the feeling that many of them (Sinn Fein) are murders with whom we cannot treat ... Still I can't deviate in my opinion that give these people a little now and they are to that extent men bribed, and men bribed are always a bit under one's thumb'.[408] Just two weeks after Sturgis's claim,

---

402   Ibid, p. 27.
403   Art O'Brien was the Sinn Fein representative in London.
404   Quoted in Gallagher, F., *The Anglo-Irish Treaty* (London: Hutchinson, 1965), 25.
405   This was Lord Justice O'Connor Master of the Rolls.
406   Sturgis, op cit, p. 107.
407   Sturgis, op cit, p. 108.
408   Ibid, p. 112.

the RIC suffered one of the most deadly attacks of the whole campaign: 'During the early days of February (1921), the RIC suffered severely in ambushes, the most disastrous of which took place at Dromkeen in Co Limerick on February 2nd when two Crossleys[409] were ambushed and ten constables killed – all the wounded were dispatched in cold blood'.[410]

At the end of March personnel changes took place in terms of the composition of the Cabinet. Bonar Law's impending retirement resulted in a more conciliatory attitude towards Sinn Fein.[411] As Sturgis recorded: 'the PM is in a much more yielding mood and is prepared, not only to make big fiscal concessions but to take the initiative and say – of course after preliminary discussion into which the Ulster people will be brought – what price he is willing to pay for peace?'[412]

During this month British casualties continued to mount. In the third week of March there were 45 and in the last week there were 46. Despite these losses, IRA's operational networks continued to be subverted. On the 24th March a major arms dump was uncovered in Mountjoy Square. Just over a month later on 27th April in Baggot Lane an IRA provincial weapons distribution centre was uncovered.[413] Then on 29th April an organised search on Blackhall Place captured 40 insurgents. Collin's own offices, the first in Mespil Rd and then at 29 Mary Street were both targets for an organised search by the end of this month.

In May 1921 the government was committed to hold elections to the devolved parliaments in Belfast and Dublin as mandated under the Government of Ireland Act. To facilitate the success of the southern parliament Lloyd George was willing to consider: 'the question of a truce during the elections in Ireland'.[414] This idea was rejected by the

---

409 Crossley Motors manufactured military vehicles between 1914 and 1945. The RIC and the British Army used them extensively in Ireland between 1920 and 1922.
410 General Remarks on the Rebellion in the 6th Divisional Area, p. 76, Strickland Papers IWM.
411 Townshend, op cit, p. 174.
412 Sturgis, op cit, p. 148.
413 For details see Townshend, op cit, p. 176.
414 From the Secretary of the Cabinet to the Chief Secretary for Ireland, 11 May 1921, F/19/4/91 Lloyd George Papers., House of Lords Library.

Coalition Cabinet. It was clear from a letter General Macready wrote to Field Marshal Sir Henry Wilson on the 14th May just after the election, the democratic process had been fatally undermined: 'the elections in the South of Ireland are all finished, as there is no contest. I am having the names checked over, because a cursory view of them indicates that the whole of the principal gunmen and the leaders of the IRA have been elected'.[415] Macready went on in the same letter to suggest that the government had created 'a Parliament of 128 red-handed murderers'.[416]

Lloyd George still harboured misplaced assumptions. Sturgis confirmed this in a conversation that he had with Miss Stevenson, the Prime Minister's secretary. There was a hope that Southern Ireland might be persuaded to work his Act without any additions whatever.[417] Sturgis also gave an insight into the extent to Cope was at the centre of this 'politico-military disconnect'. On the 17th May, he noted: 'Andy went out soon after to a very secret interview. He saw the "head lad" of Michael Collins. He gave it as the view of Michael Collins that the IRA soldiers must carry on just as ours do while negotiations are afoot'.[418]

This was compounded by the uncompromising approach to the elections taken by Sinn Fein, when the results were declared on the 25th May: 'Dail Eireann had decided to use the British election machinery as a cheap and convenient way of electing the Second Dail, which would be a larger assembly since the Government of Ireland Act provided for a lower house in Southern Ireland of 128 members, as well as representation by thirty-three members in Westminster'.[419] Sinn Fein was returned unopposed in all the Westminster seats except the four seats which had been allocated to Trinity College Dublin.

---

415 General Macready to Field Marshal Sir Henry Wilson 14th May 1921, Wilson Papers HW2/23 58A IWM.
416 Macready is referring to here to the seats in the devolved parliament that Lloyd George had wanted to set up in Dublin under the 1920 Government of Ireland Act.
417 Sturgis Diary, 11th May 1921, p. 176.
418 *The Last Days of Dublin Castle: The Diaries of Mark Sturgis*, M. Hopkinson M., ed., *The Last Days of Dublin Castle: The Diaries of Mark Sturgis* (Dublin: Irish Academic Press: Dublin, 1999), p. 178.
419 C. Younger, C., *Ireland's Civil War* (London: Fontana Books, 1970), p. 149.

This election result elicited a studied ambiguity by the Chief Secretary Hamar Greenwood. On the one hand he was proselytising the benefits of intelligence driven operations: 'The Sinn Fein Army – I attach its latest muster roll (a captured document) – is growing sullen, losing heavily and is certain to be defeated. A cessation now may mean its recovery ... The position of the Crown Forces is stronger than it has ever been and is improving every day. The extremist leaders know this well and while they are prepared to fight on if there is no alternative'.[420] Yet he reassured the Prime Minister that Cope's channels of communication remained open: 'We can get in touch with de Valera any day, indeed we keep in touch'.[421]

Cope continued to use Irishmen in Crown Service as a conduit for communications to Sinn Fein. In a letter from Seamus O'Concubair to de Valera dated 18th May; Cope disseminated intelligence on the RIC and disparaged British government policy with respect to Northern Ireland:

> I went to see Lord Justice O'Connor on his invitation not knowing that Mr Cope would be present. The latter impressed me as an able man, very adroit and pretending a full appreciation of, and some sympathy with our point of view. He stated that arrangements were already made for the withdrawal of the Auxiliary Forces, presumably as a preliminary to a truce ... he believed a settlement within the Empire, whether as a Republic within the Empire or a Commonwealth or by whatever name it might be called, would of course, have to be preceded by the scrapping of the present Act.[422] He referred contemptuously to the North-East Parliament as a Parliament that has smaller powers than an English County Council.[423]

The same day Cope called on General Macready. The latter revealed, in a letter written the following day, the extent of the opprobrium and lack of trust which existed at the highest level of political–military relations

---

420 Hamar Greenwood to the Prime Minister 11th May, F/19/4/9, Lloyd George Papers, House of Lords Library.
421 Ibid.
422 Cope meant the Government of Ireland Act which made provision for the setting up of two devolved parliaments in Dublin and Belfast.
423 O' Concubair, S., to Eamon de Valera, 18th May 1921, *Documents on Irish Foreign Policy* (Vol. 1), 1919–1921 (Dublin: Royal Irish Academy, 1998), 230–231.

in the Irish Executive: 'The self-appointed, double extra Machiavelli, otherwise Cope of the Castle came to see me late last night and was full of mystery over peace and haute politique generally. I told him pleasantly ... I would have nothing to do with politics'.[424] Macready made the simple soldier's plea of just wanting to get on with the job. Cope was interested to know what Macready thought would happen after the insurgency. His response was vague and non-committal. Cope then had two whiskeys and sodas and left.

The Military Offensive That Never Was

What was extraordinary about this exchange was the absence of any reference to a military plan Macready was to submit to the Cabinet four days later. His reticence was not surprising, Strugis judged Macready to be a complex figure: 'the simple soldier is as cunning as a bag of weasels'.[425] The Chief of the Imperial General Staff, Field Marshal Sir Henry Wilson presented an operational plan to the Cabinet on the 24th May 1921. The caveat being neither he nor General Macready could promise victory. However, he set out an operational vision of what could be achieved by the summer: first there was the need for a declaration of government will; secondly the whole of Ireland with the exception of the six Ulster counties should be placed under Martial Law, this would bring about unity of command; the Royal Navy had to deter the smuggling of arms and give assistance in watching and guarding the Irish coast; finally an active and intense propaganda campaign needed to be undertaken both in England and Ireland. He summarised the prospects of success: 'if all these things are done, we shall run a much better chance of reaching success than we

---

424 General Macready to Field Marshal Sir Henry Wilson 19th May 1921. Wilson papers IWM.
425 Hopkinson M., ed., *The Last Days of Dublin Castle: The Diaries of Mark Sturgis* (Dublin: Irish Academic Press, 1999), 210.

now have under our present plans'.[426] The first part of this plan was called 'Memo A.'[427]. It was predicated on a critical timeline, which aimed 'to take the greatest possible advantage of the weather during the summer and early autumn'. The forces Macready requested were substantial. They consisted of twenty battalions of infantry, three regiments of cavalry, armoured cars, wireless personnel and aeroplanes. In addition, Macready also showed an appreciation of one of the key challenges of this campaign; the unknown will of the enemy. This would be countered by: 'the Government deciding to throw the whole of the forces at their disposal into Ireland'.[428]

The civilian population was recognised as the centre of gravity. The proposed operations would provide a forcing function that would reinstate the civic contract with the civil population. Great importance was attached to showing the flag in districts where there were considerable number of loyalists and people who sit on the fence. The arrival of fresh troops would be an indication of the determination of the British Government to: 'see things through will encourage wavers and will make all except the irreconcilable extremists realise that the success of the rebels is out of the question'.[429]

There was an emphasis on prioritising the deployments of fresh troops to specific geographic locations. The mountainous districts were discounted, as any extremists in this area could be comparatively easily rounded up once the civilised areas have settled down. The focus was on enhancing the legitimacy and social authority: 'Another important factor is to re-establish all police posts which have been abandoned, except those which the military authorities decide need not be re-occupied'.[430] In terms of deployment of infantry units the objectives were: a focus

---

426 Memo, by CIGS Henry Wilson, 24th May 1921, CP 2965, CAB 24/123 National Archives.
427 Memo A, by G.O.C.-in-Ireland, 23 May 1921, in memo by C.I.G.S, 24th May 1921, CP 2965, CAB 24/123 National Archives.
428 Ibid.
429 Ibid.
430 Ibid.

on presence (emphasising the re-occupation of situations vacated by the RIC); information gathering by engaging with the inhabitants; and mobile columns that could move against the rebels once they have been identified.

In Memorandum 'B' Macready gave the Cabinet an assessment of the morale of the troops currently stationed in Ireland. He stressed the importance of bringing the campaign to a conclusion by October 1921. Most tellingly, he referred to the tactical consequences for morale in Ireland of the unwillingness of the British government to challenge the strategic narrative of Irish Republicanism: 'There is a feeling among them (the troops) that their efforts and the danger which hourly besets them are not appreciated by people in Great Britain. The idea is strengthened by the want of anti-rebel propaganda'.[431]

This memorandum highlighted the friction and incomprehension that the lack of a unity of effort was generating: 'It is difficult for the rank and file and junior officers to understand why it is that members of Dail Eireann are left untouched by the Government … seeing that the campaign of murder now in progress is, if not directed by the members of Dail Eireann, at all events concurred in by them'.[432]

A vital requirement for the success of any military operation is the maintenance of operational security. This did not happen. Four days later on the 28th May, Macready wrote to Wilson informing him that the press had got hold of the plan for troop levels in Ireland to be increased. Furthermore, suspicion for the leaking of this information fell on members of the Cabinet. With a hint of sarcasm Macready wrote to Wilson: 'Which of those various so-called gentlemen who were sitting round that table with us in Austen's[433] room have been good enough to tell the press?'[434]

---

431 Memo B, by G.O.C.-in-Ireland, 23 May 1921, in memo by C.I.G.S, 24th May 1921, CP 2965, CAB 24/123 National Archives.
432 Ibid.
433 Austen Chamberlain, Chairman of the Irish Situation Committee.
434 General Macready to Field Marshal Wilson 28th May 1921. Wilson Papers IWM.

Wilson came back to him two days later with the answer: 'The Secretary of State[435] tells me that it was done by the Prime Minister himself. I wonder what his object was!'[436] Senior military commanders were now dealing with a Prime Minister prepared to leak operational plans that pre-empted the Cabinet decision on the 2nd June! The programme dictated an increase in troop levels by two battalions per week. The Irish Situation Committee of the Cabinet also recommended that Martial Law should come into force in twenty-six counties of Ireland on the 14th July if the devolved parliament in the south of Ireland had failed to meet.[437] Wilson wrote to Macready on the same day, and gave a clear understanding of the requirements strategy; the importance of using force for policy ends, and the importance of avoiding what Colin Gray characterised as two dead ends: thinking up desirable policy ends or fighting skilfully. Wilson recognised the paramount importance of achieving a unity of political and military effort: 'Before I start sending troops over, I want the PM to make an announcement of the Government policy in clear terms, both in the house and in the Press, and I had another talk with Hamar (Greenwood) about this last night. His plea for a plan, the announcement of that plan, the execution of that plan, was excellent, and if the "Frocks" will hold to that, we will do our best to carry it out'.[438]

Macready could not hide his suspicions of the Chief Secretary. He informed Wilson on the 2nd June he had been stopped from executing a man in the Martial Law area. He added if there was going to be further interference then he would regard it as a resignation matter. Macready also expressed his suspicion that senior civil servants in Dublin Castle were withholding information from him: 'If they have grounds for knowing that Valera is going to come to heel I ought to be told'.[439]

---

435 This was the Secretary of State for War Worthington – Evans.
436 Field Marshal Henry Wilson to General Macready, 30th May 1921, Wilson Papers IWM.
437 Jones, T. in *Whitehall Diary* (Vol. III), (Oxford: Oxford University Press, 1971), p. 74.
438 K. Middlemas, ed., Field Marshal Henry Wilson to General Macready, 2nd June 1921. Wilson Papers IWM.
439 Macready to Wilson, 2nd June 1921, Wilson papers IWM.

Between the 14th June and the 9th July, a total of nineteen infantry battalions arrived in Ireland.[440] Over this 25-day period this was one battalion every 1.3 days. This was just one battalion short of the original target. In addition, two Royal Marine battalions, two companies of Tank Corps to form armoured car squadrons, signals personnel and Royal Engineers did not arrive before the 11th July. The Record of the Rebellion stated tersely: 'before these units had finished arriving events occurred that changed the situation'[441] and as a consequence, their despatch was cancelled.

Significantly, there was an improvement air–ground integration at the tactical level. This was a product of joint air force and army training conducted in Ireland: 'By April 1921, aircraft escort had been found to be one of the best means of preventing ambushes on either roads or railways, and the squadron diaries record almost daily co-operation with troops and police'.[442] This effectiveness was confirmed in *An T'Oglach*, the IRA's in-house journal: 'the best means that the English have at their disposal for locating our standing positions, strong points, and dumps in the country is the aerial photographer'.[443] This capability was belatedly recognised by the RAF. The first specialist photographic unit was not deployed to Ireland until the month before the armed truce in June 1921.[444]

In a letter written on the 21st June by Wilson to Macready he was still waiting to receive an indication of the political commitment needed to execute this agreed plan: 'We are still carrying on with the programme to send you troops, and tomorrow morning there is to be a Cabinet which I hope will really decide one way or the other, what they are going to

---

440 See Record of the Rebellion (Vol. I), p. 47.
441 Ibid, p. 47.
442 D. Richardson, *The Royal Air Force and the Irish War of Independence 1918–1922*. *Air Power Review*, /3, Autumn/Winter 2016, p. 27.
443 NAUK AIR 5/772. An T'Oglach, 3 June 1921. Quoted in Richardson, D., 'The Royal Air Force and the Irish War of Independence 1918–1922'. *Air Power Review*, 19/3 Autumn/Winter (2016), 27.
444 Op cit. p. 26.

do about Ireland'.[445] Exactly one week later the military offensive was unpicked by a series of choices Wilson was powerless to stop.

The Conditions of Peace and Humiliation

Four days after Field Marshal Sir Henry Wilson and General Macready had presented their military plan to the Cabinet, Patrick Moylett, the Ballina businessman, who had been involved in the aborted negotiations with Lloyd George which straddled the murders of Bloody Sunday, received an invitation from the US Consul in Dublin, Mr Dumont to meet. On the 28th May the American stated that the British were 'very anxious', to meet de Valera. Initially Moylett gave a cynical retort and suggested that if the British put an advert in the daily papers, he will certainly see it. The response of the US Counsel was to provide evidence of his bona fides: 'He then took down a file of correspondence between himself and Washington, and also between himself and Dublin Castle', which included the Chief Secretary and Sir John Anderson: 'I saw a letter from Sir John Anderson asking for Mr Dumont's good offices in bringing the British authorities and de Valera together. Having seen that, I decided to act. I knew they meant business'.[446]

This approach was discussed at a meeting of the suppressed Dail Cabinet presided over by de Valera. He viewed the offer as a trap. Yet the next day on the 29th May he agreed that Moylett should go to Dublin Castle. This information was conveyed to Mr Dumont's office. The British still had to be informed of this decision. A meeting was set up in the Shelbourne Hotel. Brigadier General Brind, GSO1 Military Intelligence, Ireland was to attend to receive the Sinn Fein response: 'I went into the lavatory in that hotel, and I found in there Mr Dumont and General Brind, the Chief Intelligence Officer for the British. I got my

---

445 Wilson to Macready 21st June. 1921, Wilson Papers IWM.
446 Bureau of Military History, Patrick Moylett WS 767.

first introduction to General Brind in that room, and that was where the information was imparted'.[447]

The next day, the 30th May 1921, Moylett presented himself at the gates of Dublin Castle. He was taken to an apartment on the ground floor where Cope was waiting. He opened the conversation by saying that the British were anxious meet de Valera. Moylett then asked Cope what his agenda was. Cope replied: 'We are willing to acknowledge that we are defeated ... We are willing to withdraw our whole establishment, from the lowest policeman to the highest judge. I [Moylett] added: and their pensions, yes, [Cope] said'.[448] This was the moment when the narrative of defeat for the British Army was conveyed to a member of Sinn Fein by a Crown civil servant.

The discussion between Cope and Moylett covered the fields of trade, currency, economics and included tariffs. What was instructive was the manner in which Cope presented his status in the British administration: 'Mr Cope told me that he had superseded both the Lord Chancellor and the Chief Secretary. They were direct representatives of Lloyd George in this country, and he said that although he was only an ordinary civil servant, he was here to make peace'.[449]

This secret meeting needs to be understood in the context of the ongoing insurgency. On the same day Irish Volunteers in Youghal launched a land mine attack on members of the Hampshire Regiment. Six soldiers were killed including two band boys. Strugis regarded these murders as an inconvenience to the policy trajectory he and Cope were committed to. His diary made a reference to: 'killing some wretched little band boys'.[450] Three weeks later on the 22nd of June, the extent of the willingness of Lloyd George's government to trade security under the rule of the law for the illusion of political reconciliation was exposed by an Army operation. de Valera was arrested in an organised search conducted by the

447 Ibid.
448 Ibid.
449 Ibid.
450 Hopkinson M., ed., *The Last days of Dublin Castle the Mark Sturgis Diaries* (Dublin: Irish Academic Press, 1999), 183.

Worcester Regiment. This represented a moment of real danger to Cope's clandestine policy. Although he initially did not give his correct name,[451] de Valera was found in possession of documents that linked him to an attack that had taken place on an army detachment seven days earlier: 'de V is responsible for all acts of the IRA. As the head of the government for which it claims to act, it is true that he doesn't organise the actual atrocities, but he has cognisance of them. Among his papers, when he was arrested last week (22/6/21) was the report, addressed to the President by the Minister of Defence on the train ambush near Dublin by the IRA against the R. W. Kent Regt (on the 16th June)'.[452] Even Sturgis referred to the 'seditious documents' found in de Valera's possession when he was arrested.[453]

The lawless actions of Lloyd George and Cope in facilitating his release can only be understood in the context of the meeting that had taken place between Cope and Moylett: 'Now Jeffries told me that the following took place. Army G. H. Q. at Kilmainham wired to his London office' and 'De Valera captured. Cope suggests release'. This telegram arrived about 7 p.m. and Jeffries took it across to the Colonial Office (Irish Office), but Hamar Greenwood had left, so Jeffries took it to Lloyd George, who rubbed his hands together and said 'Well done the military. He must on no account be released'. 'Taking this as settled, Jeffries left, but as soon as he had gone Lloyd George sends orders for de Valera to be released, which was done'.[454]

Winter, who happened to be in London at the time, requested an audience with the Prime Minister. He enquired about who ordered his release. He was told by Lloyd George: 'It was not on my orders that he was released'.[455] Sturgis gave two further insights to this episode: first desire by Dublin Castle to censor any media coverage of his arrest; secondly,

---

451   See Jeune Papers IWM.
452   Foulkes Papers 7/24, Dublin 9/7/21, Basil Liddell Hart Archive, Kings College, London.
453   Sturgis, op cit.
454   Jeune Papers IWM.
455   O. Winter, O., *Winter's Tale* (London: The Richards Press, 1955), p. 339.

Cope was intimately involved in his release. Sturgis recorded in his diary: 'Andy got on to the CS and Jonathan this morning ... they said de V was to be released at once and the fact that he was arrested at all was, if possible, to be kept out of the press'.[456]

On 24th June, the day after de Valera's release, there were two Cabinet meetings in Ireland. The first one was described by Thomas Jones: 'I got a message (very secret) to summon a group Ministers to discuss Ireland at 4.30'.[457] Among those present were Greenwood, Chamberlain, Shortt, Worthington – Evans and Balfour. Sir John Anderson and Cope were also present. The Jones omitted to state that initially, Cope was not invited. He managed to gain access due to the influence of Lady Greenwood.

Sturgis nicknamed the meeting 'the Andy Cabinet'. Cope addressed the Cabinet. His political sympathies towards the insurgents even brought a rebuke from his boss, the Chief Secretary of Ireland: 'Andy harangued His Majesty's Ministers and even on his own showing must have been pretty hysterical ... he talked failure without an offer and Greenwood told him "to curb his Sinn Fein tendencies"'.[458] When a later Cabinet meeting was called for 6 p.m. there was no Agenda. Instead, ministers were just told it would be about Ireland. When the Cabinet met a letter was in the process of being drafted. It was not to be published and there would be no communication that would give any clue to the British Government's action as that might create what was called 'special difficulties'. A personal letter from the Prime Minister to de Valera inviting him to meet him in London was signed.[459] Cope personally delivered the letter on 25th June 1921.

On the same day, the most important British agent to have penetrated Sinn Fein, at the highest level, filed a report to Sir Basil Thompson, then Director of Intelligence in the Home Office. The agent was Molly

---

456 Sturgis, op cit, p. 190.
457 T. Jones, T., in: K. Middlemas, ed., *Whitehall Diary*, (Vol. III), *Ireland 1918–1925* (Oxford: Oxford University Press: Oxford, 1971), 79.
458 Ibid, p. 192.
459 The full text of this letter can be found in Documents on Irish Foreign Policy (Vol. 1), 1919–1922, (Dublin: Royal Irish Academy, 1998), 232–233.

Childers, the wife of Erskine Childers.[460] She had access to the leadership of Sinn Fein, including both de Valera and Collins. Her report provided a candid insight into de Valera's political attitudes: 'I have frequently told you that De Valera, whatever may be said to the contrary, and is a red hot extremist'.[461] She had no illusions about the bankruptcy of negotiating with Sinn Fein, and on whom the costs would fall: 'I must again emphasise what I have repeated time after time. Any thought of compromise or conciliation with SF is absolutely unthinkable and, moreover, is impossible. You are not only wasting your time, you are frittering away the lives of valuable and gallant servants of the Crown'.[462] She identified the absence of the one thing that Cope and his colleagues assumed in the leaders of Sinn Fein: a sense of transactional reciprocity: 'In our attempts at conciliation they see only weakness and signs that they are forcing the Government to its knees, to grant them any damn thing they want'.[463]

Molly Childers' intelligence report provided an assessment of how Sinn Fein viewed the efficacy of Cope's secret negotiations and underlined the value of captured documents: 'I told you how negotiations carried on by Cope of the Castle had been scoffed at and ridiculed. They say that he was primarily responsible for D.V.s release, and that Boyd (GOC Dublin District) was all for keeping him. Is this true? The Shinners have a great wind up over some documents their august President had on him at the time of his arrest. Was anything valuable captured?'[464]

Critically her motivation as an agent was declining. The dangers and consequences of being discovered were made clear: 'you know why I took this job on, not for cash but to feel that I was really doing something to help ... I wouldn't get 10 minutes grace if they had the slightest suspicion ... As you know very well, this work is of the most trying description, no shouting or even social life for that matter, apart from the Society of these

---

460 Foy, op cit, p. 234.
461 Copy of Report from dated 25.6.21, Lloyd George Papers, F/19/5/7, House of Lords Library.
462 Ibid.
463 Ibid.
464 Ibid.

Shinners. The war was a pleasure to this, and one felt that everyone was out to win'.[465] The intelligence report was passed to the Prime Minister by Hamar Greenwood on 29th June. In the covering note to Lloyd George's secretary and mistress[466] Greenwood stressed its veracity:

> My Dear Miss Stevenson,
> This really comes 'straight from the Cow'
> HG[467]

This intelligence was four days too late in terms informing any Cabinet decision. Cope had already delivered the letter to de Valera indicating the British government's willingness to negotiate and confer legitimacy on Sinn Fein despite its status as a 'suppressed' organisation.

The issue that threatened this policy turned on a decision the British Cabinet itself had taken on the 26th May. If the southern devolved parliament in Dublin was not functioning within a fortnight of being summoned on the 28th June, then the Viceroy would dissolve it and declare martial law throughout Ireland, with the exception of Northern Ireland. The target date was the 14th July. This would provide the legal context for the planned military campaign. Senior civil servants in Dublin Castle devised a strategy to short-circuit this requirement and remove the legal context for the campaign. The solution was to enact a constitutional charade, to open and then immediately adjourn the devolved southern Irish parliament in Dublin. Sir John Ross was appointed Lord Chancellor on the 27th June. He would open the parliament on the next day and as Sturgis put it: 'address advice to himself as Lord Chancellor and President of the Senate'.[468]

Macready was drawn into this ploy as he 'was sworn today to swear Ross'. Sturgis identified his fatal character weakness: 'Macready, who

---

465 Ibid.
466 Lloyd George had installed his mistress Miss Stevenson as his private secretary in Downing Street.
467 Papers of Lloyd George, F19/5/7/ House of Lords Library.
468 Sturgis, op cit, p. 193.

always barks and then gives way good naturedly enough if pressed'.[469] Sturgis was dismissive of anticipated objections by the army, and fully embraced the choice to negotiate: 'there will be lots of talk from Junior Officers – and perhaps some senior ones! – about selling the pass and treating with the rebels but that thank God is a Cabinet affair'.[470]

On the 28th June the parliament was opened in the Council Chamber of the Department of Agriculture. Sir John Anderson and Sturgis both attended. The latter made a comment in his diary about 'the Farce, half empty room, etc.'. Cope was not at the opening. Instead, he had gone down what Macready called 'the main drain', contacting Sinn Fein to ensure a favourable response to Lloyd George's letter. More importantly Cope's activities were no longer a closely kept secret. A 6th Division Area Report indicated a realisation of what the Irish Executive had been doing: 'incredulous of the rumours that the Government were actually negotiating secretly with the leaders of the murder gang, everybody threw themselves with still greater energy into the struggle, and the campaign against the rebel Flying Columns was further intensified in June'.[471]

On the same day, Sir John Anderson, the Under Secretary at Dublin Castle sent a note to the Chief of Police. It ordered a halt to any further organised searches against the operational networks of the insurgents. More importantly the ability of Winter's organisation to monitor Cope's relationship with members of Sinn Fein disappeared: 'In view of the fact, following the Prime Minister's letter, communications are likely to pass between leading Sinn Feiners which the government are bound to respect, no raids or searches must for the time being be made on premises occupied or frequented by persons of political importance without previous reference to this office (W. Cope or myself). Please give necessary

---

469 Ibid, p. 193.
470 Sturgis, op cit, p. 194.
471 The Irish Rebellion in the 6th Div Area from after 1916 rebellion to December 1921, Strickland Papers P363 IWM, p. 112.

instructions'.[472] This intelligence capability, successfully built up over such a short period of time, was turned off like a bath tap.

De Valera's response to the Prime Minister's letter was published in the press on the 29th June. Its tone disappointed even Cope: Sturgis made a reference to de Valera's 'monkey house vanity'.[473] On the 30th of June there was yet another extension of the policy of *de facto* legal immunity to the leaders of Sinn Fein. The Record of the Rebellion referred to the 'release of extremists'. All of whom had all been charged and found guilty by due lawful process. The names were: Arthur Griffith, Professor Mc Neill, Michael Staines, E. J. Duggan. They were serving sentences in Mountjoy Jail. In addition, R. C. Barton was released from Portland Prison where he was serving a 3-year sentence for incitement to murder. Cope insisted that Anderson sanction all these releases. On the same day, Anderson wrote to the Chief Secretary suggesting that Cope was acting far beyond his remit: 'The important thing now is to preserve the note of good will and reconciliation sounded in the Prime Minister's letter. Whatever may be the outcome this is clearly right. There are people on this side who would like to trick either DV or Craig into some false move which would shift public opinion now standing with the Gov to the other side. Cope is working for himself'.[474]

Lloyd George's letter of 25th June was the catalyst for both halting British intelligence operations and facilitating the 'release of extremists' as the Record of the Rebellion called them. Cope was present at a meeting at GHQ whereby Macready agreed to halt any further reinforcements of the British garrison in Ireland. In a letter written to Lord Middleton, the head of the Southern Irish Unionists, reference was made to a conference that was held on the 8th July with General Boyd, Commanding the Dublin District, General Tudor, the Chief of Police 'at which Mr Cope[475]

---

472 Memo from Sir John Anderson to Chief of Police 28th June 1921, CO 904/188, National Archives.
473 Sturgis, op cit, p. 195.
474 Letter from Sir John Anderson to the Chief Secretary of Ireland, 30th June 1921, F/19/5/8 Lloyd George PAPERS. House of Lords Library.
475 Cope's name was underlined in the original letter.

attended'. Macready now acquiesced to the abandonment of the campaign he had planned and presented to the Cabinet with Field Marshal Sir Henry Wilson just six weeks ago: 'I have no objection from a military point of view to movement of troops from England being for the moment stopped'.[476] The emphasis was now on the unproven assumption concerning the ability of 'Mr de Valera and his supporters to give guarantees'.

Cope's role in facilitating an armed truce between the Irish Volunteers and the British government was reflected in a letter Macready wrote to Wilson on the same day as the conference: 'Just been talking on the phone to that busy little bee, Cope, to make sure that they do not carry out wholesale releases without letting me know. As already troops and police are not feeling at all happy at the release of Duggan and Staines, who are both active instigators of murder'.[477]

Later the same day Macready went to a meeting in the Mansion House and met a Sinn Fein delegation that included Griffith and de Valera to agree terms of an armed truce. Sturgis regarded Macready's participation as a strategic triumph: 'The fact that Macready is up to the neck in it himself should save *us* from much military sniping ...'.[478]

On the 9th July Cope brought Duggan and Barton, both recently released from prison to Army GHQ to discuss the terms laid down in the C in C's letter. Writing to Wilson the next day, Macready mixed social commentary, character judgements, and political observations in an effort to downplay his role in what had become a staged defeat: 'went to the Mansion House, through an extremely smelly crowd, half of whom were praying, and the other half cheering'.[479] He stressed that the conditions of peace were exactly the same as the original draft. Griffith and de Valera were characterised as political mediocrities: 'Griffith struck me as a man of no particular parts, nor, for that matter of that, did Valera, who seemed a rather fussy, small-minded man, who spends

---

476 General Macready to Lord Midleton 8th July 1921. Wilson papers IWM.
477 General Macready to Field Marshal Wilson, 8th July 1921, Wilson Papers IWM.
478 Sturgis diary, op cit, p. 201.
479 General Macready to Field Marshal Sir Henry Wilson 9th July 1921. Wilson Papers IWM.

his life concentrating on detail. I doubt he will have much chance once the "Goat" gets hold of him'.[480]

Two days later, an armed truce came into effect at 12 noon on 11th July. The concessions made by Cope on behalf of Lloyd George's government to Moylett to embrace the fiction that Britain was defeated bore little relation to the tactical realities. The Record of the Rebellion gave an assessment of the capability of the Irish Volunteers prior to the armed truce: 'The rebel organisation throughout the country was in a precarious condition, and the future from the Sinn Fein point of view may be said to have been almost desperate'.[481] They focussed their diminished material and human resources to deliver a final show of force. The period prior to the armed truce Townshend claimed was: 'one of the bloodiest weekends of the conflict, with the IRA killing some 20 people in 36 hours. The last shot was fired at a police patrol in Kingscourt, Co Cavan, at 11.55 am'.[482] Even Sturgis admitted that 'they killed right up to the Armistice'.[483]

The Consequences of the Truce

The British Army's counter-insurgency campaign effectively came to an end on the 11th July 1921. On the 12th July, Field Marshal Sir Henry Wilson wrote a letter to General Macready indicating his personal dismay at the turn of events: 'this plan of inviting over Valera and anybody he likes to bring with him leaves me in the same condition as the coster[484] who wheeled his barrow to the top of Hampstead Hill, where a passing bus knocked it over – he looked up at the bus driver and said "there ain't no bloody words for it". How anybody in their senses or out of them, can

---

480 Ibid.
481 Record of the Rebellion (Vol. 1) (Operations), p. 54.
482 Townshend, op cit, p. 198.
483 Sturgis, op cit, p. 203.
484 A coster was a seller of fruit and other wares from a barrow.

Tactics, Operations, and Lost Victories

hope to get peace in Ireland by this means passes my understanding'.[485] Wilson went on to reflect that it was a curious thing how a nation could be doped with lies until they believed they are truths, and how the doper believes in the lies himself. This was a thinly disguised attack on Lloyd George. He revealed to Macready the collapse of his professional relationship with the Prime Minister: 'I would have you know that I was never consulted and never even spoken to on any question relative to Ireland by the Prime minister or the cabinet'.[486] It was a cruel fate for this Irishman who was professional head of the British Army.

The army in Ireland now perceived itself in an 'illogical compact': 'On the one hand, the Crown agreed to refrain from action for the suppression of outrage, and on the other hand, the rebels agreed to desist from acts which under any circumstance were crimes'.[487] The Record of the Rebellion claimed the government lost, for the second time, the battle for the strategic narrative: 'not only the rebels themselves, but the Press and a large section of the public, came to look upon any outrage committed by the rebels before the agreements as a legitimate act, or at least one to be condoned, while any action of the Crown forces taken for the suppression of illegal acts after the agreement were regarded as "breaches of the truce"'.[488]

Wilson's prescience with respect to de Valera was confirmed by a series of meetings that took place in Downing Street. The first took place on the 14th July in the Cabinet Room between the Prime Minister and de Valera and his delegation.[489] There were subsequent meetings on the 15th, 16th, 18th and 21st July. There is no full record of these meetings. Tom Jones gave a sense of the difficulties Wilson first alluded to. In the initial meeting Lloyd George tried to get de Valera to concede that the 'Celts were never Republicans and have no word for such an idea'. This was the first move in a dialogue that proved to be futile: 'When after

---

485 Letter from Wilson to Macready 12th July 1921.
486 Wilson to Macready, 12 July 1921, IWM.
487 Record of the Rebellion (Vol. 1), p. 51.
488 Ibid, p. 51.
489 This consisted of Arthur Griffith, Robert Barton Austin Stack and Erskine Childers.

surveying Irish history about it and about it, it became clear that progress could only be made by the British Government tabling its own proposals. These were handed to Mr de Valera on 20th July'.[490] Until the release of the third volume of the Record of the Rebellion in 2012, it has been impossible to evaluate how the army judged its own performance in terms of the legal framework they had been working under since August 1920.[491] An insight was given to the effect Regulation 14B had on the internment of the Irish Volunteers, and the location of these camps and the numbers involved.

In terms of prosecutions there were a total of 1266 successful convictions under the Court Martial system in 1920. In 1921 the total was 1820. There was an important qualification to the latter total: 'this practically represents the work of six months, as trials after the truce were very few in numbers'.[492] The overall success of the legal process was also assessed: 'Of the total convictions under ROIR 1920, only thirty-nine were quashed for irregularities representing less than 2 per cent of the total'.[493] The concessions the government made over capital convictions was also revealed. A total of thirty-seven people convicted of the most serious offences were let off: 'On 11th July 1921 there were a total of twenty-six persons under a sentence of death by Courts Martial and fifteen under sentence of death by Military Courts. The consideration of these cases was suspended by the truce'.[494]

The use of internment had been effective in removing manpower from the Irish Volunteers. A total of 3,954 were interned.[495] This figure was broken down to four locations: Ballykinlar Camp, 1,783, the Curragh Camp 1,342, Spike Island 545 and Bere Island 284. There was an acknowledgement there had been 116 escapes 'chiefly affected by tunnelling'.

490 Jones, T., *Whitehall Diary* (Vol. 3), in K. Middlemas, ed., *Ireland 1918–1925* (London: Oxford University Press, 1971), 89.
491 Townshend's Appendix X only went up to December 1920.
492 Record of the Rebellion (Vol. III) (Law), p. 16.
493 Ibid, p. 16.
494 Ibid, p. 16.
495 Townshend claims in Appendix XII that the total interned was 4,454.

Conclusions

This chapter does not claim to provide a comprehensive account of the campaign between January 1920 and July 1921. In evaluating the elements of success and failure, the independent variables at the strategic, operational and tactical levels can be characterised as a fishing net that has provided a way to assess the historical evidence. More importantly the 'operational codes' acted a prism through which political choices can be understood and analysed.

At the strategic level, the army recognised at an early stage the importance of countering the strategic narrative of the Irish Volunteers. One of the last actions of the outgoing GOC-in-C Ireland, Lieutenant General Shaw, had been a request to the Lord Lieutenant of Ireland for greater publicity.[496] It can be argued that the army waited too long before appointing Colonel Foulkes to head up its own propaganda unit at Army GHQ in May 1921, just two months before the armed truce. A sense of frustration with Basil Clarke, a journalist appointed by Dublin Castle, was clear in a letter Macready wrote to Sir John Anderson: 'Until this question of propaganda is properly tackled by someone far more able than Basil Clarke we shall never get it right'.[497] As previously cited, a sense of frustration was clear in the last paragraph of volume two of the Record of the Rebellion: 'In one department ... namely Publicity it was unrivalled. This department was energetic, subtle, and exceptionally skilful in mixing truth falsehood and exaggeration and was perhaps the most powerful and the least fought arm of the Sinn Fein Forces'.[498] Furthermore, the security of the planned military campaign was compromised by one of the most lawless Prime Ministers of the twentieth century. Despite the successful deployment of thousands of troops to Ireland within a tight

---

496 See chapter three p. 6.
497 Macready to Anderson, 7th March 1921, Anderson Papers CO, 904 188/2 quoted in Townshend, C., *The British Campaign in Ireland* (Oxford: Oxford University Press, 1975), 168.
498 Intelligence in Ireland, 1920–1921, (Vol. 2), p. 46, Strickland Papers IWM P325.

timetable, the planned offensive was undermined and aborted by the decisions taken at the 'Andy Cabinet'.

At the operational level the disruption of the operational networks of the Irish Volunteers was a success. The decision by Anderson and Cope to stop organised searches on the 28th June 1921 was a clear mistake and dismantled a key capability that had been built up over a relatively short period of time. Winter displayed a nuanced understanding of intelligence. He acknowledged it was not a panacea, and its sustained exploitation was dependent on other factors: 'Intelligence alone cannot win a war. It is merely an aid to force, and it is only by action that the desired end can be attained'.[499] He claimed the British government used a degree of 'coercion which was not sufficiently severe'. Although he claimed they nearly succeeded.

Senior commanders like Macready, Strickland and Jeudwine recognised the need to deter the launch of attacks, reassure the public, and attrition the capability of the insurgents. The Record of the Rebellion cited a number of examples where policy decisions to release convicted prisoners, or those awaiting trial had an adverse effect on both public confidence and the morale of both the police and the Army. Successful organised searches by the Army were compromised by Cope if deemed politically expedient. Extending *de facto* legal immunity from de Valera to other members of Sinn Fein who had been convicted under the due process of the law had a corrosive effect.

General Strickland[500] one of the key Divisional commanders of the whole campaign was both despondent and disillusioned at the cumulative consequences of these choices. In the last entry in his personal diary dated 17th May 1922[501] he stated: 'And so this is the end of two and half year's toil. A year ago (May 1921) we had a perfect organisation and had "them" beat. A short time more would have completed it thoroughly. "They" knew

---

499 Ibid, p. 73.
500 General Strickland 1869–1951. He was the Commanding Officer for 6th Division from 1919 to 1922. This area covered Cork and West Cork areas of intense insurgent activity.
501 He was ordered out of Ireland on 18th May 1922.

this and got the Politicians to negotiate with the present results. *Never has the country been in such a state. No sort of order or authority in these parts. All our labours and energy have been thrown in the gutter, to say nothing of the expense and the deprivation. It almost makes one wish one had never been concerned in the show*'.[502] Winter concurred with Strickland's judgement: 'In May 1921, the IRA Commander in the south wrote to Collins to say that owing to the shortage of arms and ammunition, his men would be unable to continue much longer'.[503] Winter in his 1955 autobiography makes a reference to the achievements of the counter-insurgency campaign and the army's planned offensive which was undermined by both Lloyd George and Cope. The Crown forces: 'practically held Sinn Fein by the throat at that time and would have been able to quash the rebellion with a final offensive in the summer'.[504]

Brigadier Brind acknowledged the depleted capability of the Irish Volunteers prior to the armed truce in a secret report, submitted to Field Marshal Sir Henry Wilson, dated September 1921. Despite having facilitated the key meeting between Moylett and Cope, he now appeared to be suffering from buyer's remorse: 'three months ago the rebel organisation throughout the country was in a precarious condition, and the future from the Sinn Fein point of view may be said to have been well-nigh desperate. The Headquarters of the IRA was functioning under the greatest difficulty, many of its offices having been captured complete … it is small wonder that the rebel leaders grasped at the straw that was offered, and agreed to negotiations by cessation of activities on both sides'.[505]

Overall, this campaign failed to give consistent expression to the principles counter-insurgency. All insurgencies or terrorist campaigns are *dialectical struggles* between competing adversaries; outcomes are

---

502 Strickland Papers, P363 Pocket Diary, p. 5. IWM General Strickland 1869–1951. He was the General Officer Commanding 6th Division from 1919 to 1922. This area covered Cork and West Cork. It was an area of intense insurgent activity.
503 Winter, O., *Winter's Tale* (London: The Richards Press, 1955), p. 341.
504 Quoted in McMahon, P., 'British Intelligence and the Anglo-Irish Truce, July–December 1921', *Irish Historical Studies* 35/140 (November 2007), 526.
505 Military Situation in Ireland at the end of September 1921 (Secret) private papers FM Sir Henry Wilson (Vol. 8), HHW2/2F IWM.

determined by the interaction between opponents.[506] In this instance the British Army had to contend with the extra impediment of Ministers and civil servants, such as Cope, pursuing political initiatives with inconsistent results, and consciously undermining the security effort. This made it impossible for an integrated approach to be realised. Winter understood the consequences of these operational codes: 'The great Clausewitz said "All kinds of philanthropy in war are a gross and pernicious error"'.[507]

In July 1922, the Secretary of State for War, Sir Laming Worthington-Evans revealed the determination of the Coalition Government to ensure that any evidence which drew attention to the pernicious effect of the operational codes would have a restricted audience even inside the British Army. On the cover sheet of the draft copy of the Record of the Rebellion he wrote: 'It is proposed to give a strictly limited circulation to an account of the relations between the military and the civil authorities during 1920/1'.[508] The distribution was sparse. Only 250 copies were printed, eighty were distributed throughout the Commands, and Schools of the British and Indian Army, and the War Office. The rest, a total of 170, were 'to be kept'.[509]

The butcher's bill was not insignificant. From the 1st April 1920 to 11th July 1921, forty-three army officers were killed and thirty-five wounded. In addition, 118 other ranks were killed and 307 wounded in the same period. The two police forces took an even higher toll. From 1st January 1919 to the 11th July 1921, 405 police officers were killed and 682 wounded.

Mumford has argued that there can be identified norms with respect to the British approach to counter insurgency: 'Secret negotiations, it must be remembered, are a constant trend throughout British counter-insurgency campaigns'.[510] This is insufficiently clear as he fails to identify the proclivity to import into warfare the values of commerce.

---

506   See Gray, C. S., *Modern Strategy* (Oxford: Oxford University Press, 1999), 23–25.
507   Ibid, p. 74.
508   See WO 141/94 National Archives.
509   Ibid.
510   Mumford, A., *The Counter-Insurgency Myth* (Oxford: Routledge, 2012), 102.

This behaviour had two consequences: first an unwillingness to sustain the campaign to the finish despite intelligence indicating the Irish volunteers were unable to sustain their campaign; secondly, a predilection for indirectness and the blurring of issues such as the maintenance of legitimacy and social authority.

There are two final questions to be addressed. First, what judgements can be made about Cope's behaviour during the armed truce and beyond? Secondly, what happened to him? With respect to the first question, the 'illogical compact' that the army found itself in was greatly exacerbated by Cope. He consistently undermined the military and police authorities in Ireland. In August 1921, General Strickland sent the following message to army GHQ in Dublin: 'The motor car restrictions are a farce. Republican leaders move freely without passes in stolen cars; a case occurred of a DIV Commander IRA being arrested for this offence by the RIC. His immediate release was ordered on the telephone by an Under-Secretary at Dublin Castle, who "told off" the DI concerned for arresting him, and who chose to ignore my position as Military Governor of the Martial Law Area'.[511]

In another confidential memo sent by the Colonel Commandant of the seventeenth Infantry Brigade to General Strickland's sixth Divisional Headquarters underlined a similar pattern: 'He (Cope) said that instructions would be sent for the car which the Essex Regiment took from the rebels to be handed back to the IRA. This car is the property of Colonel LUCAS of BALLINADEE, who is the sole and lawful owner of it, and it is difficult to know how its return to the rebels can be reconciled with any sense of justice and fair play'.[512]

Cope's relationship with Macready had now frayed badly. His malleability had limits as he made clear to Wilson: 'Cope has just been in and rather lost his temper to the effect that he has had every kind of obstacle

---

511 General Strickland to Army GHQ Dublin, 22/8/1921, Strickland Papers, P363 IWM.
512 Confidential memo No. 26. Visit of Mr Cope, Assistant Under Secretary at Dublin Castle to Bandon 15th September 1921, Strickland Papers P363, Imperial War Museum.

placed in his way. I had to tell him that while I had gone a very long way in swallowing a considerable amount of dirt, there was a limit beyond which I would not go, and that while he was quite prepared to drag the Union Jack in the dirt in the hope of arriving at a settlement I could not go to that extent unless I got direct orders from the Cabinet'.[513]

The situation the RIC was placed in by Cope moved even Macready to anger: 'It is positively sickening the way in which the Police all over the country are absolutely passive, due, of course, not to any definite orders, but to their knowledge of the fact that they will be given away by Cope & Co if they try to assert themselves even in the smallest degree'.[514]

Cope's activities emerged into the public domain in September 1921 with what Mr Anderson of the Irish Office called an attack on 'Andy Cope by the Morning Post'.[515] Macready, in a letter to Wilson, was candid about the reasons for this: 'Cope's nerves and health are such that he is not fit to be in any responsible position, and I am not surprised at what appeared in the "Morning post"'.[516] In November 1921, the Unionist MP for Belfast Woodvale, Robert Lynn[517] asked the following question in the House of Commons to the Chief Secretary: 'whether any high official in Dublin Castle was supplied with a safe permit or pass by the Irish republican army or Sinn Fein, and under what conditions it was issued'.[518] Greenwood refuted the first part of the question and then claimed that the second part did not arise. Lynn responded with a supplementary: 'How is it that Mr Cope was able to go about Dublin?'[519] Greenwood

---

513 General Macready to the Field Marshal Sir Henry Wilson, 31st August 1921, Wilson Papers (Vol. 8), HHW2/2F, IWM.
514 General Macready to the Field Marshal Sir Henry Wilson, 24th September 1921, Wilson Papers, (Vol. 8), HHW2/2F, IWM.
515 The Morning Post was a right-wing paper that was published in the United Kingdom up to 1937. It was then absorbed into the Daily Telegraph.
516 General Macready to the Field Marshal Sir Henry Wilson, 23rd September 1921, Wilson Papers, Vol. 8, HHW2/2F, IWM.
517 He was MP for Woodvale between 1918 and 1922 and MP for West Belfast between 1922 and 1929.
518 Parliamentary Debates, Commons (Vol. 147), Col. 1900, 3rd November 1921.
519 Ibid.

feebly responded that Cope was a 'plucky servant of the Crown'. A more serious allegation was made by Lynn: 'whether key ciphers and confidential information regarding important matters in Ireland have been communicated by high officials in Dublin Castle to Sinn Fein Leaders; whether careful investigations have revealed the fact that not more than three officials could have been responsible for betraying the Government secrets'.[520] Cope's responsibility for the transport and communications branch of the RIC, made him a prime suspect. His final question to Greenwood revealed the consequences of Cope's actions: 'whether it is a fact that on several occasions when the police have made searches, they have found the secret key cipher before it has been communicated to the county inspector?'[521] The Chief Secretary maintained that he had no knowledge of these facts. Lynn responded that he had.[522]

Three years later, his activities burst into the public domain again. In 1924, in a House of Lords debate, the Irish peer, Lord Muskerry made a number of allegations against Cope. The context was claims for compensation by 'Irish Loyalists' for attacks launched against their properties during the insurgency. The IRA attacked Lord Muskerry's property on 4th July 1921.[523] Without using his name Lord Muskerry referred to Cope's career and the fact that he had been appointed on the personal authority of Lloyd George: 'He selected a certain person in the service of the Excise Department. ... This person was sent over to Ireland as an Assistant Under Secretary. Mr Lloyd George also sent over four other officials, but I am dealing especially with this Assistant Under Secretary'.[524] These allegations were the most serious made against Cope: 'On his arrival at the castle he took advantage of his official position to attend meetings held by heads of Departments to consider the best means of putting down these outrages and of restoring law and order. Having obtained full information, he at once proceeded to convey that information to the leaders of

---

520 Ibid, Col 1902.
521 Ibid, Col 1902.
522 Ibid, Col 1902.
523 Hansard House of Lords, 5th March 1924 (Vol. 56), Col 535.
524 Ibid, Col 536.

the Sinn Fein organisation, with the result that these plans devised by His Majesty's officers came to naught and in many cases. His Majesty's officers and men lost their lives. The result of this treachery at headquarters was to paralyse the efforts of His Majesty's officials, and crime and outrage were rampant throughout the country'.[525]

In the two weeks between this initial statement and a subsequent debate in the House of Lords, Lord Muskerry cited more corroborating evidence: 'Since that debate, I have received a number of letters from officers and ex-officers of the Royal Irish Constabulary who were in Dublin at the time, and they make the same statement. These letters are marked private and confidential, and I cannot make use of them'.[526] Lord Muskerry urged that the government should set up a committee with the power to investigate Cope's actions and take evidence as to his behaviour between 1920 and 1921. This proposal was rejected by the Lord Chancellor: 'The Government are thoroughly satisfied that no case has been shown to make Sir Alfred Cope deserving of reproach'.[527] His actions were defended by the government's chief law officer, and he had got away without a scratch.

Cope remained in Ireland until October 1922. In the same month he was knighted and became Sir Alfred Cope. This honour was conferred on him by Lloyd George. Paradoxically he never again held another post in the Civil Service. From 1923 to 1925 he was Secretary of the National Liberal Party. The Prime Minister whom he had served with such single-minded devotion brought career stopping problems for him: 'he found close co-operation with Lloyd George impossible and abandoned politics altogether'.[528]

Although he only spent two and a half years in Ireland, his actions cast a long shadow on Anglo-Irish relations. Cope acknowledged this 3 years before his death. In 1951, he was invited by the Irish ambassador to the United Kingdom, Mr Dulanty, to participate in an oral

---

525 Ibid, Col 537.
526 Ibid, Col 924.
527 Ibid, Col 924.
528 *Dictionary of National Biography 1951–1960* (Oxford: Oxford University Press, 1971), p. 252.

history project. This was the major component of the Bureau of Military History,[529] established in January 1947 by the Irish Minister of Defence, Oscar Traynor.[530] Cope's rejection letter was short, but revealed little remorse concerning the narrative of defeat he did so much to craft 30 years previously. In particular, his willingness to admit defeat to Sinn Fein representatives like Patrick Moylett: 'The I.R.A. must be shown as national heroes and the British Forces as brutal oppressors. Accordingly, the Truce and the Treaty will have been brought about by the valour of small and ill-equipped groups of irregulars. And so on. What a travesty it will be and must be'.[531] Cope displayed an indifference to the self-sustaining destructiveness he did so much to create: 'Read by future generations of Irish children, it will simply perpetuate the long-standing hatred of England and continue the work of self-seeking politicians'.[532]

Colin Gray has argued strategic culture is not only 'out here', but 'within us'. The 'operating codes' identified and assessed represent the unstated rules of conduct and norms of a policy elite. They precluded any understanding of the nature of the conflict Britain was engaged in. An entry from Sturgis's diary summarised their distorting effects: 'Yesterday (Sunday 22nd May) was uneventful save that these brutes took a poor devil they had wounded on Friday out of the Mater Hospital on a stretcher and shot him dead in the porch. If this is the sort of "military operation" which is logical to expect to continue in spite of negotiations their mentality has me beat'.[533] The two questions will be addressed in the next chapters. The extent to which these 'operating codes' persisted,

---

529 The objective of the Bureau was 'to assemble and co-ordinate material to form the basis for the compilation of the history of the movement for independence ... from the formation of the Irish Volunteers on 25th November 1913 to the signing of the Truce on 11th July 1921'. The creation of the Bureau was approved by the Irish Prime minister, Eamon de Valera. The work of the Bureau was completed in 1957. All the assembled material was then retained in the basement of the Department of the Taoiseach for 45 years. It was released in 2002.
530 Traynor ran the Dublin Brigade of the IRA between 1919 and 1921.
531 Ibid.
532 Ibid.
533 Sturgis, op cit, p. 181.

and were discernible in a new generation of policy elites? Second, did the lack of or unwillingness to articulate a strategic plan and the inability to engage with the narrative of Irish Republicanism have the same baleful influence on the effectiveness of the British Army and the Royal Ulster Constabulary as these organisations undertook yet another campaign against insurgency and terrorism?

CHAPTER 5

Assessing the Assessors – Operation Banner

Introduction

It is one thing for an army to engage in a conflict; it is a further challenge for that same army to assess the course and consequences of a campaign it was part of. How did the British Army reflect on its operations in Northern Ireland from 1969 to 2007? Did it try to identify best practice, what worked, what didn't? Was there a focus on organisational, strategic, operational and tactical issues? Was it the stated objective to avoid the same mistakes in the future?

Before analysing the dimensions of Operation Banner, it is important to mention that primary source material is now available beyond the end date of the campaign in 2007.[534] However, the Ministry of Defence still runs a Disclosure Unit designed to deter former officers, who served in Northern Ireland, from being too candid. Many documents pertaining to the late 1960s and early 1970s have been retained by the Ministry of Defence. It has been revealed by the journalist Ian Cobain that this government department has retained an archive of more than 66,000 files, including thousands of files from Army Headquarters in Lisburn, Northern Ireland.[535] Consequently, the caveat must be that any assessment of Operation Banner will be incomplete.

---

534 A small number of PREM FILES on Northern Ireland go beyond the cut-off date. PREM 49/403 PREM 49/918 and PREM 49/2076 were released in 2024. A number of Irish Intelligence files remain closed to 2076. One letter dated 14th September 1994 remains closed to 2094.
535 Cobain, I., *The Guardian* (18th October 2013).

Military Assessments: The Record of the Rebellion and Operation Banner: An Analysis of Military Operations

The two documents prepared by the British Army with respect to the campaigns in Ireland and Northern Ireland constitute the twin pillars of this book. The first, compiled in 1922, was titled *The Record of the Rebellion*, and covered the years 1920–1921. It consisted of five volumes and was withheld from the public domain until 2012, 90 years after its compilation.[536]

The origins of the first report came from a proposal made by General Macready to Field Marshal Sir Henry Wilson in January 1922. Initially, he thought about writing what he described as a 'Dispatch' but concluded that the government would not publish it if it was critical of the policy that had resulted in a British government being prepared to admit they were defeated. To have any future utility he proposed a record which could be consulted if a similar situation arose in any other parts of the United Kingdom. Furthermore, the proposed report could, with very little alteration, be made into a handbook that would form the basis of a doctrine. It would analyse the growth of insurgent activity, the difficulties the British Army had to confront, and the means taken to deal with the insurgents before the Truce was announced. Macready indicated he intended to collect all the intelligence records and arrange for the important ones to be duplicated, with the originals being sent to the War Office. Volume Two of *The Record* contains quotes from intelligence documents, and a comprehensive description of the organisational intelligence structures the army put in place.

The response Macready received from Wilson was quick and positive. He thought it was an excellent idea and would constitute a standing

---

536 The initial two volumes of the Record of the Rebellion were available in the papers of General Strickland, located in the Imperial War Museum. He was a Divisional Commander in Ireland from 1920 to 1922. The other three volumes were missing from his papers.

paper of valuable facts. This endorsement came at the end of Wilson's military career.[537] By February 1922, he had left the British Army.[538]

The second report, *Operation Banner: An Analysis of Military Operations* (hereafter *Banner Analysis*), was published in 2007. This report contained one volume broken into eight chapters. Covering a span of 37 years, it claimed to be comprehensive in terms of the sources consulted. Over 416 unit-posts, operational tour reports, were read. Several thousand other documents were reviewed. The Information Corporate Memory Analysis branch of the Ministry of Defense[539] provided thirty-four volumes of archived materials, which were analysed. 'Discussions were held with more than twenty retired or serving officers who had commanded at brigade level or above in Northern Ireland. A wide range of other individuals were also consulted, including a number who had served in Northern Ireland in 1969 or even before'.

The Foreword to the *Banner Analysis* was written by the Chief of the General Staff, General Sir Mike Jackson. A series of claims with respect to organisational learning, and the future utility of the lessons learnt were made. These were more comprehensive and ambitious than Macready's. Jackson suggested that the tactics developed during Operation Banner had already been deployed 'with considerable success ... in the Balkans, Sierra Leone, East Timor, Afghanistan and Iraq'.[540] Jackson claimed the *Banner Analysis* did not seek to capture any lessons as they had already

---

537 Wilson's comments about the consequences of the Anglo-Irish Treaty for the instigators of the rebellion were prescient. Writing from his home in Eaton Place he claimed: 'Collins has been a back number ever since he made that rotten agreement, and he will have less power as days go by'. On 22nd August 1922 anti-Treaty IRA gunmen killed Collins in County Cork. See Field Marshal Wilson to General Macready 24th February 1922. Wilson Papers HHW2/2/H, IWM.

538 In February, he was elected as a Unionist MP for North Down and became military advisor for the devolved administration in Belfast. He lived at 36 Eaton Place, and it was at this address on the 22nd June 1922, he was murdered by two IRA gunmen.

539 It has not been possible to verify this unit. It could be the Army's Tactical Doctrine Retrieval Cell which was in the former DGD&D organisation.

540 Op cit, p. 1.

been implemented; instead, the focus was on 'high-level general issues' applicable to any future counter-insurgency or counter-terrorist campaign that Britain's armed forces might undertake. It was not intended to be an official history of the campaign.

Both *The Record of the Rebellion* and the *Banner Analysis* emphasised organisational learning, and the utility of the operational experience gained in these campaigns for future counter-insurgency conflicts. A clear continuity in both reports was the call for an integrated approach between the civilian and military authorities. The contemporary report referred to the absence of an 'effective unitary campaign authority' and cited the doctrinal importance of a 'Comprehensive Approach'. However, there is no reference to the Province Executive Committee, which attempted to give expression to this approach at the operational level. Attention was drawn to the consequences of the absence of a unified authority in postponing a successful outcome of the campaign which consequently led to an increased number of casualties and fatalities.[541]

In Operation Banner, three specific continuities with the first campaign can be identified. Ministers and civil servants pursued separate political initiatives with inconsistent results. Second, both campaigns were geographically hybrid. Contact takes place in both urban and rural environments. Finally, there were continual changes in security policy, driven by ministers and civil servants.

There were also two important discontinuities. The actions of the British Army in Operation Banner were captured by television coverage from the beginning of the campaign. Self-evidently this communication media did not exist in 1919. The second discontinuity was a land boundary between Northern Ireland and the Irish Republic. This border is 310 miles (499 km) long and contains a total of 270 border crossing points.[542] It enabled the operational networks of the IRA to be sustained for the whole campaign. The strategic, operational, and tactical challenges will be addressed later in this chapter.

---

541 Operation Banner: An Analysis of Military Operations in Northern Ireland, Army Code 71842, 2006, p. 8–14.
542 The bulk of them were tarmac single lane roads.

Prior to Operation Banner, the army had formulated and disseminated counter-insurgency doctrines that were a product of previous campaigns. The 1960s produced two iterations. The manual *Land Operations Volume III: Counter-Revolutionary Operations*, which in 1969 replaced the 1963 edition of *Keeping Peace*. The former focused heavily on Malaya while ignoring operational experience in geographically hybrid environments such as Palestine. However, it did stress the importance of centrally controlled intelligence structures.[543]

A key contributor to doctrinal development in the early years of Operation Banner was Brigadier Frank Kitson. In 1970, he was appointed a Defence Fellow at Oxford University and subsequently published in 1971 '*Low Intensity Operations*'. This had influence and impact at the time.[544] It contained limited ideas about operations in urban environments in Western societies.[545] However, he produced an important innovation in September 1971 when he set up a divisional action committee to help the army liaise with the police, government departments, and the local community in Belfast. This was extended to the whole of Northern Ireland in 1972.

The Social Origins of the 'Troubles'

The 'Troubles' started in 1969. Chapter 2 of the Banner Analysis, titled 'Events', focused on the outbreak of the violence between the Catholic and Protestant communities in Northern Ireland.[546] This chapter made no mention of the 1920–1921 campaign. Although there was a reference to the 1916 rebellion in Dublin, the Banner Analysis stated Home Rule

---

543 Op cit, pp. 225–226.
544 Frank Kitson after publishing his book was appointed to command 39 Infantry Brigade in Belfast.
545 I am grateful to Major David Hazel for this insight.
546 For the best book on the origins of the Troubles see Kennedy, L., *Who was Responsible for the Troubles*, (Montreal: McGill-Queen's University Press, 2020).

was granted in 1921. By foreshortening the historical record, it neglected earlier events of genuine significance and continuity.

This chapter was highly critical of the devolved government in Northern Ireland: 'One of Stormont's early acts was to remove the safeguards for the catholic minority'.[547] It omitted to state exactly what had been removed. It was an oblique reference to the changes in electoral law for local government elections that took place in 1922 and for the Northern Ireland Parliament elections after 1925. This was a move from the Single Transferable Vote to the same practice that existed in the rest of the United Kingdom.[548] The judgement was that it disadvantaged Catholic voters.[549]

Another assumption was that Ulster Unionists demanded devolution to exercise power over the Catholic population. Yet a statement by the leader of Ulster Unionism underlined that Unionists never sought to run a devolved administration. Sir James Craig, the first Prime Minister of Northern Ireland, stated in a letter to Lloyd George dated 10th November 1921: 'As a final settlement and supreme sacrifice in the interests of peace, the Government of Ireland Act, 1920 was accepted by Northern Ireland, although not asked for by her representatives'.[550]

The academic Arthur Aughey has drawn attention to the views of Sir Edward Carson: 'As Carson[551] argued in the House of Commons,

---

547 Op cit, p. 2–2.
548 See Wilson, A., *PR Urban Elections in Ulster 1920* (London: Electoral Reform Society, 1972), i.
549 The first election in Northern Ireland in 1920 was held under the auspices of proportional representation. The impact of the change on nationalist representation at Stormont was minimal. Initially they had twelve seats and under the new system they won eleven. The main losers were Labour, and independent unionists. Their representation went from eight to four seats. See Whyte J., How Much Discrimination Was There Under the Unionist Regime, 1921–1968? in T. Gallagher, and J. O'Connell, eds., *Contemporary Irish Studies* (Manchester: Manchester University Press, 1983), 85.
550 Quoted in Lawrence, R. J., *The Government of Northern Ireland* (Oxford: Clarendon Press, 1965), 18.
551 Sir Edward Carson the Dublin born barrister who became the leader of the Unionist campaign against Home Rule.

unionists had never asked to govern any catholic but were perfectly satisfied that both Protestants and Catholics should be governed from Westminster ... These were not the words of a power-hungry supremacist'.[552] The American academic Baldy completely ignored this reality: 'Loyalists set about establishing tight political control of the province through the Unionist Party and Orange Order'.[553] What is absent from all the literature is that in enacting the Government of Ireland Act 1920 Westminster made itself the guarantor of the rights of the catholic population. The devolved government in Northern Ireland could not pass any law which would directly or indirectly: 'establish or endow any religion, or prohibit or restrict the free exercise thereof, or give a preference, privilege, or advantage, or impose any advantage or disadvantage, on account of religious belief'.[554] Sir James Craig, the first Prime Minister, of Northern Ireland declared on June 23, 1921, the day after the formal opening of Parliament, he would rule in the interests of everyone, having: 'nothing in our view except the welfare of the people. Our duty and our privilege are from now onwards to have our Parliament well established, to look to the people as a whole'.[555] The Banner Analysis also contained a misleading generalisation with respect to social conditions in Northern Ireland: 'By the early 1960s discrimination had become institutionalised'.[556] There was no mention of the singular achievement of the devolved government in the inter-war period, namely the provision of social security benefits identical to the rest of the United Kingdom, and accessible to both communities. In common with the rest of the United Kingdom poverty, unemployment, ill health, and poor housing had not been eradicated. In addition, it was still a society confronted by many deep social issues.

---

552 Aughey, A., *Under Siege* (London: Hurst & Co, 1989), 101.
553 Baldy, T., *The Battle for Ulster* (Washington, DC: National Defence University Press, 1987), 44.
554 See Government of Ireland Act 1920, c. 1.4.
555 Ibid, p. 38.
556 Op cit, p. 2–2.

The Social Conditions in Northern Ireland

What events led to the 'Troubles' and how did the *Banner Analysis* assess the significance of those events? A key question raised and addressed was identifying the catalyst for the deployment of the 1st Battalion The Prince of Wales Own Regiment of Yorkshire onto the streets of Northern Ireland on the 14th August 1969.

The answer given was the Northern Ireland Civil Rights Association (hereafter NICRA). Founded in 1967, NIRCA promoted the slogan of: 'one man, one vote, one value'. The reality was the restricted franchise in local government elections, which still existed in Northern Ireland, applied to Protestants and Catholics alike.[557] The second issue championed by the NIRCA was the allegation of systemic discrimination in the allocation of public housing.[558] The extent of this discrimination remains, a much-contested issue in the academic literature.[559] Despite accusations of discrimination, the record of the devolved government in Northern Ireland for public house building was a good one. The journalist John Morrison has claimed that:

> In England and Wales 3,298,139 new homes were completed by public authorities between 1945 and 1970 for a population of 48,500.000 people, while 116,691 were completed in Northern Ireland for 1,500,000 people. This shows that the ratio of new-post-war homes to the population was about 13% higher in Northern Ireland than it was in England and Wales.[560]

---

557 See Chapter 1, p. 5–6.
558 For a revisionist view of this issue see Gudgin, G., 'Discrimination in Housing', in J. D. Foster, and W. B. Smith, eds., *The Idea of the Union* (British Columbia: Belcouver Press, 2021).
559 For two examples of this contested literature see Hewitt, C., Grievances, 'Catholic Nationalism and Violence in Northern Ireland during the Civil Rights Period: A Reconsideration', *British Journal of Sociology* 33/3 (1981) 362–380. For an opposing view see Dochartaigh, N. O., *From Civil Rights to Armalites: Derry and the Birth of the Irish Troubles* (Basingstoke: Palgrave Macmillan, 2005).
560 Morrison, J. *The Ulster Cover-up* (Belfast: Ulster Society Publications, 1993)1.

Public house building in Northern Ireland was facilitated through the centrally controlled Northern Ireland Housing Trust (hereafter NIHT). Using money from the devolved government, the NIHT built housing on behalf of local authorities, and it could initiate housing projects of its own.

The *Banner Analysis*, in attempting to explain why the 'Troubles' began in Londonderry, claimed this city was the most deprived city in the United Kingdom with 33,000 out the 36,000 Catholic population living in the crowded 'Victorian slums' of the Creggan[561] and the Bogside, and this pattern was replicated in Belfast and many towns throughout Northern Ireland.[562] However, the 1971 census of population revealed that:

> 34.59% of all households were accommodated in unshared public authority housing units, 40.86% of all Roman Catholic households were in public authority housing. Of households other than Roman Catholic, 32.38% were in public housing, so that Roman Catholics households were shown to have been treated 25% more generously than non-Roman Catholic households in the allocation of public authority housing.[563]

These realities—the provision of public housing and the accessibility of social security benefits to everyone in Northern Ireland—were ignored by the Banner Analysis. Why was this the case? Here, one can only speculate. Government officials, including the military, often accept widespread culturally preconceived notions and base their analyses upon them. Thus, discrimination and poverty are assumed to be the causes of rioting, insurgency and terrorism. Overlooking data that contradicts this assumption frequently occurs among government officials, even those tasked with writing objective assessments of what has happened, and lessons learned.[564]

---

561 This was possibly inaccurate as a considerable amount of public housing had recently been built in this area.
562 Op cit, p. 2-2.
563 Morrison, J., *The Ulster Cover-up* (Belfast: Ulster Society Publications, 1993), 3.
564 Ofira Seliktar bases her understanding of the U.S. intelligence failure to predict the collapse of the Soviet Union on academic paradigms that imposed intellectual blinkers on the analysts. See *Politics, Paradigms, and Intelligence Failures: Why So Few Predicted the Collapse of the Soviet Union* (Routledge, 2015).

Chapter 5

Insurgency and Civil War: The Triggers

The *Banner Analysis* claimed the spark that ignited the 'Troubles' occurred in October 1968, specifically when a NICRA demonstration clashed with an Orange Order march. It has been suggested there was planning by the Irish Republican movement to initiate this violence.[565] The Analysis claimed the Royal Ulster Constabulary's (hereafter RUC) reputation was tarnished by how it reacted without adequate restraint in its use of force.[566] In November 1968 the General Officer Commanding Northern Ireland, Lieutenant General Sir Ian Harris provided a clear-eyed assessment to the Vice Chief of the General Staff of both the consequences and obligations of deploying the Army onto the streets of Northern Ireland: 'if military forces are called for, in my opinion the situation would deteriorate considerably, and the Nationalists in the North and South would make the most of it politically. However, the situation might be so serious that we must take steps to enforce law and order'.[567] He also communicated to the Ministry of Defence just how stretched the RUC were in terms of manpower: 'To give you some example of Police strength they only had 400 on duty in Londonderry on Saturday to control a crowd of about 15,000 and a large number were drafted in from Belfast and other areas'.[568]

On the previous day, a letter from the Brian Cubbon, Private Secretary at the Home Office to the Ministry of Defence revealed the conditional attitude of the Prime Minister, Harold Wilson in terms of providing military assistance to Stormont: 'The PM clearly thinks that the Ministry of Defence should be given some guidance on the extent to which our forces in Northern Ireland should accept obligations to

---

565 Interview with a former member of RUC Special Branch 13th March 2022.
566 Op cit, p. 2–2.
567 National Archives DEFE25/257. Letter from Lieutenant General Sir Ian Harris, GOC NI to Lieutenant General Sir Victor Fitzgeorge-Balfour, Vice Chief of the General Staff, dated 20 November 1968.
568 Ibid.

assist civil power'.[569] It was to be another nine months before London would accept any obligation to provide assistance to the devolved government. An Apprentice Boys march in Londonderry scheduled for 12th August 1969 was given permission to take place. It was met by a violent Nationalist response. The *Banner Analysis* suggested the RUC was overwhelmed by the scale of the violence that erupted and had to deploy half of its total strength of 3,200 to Londonderry.

These inter-communal confrontations have been assessed as being responsible for unleashing hidden forces. The Irish historian Paul Bew argued this: 'The [NICRA] marchers believed that they were participating in a protest for civil rights and socialism, in reality they had helped to unearth layers of ethno-nationalist animosity and hatred that had remained at least partly buried over previous decades'.[570] The *Banner Analysis*'s assessment failed to appreciate the unintended consequences of these confrontations, whatever the ostensible reasons for claiming a lack of civil rights, would bring inter-ethnic antagonisms to the boil.

The *Banner Analysis* acknowledged that the NICRA had become an active participant in the events by calling for 'diversions' to occur beyond Londonderry throughout Northern Ireland.[571] In effect, expanding the geographical scope of the protests and applying further pressure on the devolved government and the RUC. The report accepted the preconceptions of NICRA marchers, whose intent was to polarise Northern Ireland society by escalation.

It further stated that on the 14th August 1969, the RUC lost control of Londonderry, and the Inspector General of the RUC submitted a request for Military Aid to Civilian Power (MACP)[572] to the devolved

---

569 National Archives, DEFE25/257 Letter from the Private Secretary of the Home Office to Mr Bradshaw MOD, dated 19 November 1968.
570 Bew, P. *Ireland: The Politics of Enmity* (Oxford: Oxford University Press, 2006), 493.
571 Op cit, p. 2–3.
572 Military Aid to the Civilian Power.

government. There was no 'mutual support' from uniformed police forces in the rest of the United Kingdom.[573]

In the absence of the deployment of uniformed police from the rest of the United Kingdom to Northern Ireland, the only option was a military one. The Army had ten rifle companies available in Northern Ireland from a garrison of 2,500 troops. This was bolstered on the 15th August 1969 by the British Army's emergency stand-by battalion known as the 'Spearhead Battalion'. 3rd Battalion The Light Infantry.

Despite this deployment, violence claimed the lives of ten people between the months of July and August 1969. In addition, 368 policemen were injured. The rest of that year and the early part of 1970 were marked by what the Banner Analysis called a 'period of sporadic rioting and public disorder'.

In response to the outbreak of inter-communal violence in the previous year, Prime Minister of Northern Ireland, Lord O'Neill, set up In March 1969 the Cameron Commission. Its mandate was to investigate the disturbances in Londonderry. Reporting on the 12th September 1969, its judgements were to have significant consequences for policing. In the summary section this Commission stated the RUC used unnecessary violence, they lacked discipline and were partisan in their treatment of Catholics.

The Commission was tasked to present a report with great speed; it had no power to compel witnesses or papers; nor could it examine witnesses under oath. It was thus very dependent on what anybody chose to tell it. As a result, the Commission's findings were as the journalist John Morrison stated: 'perceptive on some matters, particularly those which related to some of the immediate events, but largely worthless when it made large generalisations about past history and the social background'.[574] It can be argued that the historical and social

---

573 This is a mechanism whereby a police force in one part of the United Kingdom can request support from another police force to reinforce its manpower. It has not been possible to establish whether a request was made to other police forces in the UK.

574 Morrison, J., *The Ulster Cover-up* (Belfast: Ulster Society Publications, 1993), 2.

generalisations were absorbed into the Banner Analysis. The result was often an incomplete and erroneous picture.

The Banner Analysis had evidence that confirmed Irish Republicans had taken an early and close interest in the Northern Ireland Civil Rights Association and been involved in producing the guidelines for the demonstrations. This has subsequently been endorsed by the Irish journalist Kevin Myers. He has claimed 12 out of the 19 members of the Executive Council of the NICRA were either hardline communists or Irish Republicans. Had these facts been incorporated into the Banner Analysis, it would have highlighted the capture of what appeared to be a public interest organisation, by political radicals and opponents of the devolved government.

The Banner Analysis attributed to the actions and speeches of Ian Paisley and Ronald Bunting a clear intent to inflame sectarian divisions. For instance, a very serious riot took place on the 3rd January 1969 in Guildhall Square, Londonderry and the malignant influence of these two speakers was highlighted. The riot resulted in considerable property damage and the police were, as the Cameron Commission stated, challenged 'to restore some semblance of order'.[575]

Given the loss of public control by the devolved government, Prime Minister Harold Wilson and James Callaghan had little option but to intervene with the deployment and use of troops. The British government's political objective was to support and endorse the reform program of the devolved government in Northern Ireland.[576] Historians, Bew and Patterson, have claimed by the beginning of 1970 there was an unrealistic optimism in the British cabinet and Whitehall departments. The *Irish Times* usually not a supporter of British government policy reflected this mood with the following words: 'The British view is that the Northern Ireland problem has been licked and that apart

---

575   Ibid, para 174.
576   See Bew, P., and Patterson, H., *The British State and the Ulster Crisis* (London: Verso, 1985). 22–23.

from odd scuffles, peace in the streets had been won and that reform will transform the north'.[577]

Events in Northern Ireland confounded these predictions. In April 1970, the first confrontation between elements of the Catholic community and the British Army occurred in the Ballymurphy estate in Belfast. There was also the expulsion of Protestants by Catholics from the nearby New Barnsley estate. These events signified the emergence of a religious conflict compounded by significant geographical and nationalist dimensions. What was developing was a conflict of national and territorial identity that was to be defined by religion.

More violence erupted in July 1970 in the Catholic/Nationalist Lower Falls area of Belfast. It can be argued the army ignored a key dimension of delivering military aid in an urban environment: creating and conveying a counter narrative at the strategic level. This was particularly pertinent with the deployment of military formations amongst an urban, civilian population. A planned house search in a Catholic area of Belfast by an infantry company escalated to a large-scale area search by four battalions. The Banner Analysis stated in effect a 'curfew was in force all that night and the next day'. The operation recovered arms, ammunition and explosives.[578] It also resulted in four civilian deaths and 68 injuries. A major failing was the inability to differentiate between those perpetuating violence and the rest of the community, which indicated a lack of tactical intelligence. The Banner Analysis acknowledged the negative consequences of this action at the strategic level: 'It handed a significant information operations opportunity to the IRA, and this was exploited to the full. The Government and Army media response was unsophisticated and unconvincing'.[579]

This operation was presented by Irish Republican propaganda as 'the Rape of the Falls'. The British Army failed to appreciate one of the

---

577 Irish Times 27th March 1970 Quoted in Bew P., and Patterson, H., *The British State and the Ulster Crisis* (London: Verso, 1985), 22.
578 A total of 107 weapons, 25 lbs of explosives and 21,000 rounds of ammunition were found.
579 Op cit, pp. 2–5-2-6.

Assessing the Assessors – Operation Banner

principles of counterinsurgency. The need to ensure the issues surrounding this operation were debated from the Army's perspective with the civilian population as the main focus was lost. Lt Col John Nagl, USA, offers an appreciation of why this aspect of counterinsurgency is fundamental. In a forward to David Galula's classic book *Counterinsurgency Warfare*[580] he stated:

> Counterinsurgency is not a fair fight, as the insurgent having no responsibility is free to use every trick, if necessary, he can lie, cheat, exaggerate. He is not obliged to prove; he is judged by what he promises, not what he does. It is essential then, for the counterinsurgent to fight an even more adroit information war.[581]

This was a lesson the British Army learnt slowly in Northern Ireland.[582] The Banner Analysis tried to place the inter-communal violence in a wider context. It highlighted changes in the structure of the IRA. Reference was made to a central council meeting of the IRA held in Dublin on 10th and 11th January 1970. As a result of this meeting it was subsequently announced the hardline activists had split from the main body and set up the provisional wing, known as the Provisional Irish Republican Army (PIRA). By early 1971 the Banner Analysis stated: 'there was no doubt that the IRA, and especially PIRA was the principal threat'[583] to peace and stability in Northern Ireland.

---

580 David Galula's book, Counterinsurgency Warfare: Theory and Practice was reissued by Praeger Security in 2006.
581 Galula, D., *Counterinsurgency Warfare: Theory and Practice* (Westport: Praeger Security International, 2006), ix–x.
582 By contrast Generals Shaw and Macready displayed a firm grasp of its importance between 1920 and 1921. The problem being they were poorly served by Basil Clarke in Dublin Castle, and the army left it too late (May 1921) to organise its own information campaign.
583 Op cit, p. 2–6.

Chapter 5

Intensifying Insurgency and the British Response

The Banner Analysis identified 1971 as the year when several important milestones in the developing insurgency occurred. On the 6th February the first British soldier was killed; the first incendiary bomb attack took place, and the first anti-personnel devices were used.

Polarisation and escalation of the conflict ensued. Internment (known as Operation Demetrius) was introduced on 9th August 1971.[584] The Prime Minister of Northern Ireland, Brian Faulkner persuaded the British Prime Minister Edward Heath to support the policy. The Banner Analysis stated that this was 'contrary to military advice'.[585] The RUC also advised against this tactic at this time.[586]

Tactical tempo was achieved by Operation Demetrius. There was a decrease of 400 active insurgents who were at large. It provided a new source of intelligence for the police and the army. This operation resulted in fifteen people being selected for deep interrogation techniques which had been 'developed in other theatres during the 1950s and 1960s'. The Banner Analysis claimed the security forces generated an important tactical advantage because of interment, and they were able to erode the capability of the IRA through the rest of 1971 and early 1972.

Despite these tactical successes, Operation *Demetrius* was interpreted strategically as a failure: 'Both the reintroduction of internment and the use of deep interrogation techniques had a major impact on popular opinion across Ireland, in Europe and the US. Put simply, on balance and with the benefit of hindsight, it was a major mistake'.[587] The academic Mockaitis, has claimed the RUC used its control over intelligence to manipulate the Army to act in a particular way: 'By providing

---

584 See McCleery, M., *Operation Demetrius and its Aftermath: A New History of the use of Internment without Trial in Northern Ireland 1971–1975* (Manchester: Manchester University Press, 2015).
585 Op cit, p. 2–7.
586 Interview with a former member of RUC Special Branch, 13th March 2022.
587 Op cit, p. 2–7.

the right sort of information on the existence of arms caches Stormont could force the troops into action despite their better judgement'.[588] In addition, the cutting edge of the intelligence operation, RUC Special Branch, was alleged by the military historian Hew Strachan to have collapsed.[589] Both these assertions are insufficiently correct.

The RUC Special Branch was to play a critical role in countering paramilitary activity as attested by a senior army intelligence officer: 'During Operation Banner the intelligence infrastructure gradually developed by military and civilian intelligence agencies was powerful and effective. Integrated into this infrastructure was the considerable contribution provided by the RUC Special Branch. This contribution was uniquely important, as branch officers had the advantage of continuity and a long-time knowledge, understanding and record of the history, political motivations and personality details of men and women of violence on both sides of the community'.[590]

The escalating political violence of the early 1970s provided the context for political choices. The initial motive was for Westminster to have its own channels of reporting and communication that were separate from the devolved government in Northern Ireland. In August 1969, the same month the army was deployed on the streets, Prime Minister Harold Wilson established the Office of the UK Representative (UKREP). Officially it was to do two things: first to monitor political developments; second, to assess the progress of Stormont's program of reform. All three of the holders of the post before Stormont's suspension were Foreign and Commonwealth Office civil servants of ambassador rank.[591]

The UKREP was based in the Conway Hotel in southwest Belfast.[592] The first holder of the post, Oliver Wright, used the Foreign Office format

---

588 Mockaitis, T. R., *British Counterinsurgency in the Post Imperial Era* (Manchester: Manchester University Press, 1995), 102.
589 See Strachan, H., *The Politics of the British Army* (Oxford: Clarendon Press, 1997), 183.
590 Interview with a former senior military intelligence officer 9th December 2022.
591 They were Oliver Wright, Ronnie Burroughs, and Howard Smith.
592 See Patterson, H., 'The British State and the Rise of the IRA, 1969–1971: The View from the Conway Hotel', *Irish Political Studies* 23/4 (2008) 491–511.

to report on the devolved government. These reports were passed around Whitehall in what became known as the 'Irish Net'.[593] This would have two consequences. First, it created an alternative channel of information on Northern Ireland uniquely detached from sources supplied by or through the Northern Ireland government.[594] Second, by the time it moved to Laneside on the shores of Belfast Lough in the summer of 1971, it had evolved into a 'professional base where people could meet and speak with British officials'. Perhaps even more important was the decision by the new incoming Prime Minister Edward Heath in the same year. He: 'instructed MI6[595] to lead in Northern Ireland ... A major strategy was to open negotiations with opponents'.[596]

This institution evolved further in October 1971 with the arrival of a career SIS officer Frank Steele as Deputy UKREP. His task was to extend the British Government's contacts into local communities. During the early 1970s this meant engagement with the Official and Provisional IRA.

The former military intelligence officer, Michael Smith, characterised these choices as 'Parallel Diplomacy': 'the establishment of channels of communication with the enemy that would be too dangerous, both physically and politically, for ministers or ordinary civil servants to contemplate'.[597] There is evidence to show that choices for political action went far beyond establishing channels of communication. They entailed negotiations with insurgents that undermined the unity of effort a security policy must have when facing an emerging insurgency. In terms

---

593   This was a term used by Whitehall Departments that dealt with Northern Ireland. Revealed in an interview by Tony Craig with Kelvin White, Undersecretary at the Republic of Ireland Department 1969–1974, 25th October 2007. See Craig, T., From Backdoors to Back Lanes to Backchannels: Reappraising British Talks with the Provisional IRA, 1970–1974, *Contemporary British History* 26/1(2002).

594   See Craig, T., 'From Backdoors to Back Lanes to Backchannels: Reappraising British Talks with the Provisional IRA, 1970–1974', *Contemporary British History* 26/1 (2012), 101.

595   MI6 is also known as the Secret Intelligence Service.

596   van de Bijl, N., *Operation Banner* (Barnsley: Pen and Sword Military, 2009), 103.

597   Smith, M., *The Spying Game: The Secret History of British Espionage* (London: Politico's, 2003), 365.

of strategic culture,[598] it represented what Liddell Hart had termed the 'businesslike tradition in the conduct of war'.[599]

On the 13th March 1972, eleven days before Stormont was suspended; Harold Wilson led a delegation,[600] with the permission of the Prime Minister, Edward Heath, to Dublin and met with three senior members of the IRA: David O'Connell, Joe Cahill and John Kelly. Unsurprisingly nothing came of these talks. However, Mumford correctly assessed their significance. They represented: 'the establishment of cross-party consensus as to the need to engage in a dialogue with the IRA if the peace process was to be moved on politically'.[601] The impact of these choices would be as profound as it had been between 1919 and 1921.

Bloody Sunday, Direct Rule and the Operating Codes

The reaction to internment provided the context for 'Bloody Sunday'. The origins of this tragic event can only be understood through the lens of the politics of the British Army's counter-insurgency tactics and crowd control doctrine in Northern Ireland. In December 1971, Major General Ford[602] had produced a paper titled 'Future Military Policy for Londonderry'. He had outlined three options with respect to the deteriorating security situation in Londonderry. The first was to do nothing; the second was a limited operation to dismantle barricades; the final one was to take a more coercive approach towards establishing a greater civil-military footprint in the city. This option was designated as the 'correct

---

598 For an extended discussion of this phenomena see Gray, C. S., *Modern Strategy* (Oxford: Oxford University Press, 1999), 129–151.
599 See Basil Liddell Hart, *The British Way in Warfare* (London: Penguin, 1932), 29.
600 He was accompanied by Merlyn Rees, Joe Haines and Tony Field.
601 Mumford, A., 'Covert Peacemaking: Clandestine Negotiations and Backchannels with the Provisional IRA during the Early Troubles, 1972–1976'. *The Journal of Imperial and Commonwealth History*, 39/4 (2011), 636.
602 He was the Commander of Land Forces (CLF) in Northern Ireland.

military solution' and proposed occupying the Bogside and the Creggan. He tempered this proposal by declaring that probable mass resistance precluded this action. The academic Hew Bennett has claimed: 'attention shifted to Derry in mid-January as progress against the IRA in Belfast stalled'.[603] In the second half of this month the security forces in Londonderry were dealing with a growing insurgency. As Bennett states they 'came under fire on sixty-one occasions and had fifty-two nail bombs thrown at them. IRA opened fire several times from behind civilians'.

What was missing from the Banner Analysis was a failure of the Army to recognise the vital importance to formulate, disseminate, and apply province wide a tactical doctrine that provided both training and instructions as to how all units could respond to crowd control. The chief RUC officer in Londonderry, Chief Superintendent Lagan,[604] and his army counterpart, Brigadier MacLellan wanted to enact a non-confrontational doctrine in terms of crowd control. The planned NICRA protest march in Londonderry against internment was perceived as best handled by taking this tactical approach. By contrast the Army high command in Northern Ireland wanted to stop the marchers reaching their intended destination and wanted to make arrests. Lagan still wanted the march to proceed without arrests.

This was compounded by an intelligence report classified as 'reliable and detailed' that the IRA planned to attack the security forces during the march.[605] The key point about intelligence is that it cannot eliminate uncertainty, it can only help to manage uncertainty. MacLellan had in his plan 'Operation Forecast' for paratroopers to be available as an arrest force, but only on his orders. The Banner Analysis noted that NICRA's

---

603 Bennett, H., *Uncivil War: The British Army and the Troubles, 1966–1975* (Cambridge: Cambridge University Press, 2024), 144.
604 For an excellent summary of the importance of this senior RUC officer in driving security policy up to and including Bloody Sunday See Dochartaigh, N. O., 'Bloody Sunday: Error or Design', *Contemporary British History* 24/1 (2020) 94–96.
605 TNA DEFE 70/1067, Ministry of Defence Monthly Operational Summary, 10 February 1972. Quoted in Bennett, H. *Uncivil War: The British Army and the Troubles, 1966–1975* (Cambridge: Cambridge University Press, 2024), 145.

response to a ban was to hold a march illegally, seek confrontation, and attract favourable publicity. The Army's objective was to try and prevent the marchers from reaching the commercial centre and, if rioting broke out, to undertake arrest operations and pick up the ringleaders. In addition, it was hoped that this action would deter further illegal marches.

The subsequent unfolding of events has been subject to two judicial inquiries. The second was set up in 1998 by Prime Minister Tony Blair and led by Lord Saville of Newdigate. It finally published its findings on 15th June 2010. As a result, David Cameron, the serving Prime Minister, acknowledged in the House of Commons that the paratroopers of the 1st battalion, The Parachute Regiment had fired the first shot. Furthermore, they had fired on unarmed civilians. It also exonerated Martin McGuiness a senior member of PIRA. It stated he was probably in possession of a Thompson sub-machine gun, although he 'did not engage in any activity that provided any of the soldiers with any justification for opening fire'.

The Banner Analysis cited a Brigade operational order that anticipated arrest operations would take place on foot. On 30th January 1972, Brigadier MacLellan, the commander of 8th Infantry Brigade, delayed giving an order for an arrest operation because: 'he was correctly concerned that there should be separation between the rioters and peaceful marchers before launching an operation to arrest the former'.[606] At 16.07 Brigadier MacLellan gave 1 Para orders to mount an arrest operation by sending one company through barrier 14. They were ordered not to conduct a 'running battle' down Rossville Street. Lieutenant Colonel Derek Wilford, the CO of 1 PARA, disobeyed orders and deployed, without authority, Support Company in vehicles through Barrier 12 along Rossville Street and into the Bogside. The nexus of the problem was by this time it was impossible to distinguish between the marchers and the ringleaders and critically there was: 'no means whereby soldiers could identify and arrest only the latter'.[607] This was the context in whereby a total of 13 people were killed.

---

606 The Saville Inquiry. Principal conclusions and overall assessment of the Bloody Sunday Inquiry 15th June 2010, para 3.15.
607 Ibid, para 3.18.

The Banner Analysis referred just moments before this operation to 'a high velocity shot' was fired at the soldiers from the area of the rioters. The Saville Inquiry identified two Official IRA gunmen: 'In our view these two Official IRA members had gone to a pre-arranged sniping position in order to fire at the soldiers; and probably did so when an opportunity presented itself'.[608] What was omitted from the findings of the Saville inquiry was a statement given by Colonel Roberts of the Parachute Regiment who held the post of the Regimental Signals Officer working the battalion radio net from his 'command post' which was a canvas-sided Bedford 3 ton lorry relatively close to the action: 'several high velocity bullets ripped through the canvas – but although Roberts and a fellow officer gave evidence of this IRA gunfire to the Bloody Sunday Inquiry headed by Lord Saville, they were disappointed when it appeared to be ignored'.[609] Did this event confirm the intelligence report received prior to the march taking place?

Inconsistency in terms of the tactical doctrine of crowd control and counter-insurgency the army applied in Londonderry prior to Bloody Sunday was the nub of the problem: 'In late 1971, British troops launched repeated night-time raids into the no-go areas of Derry, deep inside the barricades. In the middle of the night, they faced large crowds of rioters several hundred strong, were attacked with petrol bombs and blast bombs, and came under fire as they carried out search operations ... but despite the intense violence and the unpredictable conditions just one civilian was killed in these raids'.[610] These raids were stopped by the 10th December 1971, and the army reverted to a policy of relative restraint. MacLellan subsequently put an emphasis on searches and 'quick lifts' being carried out 'if' there was hard intelligence. A statement made to the Saville Inquiry by Lt Col Wilford conveyed an absence of understanding the different tactical approaches being used in Londonderry:

608 Op cit, para 3.12.
609 See Daily Telegraph, 8th September 2022.
610 Dochartaigh, N. O., 'Bloody Sunday: Error or Design', *Contemporary British History* 24/1 (2020), 94–96.

he wanted to demonstrate that the way to deal with rioters in Londonderry was not for soldiers to shelter behind barricades like (as he put it) *'Aunt Sallies'* while being stoned, as he perceived the local troops had been doing, but instead to go aggressively after rioters, as he and his soldiers had been doing in Belfast.[611]

The Banner analysis acknowledged the strategic impact of these killings: 'The consequences ran around the world and could still be felt more than 30 years after the event'.[612] The devolved government in Northern Ireland was to pay the political price for these events. The fatalities in Londonderry were acutely embarrassing for the government in London. Critically the lethal shots had been fired by the Army *not* the RUC. The Army was the responsibility of the government in Westminster *not* the devolved government, although this was never explicitly acknowledged. The apparent inability to deliver institutional reform was cited in the Banner Analysis as the reason for ending devolved government in Northern Ireland: 'Whitehall had come to realise that the conditions of the 1969 Downing Street Declaration were not going to be met by Stormont'.[613] The shifting responsibility for these killings to Stormont required the crafting of a new strategic narrative.

On the 3rd February 1972, four days after Bloody Sunday a Top Secret Cabinet paper concluded: 'It was desirable that movement towards some political solution of the conflict should be seen in prospect'.[614] Just one month later the Foreign Secretary Sir Alec Douglas-Home sent a letter to the Prime Minister[615] It illuminated two things: a process had begun whereby another generation of the policy elite began to distance Westminster from the need to defend the political integrity of the United Kingdom; secondly it showed a profound ignorance of the human associations that existed within the geopolitical configuration of the British state, and highlighted the nature of the political change that

---

611   Op cit, para 4.16.
612   Operation Banner report, p. 2–8.
613   Operation Banner report, p. 2–8.
614   CAB 128/48, 3rd March 1972. National Archives.
615   It was also sent to other key members of the Cabinet.

was coming:[616] 'I really dislike Direct Rule for Northern Ireland because I do not believe that they are like the Scots or the Welsh and doubt if they ever will be. The real British interest would I think be served best by pushing them towards a united Ireland rather than tying them closer to the United Kingdom. Our own parliamentary history is one long story of trouble with the Irish'.[617]

The choices for action had been made. All that remained was for perfidy to play its part. The first act came in the form of a telegram sent by Edward Heath to Brian Faulkner and read out at a meeting of the Ulster Unionist Council in the first weekend of March: 'You will have seen various articles in the press today claiming to describe the views of the United Kingdom Government on constitutional change in Northern Ireland. These articles are pure speculation, and we have made this clear to the press'.[618]

The second act was a telephone call between Heath and Faulkner on the 15th March 1972. This was in preparation for a meeting Heath wanted to hold a week later. The Prime Minister stated: 'I always said that we would have consultations with you before we finally settled anything for announcement. So I was regarding this as a good "going over the ground". It rather depends on where we get to as to whether there are decisions for announcement immediately or not'.[619]

The final act came exactly one week later on the 22nd March 1972, when Faulkner arrived in London. The consultations he anticipated had been transformed into a Cabinet decision to take control of law and order in Northern Ireland. There was no relationship between the exercise of this function and the shootings in Londonderry, which were

---

616   The two geopolitical axes being the human associations existing England and the south of Ireland, and Scotland and the north of Ireland. As a consequence, the border between Northern Ireland and the Irish Republic marks off in a cultural sense the Scottish part of Ireland from the Anglicised part.
617   Letter from the Foreign Secretary, Sir Alec Douglas-Home, to the Prime Minister, 13th March 1972. PREM 15/1004, National Archives.
618   Quoted in Morrison, J., *The Ulster Cover-up* (Belfast: Ulster Society, 1993), 106.
619   Record of telephone conversation between the Prime Minister and Prime Minister of Northern Ireland, 15th March 1972. PREM 15/1004. National Archives.

a result of the Army's actions. It was designed to deflect attention from the Westminster government's responsibility for the deaths that had occurred. Not surprisingly, Faulkner and his colleagues rejected this demand, and the Northern Ireland Cabinet resigned.

On 30th March 1972, the Government of Northern Ireland was suspended for one year and the powers of the devolved government were transferred to London. In addition, a Secretary of State for Northern Ireland was appointed to head a Northern Ireland executive. The journalist John Morrison summed up the process that had been enacted: 'By a variety of dishonest devices, the victims were to be represented as the culprits'.[620]

Direct rule from London resulted in the Cope genie being uncorked from the bottle it had been in for the last 51 years. The operating codes to pursue separate political initiatives with inconsistent results manifested itself on the 20th June 1972, when P. J. Woodfield a Northern Ireland Office civil servant and Frank Steele, a serving SIS officer met two senior members of PIRA, David O'Connell and Gerry Adams.[621] Authority for this meeting is clear in the report and was classified as Top Secret: 'on the instructions of the Secretary of State[622] I met representatives of the Provisional IRA'.[623]

The key issue discussed was an offer from PIRA representatives for a permanent ceasefire. A condition of this being that raids, searches and arrests would not take place. The British side agreed to this. There was also a demand for 'political status' for convicted prisoners. The response was to say this category did not exist in law, but they were willing to make concessions in terms of prison conditions. There was also a request that the Secretary of State meet the representatives of the Provisional IRA.

---

620 Op cit, p. 108.
621 The meeting took place at Ballyarnet the home of Colonel and Mrs MacCorkell. They were present when the meeting took place The house was located close to the border between Co Donegal in the Irish Republic and Co Londonderry in Northern Ireland.
622 William Whitelaw was the Secretary of State for Northern Ireland.
623 See PREM 15/1009, 20th June 1972. National Archives.

A future meeting was agreed to by Woodfield and Steele. The caveat being that there had to be an effective ceasefire. The businesslike tradition was illuminated by a statement in the subsequent report that 'there was a good deal of haggling about the time a ceasefire would last before a meeting would take place'. In the end, a bargain was struck for ten days!

The final paragraph of Woodfield's report is insightful as it revealed an understanding of the role that these two PIRA representatives had in directing the insurgency and how contrasted with their behaviour at this secret meeting: 'Their response to every argument put to them was reasonable and moderate. Their behaviour and attitude appeared to bear no relation to the indiscriminate campaign of bombing and shooting in which they had both been prominent leaders'.[624]

On 7th July, William Whitelaw and Paul Channon held a secret meeting with six senior members of the Provisional IRA in Cheyne Walk in Chelsea. They were Ivor Bell, Seamus Twomey, Gerry Adams, Martin McGuiness, a PIRA Army Council member, and the PIRA Chief of Staff Sean MacStiofain. These talks failed to produce anything of lasting value. PIRA gave British government an 18-month notice to withdraw from Northern Ireland.[625]

The nemesis of this meeting came two weeks later on Friday 21st July 1972, when PIRA exploded 22 no-warning bombs within a one-mile radius of Belfast city centre killing 11 people and injuring 130 in just under an hour. This event became known as 'Bloody Friday'. The Banner Analysis conceded the victims were 'mostly protestant civilians'. Shooting incidents had gone up from 399 in March, the month Stormont was suspended, to 2,718 in July.[626] In addition there had been 95 terrorist-related deaths in July.

In the months leading up to 'Bloody Friday', the army had been given new orders: 'The Army was directed, and agreed, to take a low-key approach ... The Army's posture had little effect on weaning the

---

624 Ibid.
625 For a brief description of the conversation between Whitelaw and the IRA leadership see, National Archives CI 4/1456. 'Top Secret'.
626 These figures are taken from the Banner report.

Catholics from supporting the IRA. PIRA regrouped, retrained, and reorganised'.[627] Minister and civil servants were unwilling to take an integrated approach to counter-insurgency and coordinate political and military efforts. PIRA was able to demonstrate the failure of the army to do three things: attrition the insurgent capability, deter bombing attacks, and reassure the public that lives, and property were being protected. It was the most violent year of the whole campaign. All the independent variables that defined success at the strategic, operational and tactical levels flashed failure on the dashboard of counterinsurgency.

Operation Motorman: The Changing Characteristics of an Insurgency

The British government's response to 'Bloody Friday' was Cabinet approval on the 27th July 1972 for a military operation to remove the barricades and safe havens of PIRA in both Belfast and Londonderry. They had become locations from where attacks could be planned, and influence exerted. On the 31st July 1972 Operation Motorman was launched with 22,700 regular troops now deployed in Northern Ireland, supported by 5,300 troops of the Ulster Defence Regiment. PIRA were given a choice of fighting to defend these havens or withdraw. They choose the latter.

Despite these troop levels, on the same day, PIRA was still able to explode three no-warning car-bombs in the small town of Claudy in County Londonderry. Six adults and three children were killed. The bombing was planned by a Catholic priest, Father James Chesney.[628]

When Operation Motorman was formally closed on 1st December 1972, the Banner Analysis assessed it as a turning point. The judgement was the character of the campaign had changed from a counter-insurgency to a counter-terrorist operation. However, it was not stated

---

627 Op cit, p. 2–8.
628 See RTE Archives assessed 2/1/23.

what the difference between the two might be. At the strategic, operational and tactical levels the British Army judged it a success.[629]

Following Operation Motorman, the army claimed PIRA were in disarray.[630] The OIRA had declared a ceasefire in 1972. The following year it was asserted that PIRA had been 'badly beaten'. The statistics were impressive: 'Between May and December 1973 1,798 members of PIRA were arrested. One PIRA company had to be disbanded. Arrests included one brigade commander, eight battalion commanders and 39 members of IRA HQ staff'.[631] These statistics require some qualification.[632]

In 1973, the army had conducted 74,556 searches of premises, and in 1976 had arrested 8,321 people.[633] It is uncertain what effect this activity had given a legal situation whereby those the army arrested had to be quickly released as there was no evidence to hold and prosecute them. The proclivity to use these arrests for political purposes was commented on in the Banner analysis: 'the release of numbers of internees as a part of a political process with the eventual goal of the reintroduction of self-government. It was intended that internment would be phased out as part of the process'.[634]

In early 1975, a ceasefire was announced by the PIRA, which lasted for most of the year. However, the PIRA did not adhere to it as they averaged 'one explosion, one device neutralised and four shootings per day'. During the last three months of 1975, 17 members of the security forces had been killed and 57 wounded. This year also witnessed PIRA and the British Army adapting and evolving. Between 1975 and 1978, the PIRA developed a cellular structure called 'Active Service Units' (ASU). The rationale being that it would provide better security.

---

629 Op cit, p. 2–11.
630 Op cit, p. 2–11.
631 Op cit, p. 2–11.
632 Often volunteers spent short periods of time doing these jobs and sometimes left for domestic reasons. I am grateful to a former RUC Special Branch officer for this insight.
633 Strachan, H., *The Politics of the British Army* (Oxford: Clarendon Press, 1997), 183.
634 Op cit, p. 2–11.

In the rural areas they operated in larger groupings: 'South Armagh was a large group which we in the RUC SB divided up into two main groups. These were Crossmaglen/Silverbridge and North Louth/Drumintee [Drumintee being in the North]. One in the West and one in the East of South Armagh but we made this attribution not for geographical convenience but according to how we saw them operating. Although elements of both groupings did from time to time come together to mount big operations [generally mounted from the Republic] for day-to-day ops they appeared to operate separately, hence the attribution'.[635] South Armagh IRA sometimes referred to themselves as the South Armagh Brigade of the IRA but they did not retain the older order of battle organisational structure of platoons and companies.

There was according to the Banner analysis a qualitative shift in the character of the violence they could inflict: 'PIRA's attacks were fewer; but more selective, better conducted and more effective. This period demonstrated the emergence of PIRA as a highly effective terrorist organisation'.[636] The Banner Analysis estimated there were between '200 and 300 active members with no shortage of experienced men and women to draw upon'.

In the second half of the 1970s the SAS were deployed to Northern Ireland. Initially in South Armagh, from 1976, and then throughout the rest of the province. They remained in the form of the Special Reconnaissance Regiment up until the end of Operation Banner. Skills of gathering and processing of intelligence had now been disseminated to tactical level: 'soldiers were taught to turn "background" information into "contact information"'.[637]

During the late 1970s, the British army began changing how it worked with the RUC. The key policy change was a move towards 'police primacy'. This was instigated officially on the 25th of March 1976. This change was a product of the findings of the Bourn Committee's Way

---

635 Interview with a former member of Special Branch RUC, 12 March 2023.
636 Op cit, p. 2–12.
637 Mockaitis, T. R., *British Counterinsurgency in the Post-Imperial Era* (Manchester: Manchester University Press, 1995) 107.

Ahead blueprint.[638] London took the decision to invest in the RUC under the slogan of Ulsterisation. There were real advantages to be gained from this change in policy: 'After the period of military primacy between 1970 and 1976 I think it was realised that the more appropriate way of dealing with a criminal insurgency against democracy is for the police to have primacy operating within the criminal justice system. Of course, because of the level of violence exhibited by both republican and loyalist terrorists the police continued to need significant military support up to the end of Operation Banner'.[639]

There is evidence from the correspondence between Roy Mason and Fred Mulley[640] that the government understood how the character of the PIRA threat had evolved: 'The problem has ceased to be one of large confrontations with rioters and is one of identifying and tracing and finding evidence against small groups of terrorists'.[641] The academic Neumann has questioned whether police primacy actually happened.[642] He failed to understand that the RUC from the top of the province wide security structure down to the Sub-Division Action Committees were in charge. They were also in the lead with respect to the collection and collation of intelligence. Obviously in hard republican areas: West Belfast, the Bogside and the Creggan in Londonderry, Shantallow and South Armagh it was necessary to station the army in these areas to afford the police the protection they needed to operate.

The most important institutional developments in terms of developing an integration army and RUC efforts occurred from 1976 onwards: 'establishment of the Tasking and Coordination Groups, each one responsible for a geographic portion of the province and commanded by

---

638 This was a committee chaired by Sir John Bourn, when he was Deputy Under Secretary of State in The Northern Ireland Office.
639 Interview with a former senior officer in the RUC, 3rd December 2023.
640 Roy Mason was then Secretary of State for Northern Ireland and Fred Mulley was Secretary of State for Defence.
641 Correspondence from Roy Mason to Fred Mulley, dated 18th May 1977, DEFE11/918, The National Archives.
642 See Neumann, P., *Britain's Long war: British Strategy in the Northern Ireland Conflict 1969–1998* (Basingstoke: Palgrave Macmillan, 2003).

a Special Branch officer of Detective Chief Superintendent rank'.[643] The Banner report makes no direct reference to the TCGs. It merely stated the RUC: 'had recovered its operational effectiveness to the point where the operational primacy of the RUC in security operations was formally re-established in 1976'.[644]

It is important to understand the background and importance of this change. The Hunt report commissioned by the British government, after the public disorder of the late 1960s recommended that the 'security situation' in Northern Ireland should be the primary responsibility of the army and the RUC be an unarmed force. This remained the policy until 1976: 'when the Chief Constable and the Army General Officer Commanding (GOC) drew up a strategy to initiate "primacy of the police", with the Army in support. This process is possibly what gave rise to the need for means of coordinating the activities of the two organisations, including the creation of the concept of the "Tasking, Coordinating Group"'.[645]

MI5 and the Metropolitan Police Special Branch engaged in a continuing review of the performance of the RUC's Special Branch. The failure of the Banner Analysis to deal substantially with this change was compounded by the need to omit any reference to the strained relationship between the then GOC for Northern Ireland Lieutenant General Sir Timothy Creasey and the Chief Constable of the RUC, Sir Kenneth Newman. Their 'disagreements came to a head in 1979 with the general demanding that the Army take over responsibility for policing'.[646] The murder of Lord Mountbatten and the killing of eighteen soldiers in Warrenpoint in the same year brought this relationship to an all-time low. In the end, a law enforcement response to combating PIRA

---

643 Edwards, A., 'A Whipping Boy If Ever There Was One? The British Army and the Politics of Civil–Military Relations in Northern Ireland', *Contemporary British History* 28/2 (2014) 183.
644 Op cit, p. 2–13.
645 Interview with a former senior officer RUC 3rd December 2023.
646 Obituary of Lieutenant General Sir Timothy Creasey, The Times 7th October 1986.

remained in pole position. However, there was one issue that remained impervious to this new policy, and that was the issue presented by the United Kingdom's land boundary with the Irish Republic.

Banner Analysis and the Border

Chapter 2 of David Galula's book on Counterinsurgency Warfare identified four criteria for an insurgent victory: A cause, weakness of the counterinsurgent, geographic conditions, outside support.[647] The importance of geography was clearly explained: 'the role of geography, a large one in ordinary war, may be overriding in a revolutionary war. If the insurgent, with his initial weakness, cannot get any help from geography, he may well be condemned to failure before he starts'.[648] Furthermore, he identified eight component elements that constituted these geographic conditions.[649] The configuration of a border was also judged by Galula to be of importance. 'The length of the borders, particularly if the neighbouring countries are sympathetic to the insurgents, as was the case in Greece, Indochina and Algeria, favours the insurgent'. The Banner Analysis attempted to evaluate the geographic conditions of the border and briefly examined outside support. Galula identified five dimensions of outside support: moral, political, technical, financial and military. PIRA was in receipt of outside support that encompassed all five categories. There was a diversity in this support: the Libyan Government, organisations such as Noraid in the United States and the Irish Republic. The moral and political support for the PIRA's campaign existed in the Irish Republic.

---

647 See Galula, D., *Counterinsurgency Warfare* (Westport: Praeger International, 1964), 11–28.
648 Galula, D., *Counterinsurgency Warfare* (Westport: Praeger International, 1964), 23.
649 There were: location, size, configuration, international borders, terrain, climate, population, economy.

This has been calculated as running as high as 62%.[650] The political choices made by successive Irish Ministers of Justice to prevent the Irish police from co-operating with the RUC on cross-border security were a serious impediment to counter-insurgency at the operational and tactical levels.[651] Financial and technical support from the Irish government began in 1969 but had faded by 1972 largely due to the arms trial of Irish Government ministers and a former Irish Army intelligence officer.[652] There was also institutional support for PIRA[653] in the Irish Republic.

Did the British Army acknowledge the significance of the land boundary, and how successful was it in dealing with the challenges presented? Given the importance of the boundary between Northern Ireland and the Republic of Ireland, one curiosity of the Banner Analysis is that only four paragraphs out of 856 paragraphs were devoted to the border. However, these paragraphs were candid in their analysis but failed to identify one of the key issues at the strategic level.

The initial statement correctly identified the scope of the issue: 'The Border with the Irish Republic was a problem at the strategic, operational and tactical levels'.[654] From August 1969 to the later stages of the campaign the Republic was a 'safe haven'. By the late 1970s, the judgement was that the PIRA could not have survived without refuge in the Republic. The PIRA took full advantage of cross-border activities which included fund raising opportunities and smuggling.

British governments made a choice that persuading successive Dublin Governments to change their policies on cross border cooperation was too difficult. It would have entailed enacting sanctions against the Irish Republic. Ireland's neutrality in the Cold War and

---

650 An opinion survey done by in 1979 by the Economic and Social Research Institute in Dublin found that 20.7 of respondents in the Irish Republic supported IRA activities and 41.8 sympathised with IRA motives. Irish Times 16 October 1979.
651 Interview with a former member of the RUC Special Branch 12th March 2023.
652 For an extensive account of these events. See Heney, M., *The Arms Crisis of 1970* (London: Head of Zeus, 2020).
653 See O'Faolean, G., *A Broad Church, The Provisional IRA in the Irish Republic 1969–1980*, (Newbridge: Merrion Press, 2019).
654 Op cit, p. 4–4.

the United Kingdom's application to join the EU were cited as strategic reasons for not doing more to enhance security on the border.[655] This inaction did not preclude the claim being made that: 'local cooperation between the RUC and the Garda improved progressively'.[656] The question remained, did the British Army believe cooperation between the RUC and the Irish police was steadily improving?

The Banner Analysis stressed the border's operational importance, but ignored strategic failure.[657] Nevertheless, it did acknowledge the impossibility of finding lasting solutions at the operational and tactical level: 'The question of the Border was revisited by GOCs and CLFs[658] on several occasions, but few lasting military initiatives resulted'.[659] The report went on to state the same candidate solutions were considered and discarded three times at roughly 5-year intervals.

The Banner Analysis explained this 'reinvention of the wheel' was a product of two things: the absence of a single unifying authority, and a lack of understanding of the operational level of war in the British Army at the time. The first option was the sealing of the border with a fence and the deployment of a security force. It was estimated that 29 battalions would be required for this option. The second option was to lay minefields along the border. This option was always quickly dismissed, presumably on humanitarian grounds. The Banner Analysis noted: 'an operational estimate of the campaign as a whole might have identified that the Border *area* was critical to the conduct of PIRA operations and therefore should have been the geographical focus of the campaign ... where, in operational terms the PIRA was to be engaged and defeated'.[660]

The Banner Analysis identified a critical problem: 'In the mid-1980s PIRA was organised into sixteen principal ASUs of which ten were

---

655 A former RUC Special Branch officer has calculated that a total of 153 murders took place along the border with the Irish Republic and were planned from the Irish Republic.
656 Op cit, p. 4–5.
657 Op cit, p. 4–5.
658 General Officer Commanding and Commander Land Forces.
659 Op cit, p. 4–5.
660 Op cit, p. 4–6.

based South of the Border'.[661] In addition, it created and sustained 'efficient intelligence, quartermaster, finance and engineering branches' in the south. These operational networks would not have remained functional without the acquiescence of successive Irish Governments. A good example of this was the PIRA engineering department. It manufactured home-made weapons and IEDs and consisted of seven full-time employees. This required constant funding from PIRA, and the indulgence of successive Irish governments. All meetings of PIRA'S Army Council were held in the Irish republic. In addition, there were two extensive arms dumps which supplied weapons for the campaign along the border area and access to these dumps was never impeded by the Irish authorities over a 20-year period. All the deep hides which held the weapons smuggled from Libya were located south of the border. In summary the territory of the Irish Republic could be characterised as an active sanctuary.[662]

Theses real tactical and operational challenges were compounded by an unwillingness of the policy elite to articulate a strategic counter narrative that challenged the Irish Republican one. They accepted the assumption that the geographical configuration of Ireland presupposed political unity. In short, geography was political destiny. The absence of a counter narrative meant the security forces were deprived of the legitimacy and guidance so critical at the operational and tactical level.

After the operational and tactical success of Operation Motorman. The Northern Ireland Office published a discussion paper in October 1972; seven months after Stormont had been suspended. The key phrase coined was the 'Irish Dimension'.[663] Geography was presented as political destiny. While careful to underline that the status of Northern Ireland could only be changed by consent, a distancing process from the rest of the British state was set in motion: 'A settlement must also recognise Northern Ireland's position within Ireland as a whole ... it is a fact that

---

661 Op cit, p. 3–2.
662 Interview with a former member of the RUC Special Branch, March 2021.
663 *The Future of Northern Ireland: a paper for discussion*, London: HMSO, 1972, p. 33.

Northern Ireland is part of the geographical entity of Ireland'.[664] This discussion paper went further and stated that: 'No United Kingdom Government for many years has had any wish to impede the realisation of Irish Unity'.[665]

The operational and tactical successes of Operation Motorman were negated by the absence of this counter narrative. An integrated political–military approach, so vital in all insurgencies, was like a mirage, ever receding into the horizon.

Conclusions

This chapter highlighted three challenges. First, the British Army was not provided with a strategic plan for success. Initially, the Army interpreted its role as non-aligned with respect to both the Nationalists and Loyalists. The GOC of Northern Ireland, Lieutenant General Sir Ian Freeland saw his immediate task to 'hold the ring' in 'a completely impartial manner'.[666] This had changed by the early 1970s. In the previous campaign, the Army saw itself as defending the integrity of the British state in Ireland. Now the aim was to maintain order, but not to defeat an insurgency – the antithesis of the principles of war. Second, initially, the British Army used some tactics from earlier counter-insurgency campaigns, despite their inappropriate nature. Finally, the border represented a challenge at all three levels.

These challenges were compounded by the resurrection of the operational codes of pursuing separate political initiatives with inconsistent results. Eleven days before the suspension of Stormont, the two main political parties in Britain established a cross-party consensus to engage

---

664 Ibid, p. 33.
665 Ibid, p. 33.
666 See Edwards, A., 'A whipping Boy If Ever There was One? The British Army and the Politics of Civil Military Relations in Northern Ireland, 1969–1979', *Contemporary British History* 28/2, 168.

in a dialogue with the IRA. After March 1972, the operational codes informed choices of a new generation of policy makers and civil servants.

The problem was these codes conferred no benefits on an army facing a growing insurgency. There was no strategic narrative that could provide, as previously stated, both guidance and legitimacy. Instead, it was 'under additional pressure to suppress violence and restore order'.[667] Despite its successes during Operation Motorman, as measured by the statistics presented in the Banner Analysis, the continued incidence of violence created a disconnect between tactical and operational achievements and strategic objectives.

Previous post-1945 counter-insurgency campaigns undertaken by the British army were conducted in colonial settings, and in predominantly rural environments. The deployment to Aden between 1963 and 1967 had some similarities to Operation Banner. Commenting on this past operational experience, one academic indicated that British Army was 'ill-prepared' for what General Sir Rupert Smith described as a multiphase confrontation: 'The troops had little internal security training'.[668] Ironically, the last time it faced a geographically hybrid insurgency containing both urban and rural dimensions was in Palestine in 1947.

The key difference from Palestine was that Northern Ireland was an integral part of the British state. The last time this had occurred was the campaign between 1919 and 1921. However, there were two important differences. First, there was now an international border. The Banner Analysis acknowledged the army interpreted the border too narrowly: 'In practice excessive importance was attached to the immediate tactical aspects of the Border itself, rather than to the theatre level aspects of cross-border operations'.[669] Second the unstated policy of successive

---

667 Mumford, A., 'Covert Peacemaking: Clandestine Negotiations and Backchannels with the Provisional IRA during the Early Troubles, 1972–1976', *The Journal of Imperial and Commonwealth History* 39/4, 6486.
668 Mockaitis. T.R., *British Counterinsurgency in the post-Imperial Era* (Manchester: Manchester University Press, 1995), 98.
669 Op cit, p. 4–6.

Irish governments meant that the ability to subvert, divert and possibly destroy the operational networks of PIRA was seriously impaired for over thirty years.

From the late 1970s the British Army's role changed and it accommodated itself to police primacy. The Royal Ulster Constabulary now had the task to erode the operational networks and tactical ability of PIRA inside Northern Ireland. However, the operating codes meant a counter-narrative was always absent. The next chapter will assess how the operating codes defined the final phase of Operation Banner.

CHAPTER 6

Successes and Failure: A Judgement on Operation Banner

Introduction

It is often assumed that Operation Banner ended in 1998, the year the Good Friday Agreement was signed. In fact, Banner did not formally end until 2007, some 9 years later, and 38 years after it began in 1969. The reason being PIRA did not stand down its units until 2005.[670] The Banner Analysis did not refer to this except to acknowledge until that year, Army Ammunition Technical Officers were clearing about thirty explosive incidents a month.[671] A year later, in 2006, the report stated there were still areas of Northern Ireland out of bounds to soldiers.

This chapter will assess the judgements from the analysis made concerning the latter half of this campaign. It will assess the extent to which the systematic infiltration by RUC Special Branch, and the application of military force modified the will of PIRA? There is evidence to suggest that by the 1990s intelligence driven counter-terrorism operations had taken their toll: 'Thanks to intelligence operations, just before the beginning of the peace process, more than 40 per cent of PIRA members had been convicted and over 70 per cent of PIRA operations were aborted'.[672]

---

670 See Bradley, G., and Feeney, B., *Insider: Gerry Bradley's Life in the IRA* (Dublin: The O'Brien Press, 2009), 173.
671 Operation Banner, An analysis of Military Operations in Northern Ireland, Army Code 71843 (2006), 2–16.
672 Transcript from Capturing the Lessons of Northern Ireland Seminar held at the University of Reading, 30th January 2013.

Other estimates put the number of PIRA operations either stillborn or aborted at a much higher figure.[673]

The culminating point of Operation Banner came at 5.36 p.m. on Good Friday on the 10th April 1998. On that date Senator George Mitchell declared: 'I am pleased to announce that the two governments and the political parties in Northern Ireland have reached an agreement'.[674] This agreement has been the subject to a vast and still unfolding literature.[675] It is not intended to assess all aspects of the Good Friday Agreement.[676] One of the most contentious issues was the release of convicted terrorists. The former army intelligence soldier Nick van der Bijl has argued that prisoner of war releases are an aspect of any modern peace talks. Northern Ireland was different in that these prisoners were convicted criminals. By the 30th June 1998, 426 prisoners had been released: 'many of them high profile terrorists, including the killers of Lance Bombardier Restorick Guardsmen Wright and Fisher and Trooper Clarke'.[677] These releases did little to temper the outlier elements of the Republican movement. Individuals from a number of different Irish Republican factions combined to place and detonate[678] a massive car bomb outside the Omagh Courthouse on the 15th August 1998. The result was the death of twenty-eight people and the injury of 220 people. The assumptions, the policy elite and their civil servants made about reciprocal behaviour and

---

673 Interview with a former member of the Royal Ulster Constabulary Special Branch, 14 March 2023.

674 Quoted in van der Bijl, N., *Operation Banner*, Barnesley: Pen and Sword Military (2017), 217–218.

675 This is a small sample of the literature. See for example: Aiken, N., *Reconciliation, and Transitional Justice* (New York: Routledge, 2014). Cox, M., Guelke, A., and Stephen F., eds., *A Farewell to Arms? From 'Long War' to Long Peace in Northern Ireland* (Manchester: Manchester University Press, 2000). Jarman, N., *Managing Violence and Building peace from Below* (Belfast: Northern Ireland Community Relations Council, 2013).

676 This can accessed at The Belfast Agreement, UK Government Policy Papers, 10 April 1998, Available at <www.gov.uk/government/publications/> the Belfast agreement assessed 12 June 2023.

677 Op cit, p. 218.

678 This was the Dissent IRA, Real IRA, Continuity IRA, and the INLA.

a business-like tradition in dealing with political violence were brutally underlined yet again.

One of the most insightful critiques of the agreement has come from the American academic Amanda Hall. She cited John Galtung's concept of a 'negative peace' as a way of understanding the outcome of the Good Friday Agreement. It managed and reduced the violence, rather than transforming the conflict and Northern Ireland society.[679] Another insight was the agreement had formalised divisions exacerbated by the conflict. This manifested itself by the restructuring and return of devolved powers based on creating a highly structured framework for a power sharing democracy. Ten years previously, the academic Frank Wright had argued this format[680] was a flawed concept: 'it only worked when it isn't very necessary (or indeed when it isn't strictly necessary at all)'.[681] Wright argued this artifice would have a negative effect in Northern Ireland, and would encourage extremism by the leaders of the sectarian parties[682] and their followers to maintain influence.[683] Mutual deterrence from violence was seen by Wright as the best way of maintaining tranquillity. Hall has summarised the paradox that lies at the heart of the agreement: 'The legacy of the Good Friday Agreement is therefore one of blighted potential: succeeding just enough not to fail but failing to bring about a truly sustainable peace'.[684]

---

679 For a statement of this concept of negative peace see Galtung, J., 'An Editorial', *Journal of Peace Research*, 1/1 (1967), 1–4.
680 It is also referred to in the academic literature as consociationalism.
681 Wright, F., *Northern Ireland a Comparative Analysis?* (Rowman & Littlefield, 1988), 274–275.
682 By this, I mean the leadership of Sinn Fein and the Democratic Unionist Party.
683 The prescience of Wright's analysis is pertinent in that 35 years later as in the local elections of 2023 moderate parties on both sides, such as the SDLP and UUP, suffered heavy electoral losses.
684 Hall, A., 'In complete Peace and Social Stagnation: Shortcomings of Good Friday Agreement', *Open Library of Humanities* 4/2 (7 August 2018) 28.

The Evolution of Operation Banner

The Banner Analysis assessed how the characteristics and scope had changed from the early 1980s to its termination in 2007: 'The British Government's main military objective in the 1980s was the destruction of PIRA rather than resolving the conflict'.[685] The academic Caroline Kennedy-Pipe has claimed that by the end of the 1980s there had arisen a: 'situation of what we might term a military stalemate'.[686] The Analysis gave a detailed account of the conduct of operations. At the tactical level, it was a fusion of overt and covert operations. The bulk of the Army and the Ulster Defence Regiment carried out 'framework operations'. The aim was to reassure the public, protect property and deter the terrorists. The deployment of army units had evolved to a pattern of stability, in contrast to the early 1970s: 'six regular battalions were stationed in Northern Ireland on two-year tours. Three further battalions undertook *Roulement Tours* of four and a half months'.[687] These *Roulement* battalions operated in the most 'active areas' of Northern Ireland.[688] In addition, the UDR[689] operated across areas of Northern Ireland like North Down where there was comparatively little terrorist activity.

Covert activities had a focus on intelligence gathering through human and technical surveillance, and what was described as 'human Intelligence collection' now referred as Humint. By the 1990s, surveillance methods were sophisticated and effective as: 'satellite surveillance, electronics, real-time heli-telly from helicopters, bugging devices, and covert video cameras disguised as stones, tree stumps, or fallen branches, and advances in computing and telecommunications were leaving the

---

685 Ibid, p. 2–15.
686 Kennedy C., 'Pipe, From War to Peace in Northern Ireland', in Cox, M., Guelke, A., Stephen F., eds., *A Farewell to Arms? From 'Long War' to Long Peace in Northern Ireland* (Manchester: Manchester University Press, 2000), 34.
687 Ibid, p. 2–13.
688 This meant South Armagh and West Belfast.
689 Ulster Defence Regiment.

IRA's experts behind'.[690] Human intelligence had become equally effective with respect to both PIRA and Loyalist paramilitary organisations. Gerry Bradley a member of PIRA claimed extensive penetration, from the mid-1980s, and outlined the impact they were having: 'Increased undercover work by locally recruited agents who had infiltrated the IRA ... made it difficult to know who to trust or where was safe. A significant number of men in key positions in Sinn Fein and the IRA, including men who acted as body guards to Gerry Adams – and even his driver had been 'turned' by British Intelligence'.[691] However, a RUC source has stated these claims must be treated with a degree of caution: 'the percentages quoted in respect of 'recruited agents' are widely excessive'.[692] According to one estimate, around 85 per cent of IRA operations in the late 1980s had to be aborted either the security forces had detected them, or the IRA itself chose not to go ahead because of fears that they had been compromised by agents within their organisation.[693] Infiltration by turning existing PIRA members remained the most effective way of undermining the organisation. The raison d'etre was to convert intelligence into evidence that could be used, where possible, to prosecute terrorists in the courts.

There were references to operations designed to intercept terrorists 'intent on committing violent offences'. Little granular detail was included, although an insight was given to the scale of such operations. The small number underlined the challenge of gaining and exploiting intelligence on imminent terrorist operations: 'Terrorists were killed on about 13 or 14 such operations and arrested in a number of others. The most famous was at Loughgall on 8 May 1987, when eight terrorists died'.[694] The Banner Analysis stated that a total of forty terrorists were

---

690 Op cit, p. 283.
691 Op cit, p. 284.
692 Interview with a former senior officer of the RUC, 3rd December 2023.
693 Interview with Bill Lowry, former Head of Special Branch, Northern Ireland Police service. Quoted in Neumann, P., 'The Bullet and the Ballot Box: The Case of the IRA', *Journal of Strategic Studies* 28/6, p. 969.
694 Op cit, p. 2–15.

killed in these operations, including many of their most experienced operators. Furthermore, it was claimed that PIRA never found an adequate response to this covert tactic.

The report claimed the attrition of individual terrorists 'of itself' had little effect on the outcome of the campaign. Instead, covert tactics were seen as pivotal: 'PIRA seem to have been brought to believe that there was no answer to Army covert operations, and that they could not win through violence. That was probably a key factor'.[695]

The capability of PIRA Active Service Units, even though the bulk of them were based in the Irish Republic was eroded by the RUC Special Branch, supported by Army intelligence and Special Forces: 'Operations were foiled repeatedly. The RUC Chief Constable in the early 1990s said the security forces were foiling four out of five IRA operations. Gerry Bradley says perhaps more, maybe nine out of ten'.[696] The cumulative effect of this activity was that the number of IRA operators was drying up.[697]

What remained substantially unchanged from the beginning of the campaign to the end was the challenge posed by the Irish border. This geographical dimension, which David Galula cited as one of the prerequisites[698] for a successful insurgency, was never decisively addressed.[699] The reason for this was the lack of sustained co-operation from successive Irish Governments. This was despite efforts to 'talk up' the nature of the co-operation being received by British governments from 1985 onwards.[700] For a total of 29 years, the Irish Republic made no meaningful contribution to cross-border co-operation: 'Cross-border police contact only provided worthwhile and effective intelligence after the Good

---

695 Op cit, p. 2–15.
696 Op cit, p. 293.
697 Op cit, p. 284.
698 The others were: a cause, weakness of the counterinsurgent and outside support.
699 See Galula, D., *Counterinsurgency Warfare* (Westport: Praeger Security International, 2006), 23–25.
700 This being the date of the Anglo-Irish agreement.

Friday Agreement. From 1969 to 1998, the Gardai had good intelligence but were prohibited from sharing it by their political masters'.[701]

One way of compensating, but not replacing, this void of intelligence was the decision in the mid-1980s to erect a series of permanent hilltop observation posts across South Armagh. The Banner Analysis cited four benefits of these new observation posts: they provided 24-hour weather and bullet proof cover for surveillance operations; they facilitated the use of sophisticated surveillance equipment, such as high-powered optics and MSTAR radar; they supported the development of an advanced communications network; finally, they facilitated a continuity of observation across wide rural areas. In addition, the deterrent effect of the towers on PIRA activity cannot be understated. Sightings of terrorists as they moved across the border could be passed from tower to tower, and it facilitated a possible interception before their bombs and ASUs reached urban areas.

The Debacle of Information Operations

In the previous chapter, the Banner Analysis acknowledged that the army learned some hard lessons regarding media handling in the 1970s and responded to them. It omitted to state that in September 1971, the Army appointed Lt Col Maurice Tugwell to head up an Information Policy Unit at HQNI. This was done largely as a reaction to the absence of a counter-strategic narrative from the British government. Unfortunately, the Army could not perform this task on its own. This absence had consequences. The nadir was an attempt by the Thatcher government to erode the narrative of Irish Republicanism by having actors voice over Sinn Fein media statements. This was no substitute for a systematic narrative from the British Government.

---

701 Capturing the Lessons of Northern Ireland, Seminar held at the University of Reading 30th January 2013, p. 9.

The Banner analysis claimed information operations were poorly conducted and ill-coordinated with other government bodies. The approach was reactive and often missed significant opportunities. This was exploited by terrorists with operational and strategic consequences: 'Constant criticism in the republican media, notably the *An Phoblacht* newspaper, was not seriously challenged by Government, NIO or Army Information operations'.[702] Two reasons were identified for this failure: the lack of a single unitary authority for the campaign. This absence was referred to a number of times in the Banner report; second, and more critically, there was no 'joint forum to agree Information Operations priorities, messages and means of dissemination'.

There was a strong continuity from the first campaign. In a memorandum titled: 'The Secrets of Crew House', Colonel Foulkes, appointed in May 1921, to run the army's propaganda effort from GHQ at Parkgate, Dublin, identified similar challenges. Furthermore, the remedies were identical to those highlighted in the Banner report. He asserted that 'Co-ordination of propaganda is as necessary as unity of command'. In addition, he recognised the 'vital connection between propaganda, policy and military operations'.[703]

Colonel French at GHQ in Dublin developed these themes in what was described as a 'Draft Circular' dated July 1921, the month the armed truce was announced. It contained a number of practical proposals to take over the printing press of the 'Weekly Summary' based in Dublin Castle. In addition, he wanted to use Basil Clarke[704] and Captain Darling (Private Secretary to General Tudor, Head of the RIC) as writers. Apart from maintaining a Press Branch at Dublin Castle (with its Chief), all propaganda branches should be collected together.[705] The 'Draft Circular'

---

702 Op cit, p. 7–6.
703 The Secrets of Crewe House May 1921, Foulkes Papers 7/1 Basil Liddell Hart Archives, King's College London.
704 Basil Clarke was the Head of the Press Office in Dublin Castle. As a journalist he was largely ineffective when compared to his Sinn Fein equivalents.
705 Colonel French Draft Circular dated 24th July 1921. Foulkes Papers 7/1 Basil Liddell Hart Archives, King's College London.

had a clear understanding of what the key aim should be: 'The object of propaganda is to induce everyone to think and talk about all questions from *Your* point of view'.[706] (Emphasis added) The importance of political propaganda was acknowledged in Army Quarterly, six years after the end of the campaign. Major Denning stated: 'Guerrillas have in fact, today, a new weapon, political propaganda, which draws blood upon the home front of the Great Power'.[707]

Successive British governments failed to develop and sustain a strategic narrative over the entire period of Operation Banner. Just 10 months before the PIRA ceasefire,[708] the extent of this failure was illuminated by the minutes of the Security Information Group dated 10th November 1993. A member of the group Mr Wood, a civil servant, had produced a paper titled 'Security Information: The Outline of a Way Forward'. Sir John Wheeler, a junior minister in the Northern Ireland Office, was in full agreement with the 'Plan for Information Strategy on Security'. He also recognised: 'The Government was failing to win its case. There was a depth of ignorance among important opinion formers, particularly, members of the House of Commons, where this extended to the new intake of MPs, longer-standing Members and those who had an interest in Northern Ireland matters'.[709]

Failure pivoted around the inability to resolve the issues of resources and institutional responsibility: 'The crucial question of the additional resources required to set up a dedicated information unit, and where it might be located, still remain unresolved. It was necessary for long-term strategic thinking to have fully resourced mechanisms in place'.[710] It was recognised as essential to address international Irish diasporas with respect to information operations. In this context, the only positive proposal came from the British Embassy in Washington. A response

---

706 Ibid.
707 Denning, B. C., 'Modern Problems of Guerrilla Warfare', *Army Quarterly* 13 (1927), 349.
708 This was announced on 31st August 1994.
709 PRONI cent/1/22/11A. Belfast PRONI.
710 Ibid.

to a letter from Mr Wood they suggested Congressman Newt Gingrich 'might be a possible candidate for a sponsored visit to Northern Ireland'. There was an acknowledgement how important these constituencies were: 'The United Kingdom was very poor at recognising the need to shape people's understanding. Yet the diasporas had an important role in shaping the understanding of the events in Northern Ireland'.[711] Tony Blair when Prime Minister failed to address this in the United States to the puzzlement of the British Ambassador at the time: 'No. 10s inability or unwillingness to match the implacability of the Sinn Fein negotiators, contributed to a peace deal which posed almost as many questions as it was meant to answer'.[712]

The minutes of the meeting contained the misguided assumption that 'Highlighting successes might be counter-productive'. The perverse logic being it could illuminate the successes of the terrorists. Most damaging of all was the ability of Sinn Fein propaganda to prompt the British government to respond to allegations of collusion between protestant paramilitaries and the RUC on their terms: 'the RUC has been able to highlight the fact that more Loyalist than Republican terrorists had been charged in 1993, to counter claims of collusion by the security forces'.[713] This was judged to be 'extremely effective' in the minutes. The Chief Constable of the RUC was listed as present at this meeting, in addition to two senior Army officers from HQNI.[714] The failure of Information Operations persisted to the end of Operation Banner. The deeper reasons for this failure will be accessed later in this chapter.

---

711 Transcript from a seminar titled: 'Capturing the Lessons of Northern Ireland', held at the University of Reading 30th January 2013.
712 Meyer, C., *DC Confidential* (London: Weidenfeld and Nicolson, 2005), p. 114.
713 Ibid.
714 They were named as Brigadier Strudley and Lt Colonel Hicks.

The Enemy Has a Vote

The German theorist of war Carl von Clausewitz coined a metaphor that expressed how the character of a conflict evolves:

'War is more than a true chameleon that slightly adapts its characteristics to the given case'.[715] He identified a 'paradoxical trinity' of violence and enmity, the play of chance, and its 'element of subordination' as an instrument of policy. This made it subject to reason. It is this trinity that provides a template for understanding how the latter part of the campaign evolved.

An academic seminar concluded the campaign had failed to adapt with sufficient rigour with respect to both organisational learning and after-action reviews: 'Northern Ireland demonstrated the need for the army and the police to adapt to become learning institutions quickly. The campaign as a whole demonstrated a lack of reflection on previous principles, practices and experiences. Competition between different governmental departments was an obstacle to progress'.[716]

However, the Banner Analysis stressed the degree to which the Army and the RUC had evolved in terms of their tactical and operational competence. It underlined the considerable advances made in surveillance and human intelligence. Despite these changes from the early 1980s to the mid-1990s, PIRA demonstrated its ability to broaden the geographical scope of its campaign, and craft a strategy based on a paradox. It was 'a two-track approach': 'a ballot box in one hand and an Armalite in the other'.

It was announced by PIRA in 1991 and marked a shift towards politics led by Gerry Adams. There was ambivalence in the Banner Analysis about this change. It could not decide if it should be interpreted as a milestone towards polarisation of the extremes, or a process of moving extreme

---

715   von Clausewitz, C., *On War* M. Howard, ed. and tran. and Peter Paret (Princeton: Princeton University Press, 1976), 89.
716   Transcript from a seminar titled: 'Capturing the Lessons of Northern Ireland', University of Reading 30th January 2013, p. 8.

republicanism towards 'legitimate political activity'. It was suggested that it was a: 'factor in the signing of the Good Friday Agreement'.[717] That was the only mention of the agreement and the events leading up to it.

This twin track approach underlined the key challenge any terrorist strategy has to confront. The academic Lawrence Freedman has drawn attention to the reality that the gap between violent capacity and the desired end is often a wide one.[718] How this gap was closed will be examined later in this chapter. The operational aim of PIRA was summarised by M. L. R. Smith: 'Using the military effort to undermine stability in Northern Ireland, the movement could attract notoriety which it could use to further publicise its social, economic and cultural policies'.[719]

The Banner Analysis argued there was a recognition, as in all forms of insurgencies or terrorist violence, of a dialectical struggle between competing adversaries; the outcome was determined by interaction between opponents:[720] 'Conflict is complex, adversarial and evolutionary, which suggests that in the longer term, the advantage goes to the side whose military and non-military processes adapt and evolve fastest'.[721] Two processes were identified by the report: first there was a 'closely linked loop' responsible for the development of counter terrorist response measures under the command of HQ Northern Ireland; second, there was a process of military appreciation or estimate. This was a detailed review of military decision-making. The report cited examples of poor decision-making that had operational and strategic consequences during the campaign: the first was the Balkan Street search and subsequent curfew of 1970. The second was the tactics of the arrest operation on Bloody Sunday.

The Banner Analysis provided an estimate of PIRA's strength in the early 1980s. It stated, there was a core of 30 leaders plus 200–300 active

---

717 Op cit, p. 2–15.
718 See Freedman, L., 'Terrorism as a Strategy', *Government and Opposition* 42/3 summer (2007). Special Issue on Politics in the Age of Terror, p. 319.
719 Smith, M. L. R. *Fighting for Ireland the Military Strategy of the Irish Republican Movement* (London: Routledge, 1995), 165.
720 For a more detailed exposition see Gray, C. S., *Modern Strategy* (Oxford: Oxford University Press, 1999), 23–25.
721 Op cit, p. 8–7.

terrorists. In this period, the large-scale house searches of the 1970s had been abandoned. They were no longer needed as intelligence made a more focused approach viable: 'By 1983 it was 1,500 (house searches). They no longer needed speculative searching. By the end of the 1980s, the IRA went for a period of 2 years without being able to detonate a single bomb in Belfast city centre'.[722]

As previously mentioned, during the 1980s PIRA demonstrated a capability to expand the geographical scope of its operations. This resulted in attacks on continental Europe against Army and RAF bases in West Germany,[723] Holland and Belgium. It must be emphasised that these attacks only needed a handful terrorist operatives. The most dramatic example of this expanded reach and capability was the disrupted attack on a British Army band parade in Gibraltar in March 1988. Three members of PIRA were ambushed and killed by a SAS team.

An important dimension of this dialectical struggle was the ability of PIRA to source new supplies of explosives, arms and ammunition. By far, the most important development was the willingness of Colonel Gaddafi's Libyan Government to supply PIRA with weapons, ammunition and explosives.[724] This had a lasting impact in two ways: it provided the means for their strategic aspiration of a long war,[725] and plan for a 'Tet Offensive;' second, as Patterson has argued[726] these weapons were to enable the PIRA to maintain their campaign at a level which provided them with powerful leverage when it came to the negotiations that led to

---

722 Ibid, p. 239.
723 For example, PIRA attacked Rheindahlen barracks in March 1987 and Roermond and Nieuwbergen barracks in March 1987 and Osnabrueck barracks in 1987.
724 This was in direct retaliation for Mrs Thatcher allowing US war planes to use British bases to bomb targets in Libya.
725 In essence it was a strategy of attrition that would take two decades and was designed to break the will of the British government to remain in Northern Ireland.
726 See Patterson, H., *Ireland's Violent Frontier*, p. 118.

the Good Friday agreement. The 'Tet Offensive' plan[727] was aborted as a consequence of the interception of the *MV Eksund*[728] by the French Navy on 31 May 1987: 'Tet' was to be fought with the *Eksund's* cargo. Once unloaded, the plan was for these weapons to be stored temporarily in a single bunker in Arklow, County Wicklow, and then distributed to the ASUs who would lead the offensive north of the Border and elsewhere in Britain and Europe'.[729] The Banner Analysis claimed in an understated manner: 'The French authorities believed that Libya was involved in the provision of this material'.[730]

What was omitted was how the relationship between the Libyan Intelligence Service and PIRA was enhanced between late 1984 and early 1985. This was symbolised by an invitation from Joe Cahill, a PIRA member, to the Libyans to visit the Irish Republic for face-to-face meetings with PIRA. Colonel Gaddafi sent Nasser Ashour, the third most senior officer in the Libyan Intelligence Service. He made at least two undetected visits to the Irish Republic to meet the Army Council of PIRA.[731] He offered the organisation $10 million and 300 tons of modern weapons and explosives. If this money and weapons got through it would, at a stroke, transform the viability of PIRA's 'long war' attrition strategy.

The first of these shipments took place in July 1985 when a 65-foot Irish fishing boat named the *Casamara* successfully transferred 7 tons of weapons from a Libyan ship in the Mediterranean and landed them off Clogga Strand in County Wicklow. The weapons were loaded onto lorries and taken to dumps throughout the Irish Republic. This pattern

727 The plan was modelled on the Tet offensive launched by the Vietcong in January 1968. The offensive is credited with convincing a key section of the U.S. public that the war against North Vietnam was unwinnable. The IRA hoped to have the same impact on the policy elite and the British public.
728 The Eksund was carrying 3,500 crates of arms and ammunition, including 20 SA7 missiles, 1,000 AK 47 rifles, ten DshKM heavy machine guns and 2 tons of Semtex explosive.
729 Moloney, E., *A Secret History of the IRA* (London: Penguin Books, 2002), p. 21.
730 Op cit, p. 3–7.
731 For a more granular description of the cover Ashour used for these trips, see Moloney, E., *A Secret History of the IRA* (London: Penguin Books, 2002), 15.

was repeated in July 1986, when the *Casamara* now renamed the *Kula*, brought 14 tons of weapons, plus the first consignment of SAM-7 missiles. The third shipment was in October 1986. The ship used was the *Villa*, a former oil rig standby vessel. It transported 105 tons of weapons, including forty general purpose machine guns. The most important item in this shipment was 5 tons of Semtex, a high-quality explosive developed by the Czech arms industry. The journalist Ed Moloney has claimed that British security forces estimated that the value of the shipments came to a total of $40 million. This was five times the PIRA's total annual budget. There were enough arms in the *Villa* shipment alone to keep PIRA's campaign going for at least 20 years.[732] The uninterrupted landings and subsequent distribution of these arms across the Irish Republic underlined the lack of effort and resources, the Irish state committed to any prevention measures. It represented a huge failure of intelligence.

The Banner Analysis also focused on the United States. It was the 'biggest foreign contributor to Northern Ireland'. For example, £100,000 was raised in 1974 alone. During the hunger strikes in the early 1980s the sum of about $250,000 was raised in 6 months. However, there was no mention of George Harrison an IRA member based in New York. He was responsible for sending up to 300 guns a year to PIRA. Moloney cited an estimate that he sent a total of 2,500 weapons across the Atlantic plus a million rounds of ammunition.[733] It was not until the early 1980s that the Reagan Administration, under pressure from Mrs Thatcher, directed the FBI to investigate Irish Republican fund-raising activities. This resulted in a director of NORAID being charged in the United States with terrorist related activities in October 1981. The Banner Analysis credited the terrorist attacks of 11th September 2001 with having a severely detrimental effect upon support for PIRA. These attacks: 'largely removed American sympathy for terrorism world-wide, and this effect, keenly felt in Northern Ireland, forced Irish republicans further towards pursuing their cause in the political rather than in the military arena'.[734] Despite the impact of the terrorist

---

732 Ibid, p. 20.
733 Ibid, p. 16.
734 Op cit, p. 3–8.

attack on the twin towers in New York, PIRA thanks to the support of the Libyan government, remained a well-armed terrorist organisation right up to the announcement of a ceasefire in August 1994.

Missed Opportunities

A reflective aspect of the Banner Analysis was an attempt to identify decisive points in the campaign. Could the campaign have been concluded earlier? Three critical periods were identified: a few months after the breakdown of public order in 1969; in the mid-1970s when the defeat of the insurgency could have neutralised PIRA before it became a 'skilled terrorist organisation'; finally, enhanced legal powers could have been sought in the 1980s to remove the top echelons of PIRA when the organisation was able to exist independently, in logistic terms, from the catholic nationalist community. This last point was qualified by two factors. The challenge of implementing selective long-term internment. The Irish border was also identified as important. The lack of support of successive Irish governments was critical. This meant that: 'PIRA leaders in the Republic could not have been removed and a clean sweep could not have been achieved'.[735] The Banner Analysis stressed the 'Decisive Points' assessment was not a mere academic exercise as over 1,400 people died in the 25 years after 1980.

Down the Main Drain Again

Going 'down main drain' was a phrase coined by General Macready to describe Alfred Cope's persistent behaviour of passing information to and sustaining secret communications with Michael Collins and other

---

735   Op cit, p. 8–14.

leaders of the insurgency.⁷³⁶ This proclivity was identified in the Record of the Rebellion as explaining the unwillingness and inability of the government to articulate and disseminate a strategic counter-narrative. The mediocre media talents of Basil Clarke, based in Dublin Castle were also a factor. The *Record of the Rebellion* rightly claimed this was the least fought aspect of the insurgency. The persistent result was the pursuit of separate political initiatives with inconsistent results. The *Record of the Rebellion* made a direct reference to the 'conciliatory attitude' of Sir Hamar Greenwood, the Chief Secretary of Ireland.

Where the same operating codes discernible, and did they have the same effect in the latter part of Operation Banner? The answer was multiplied in its complexity in comparison to the first campaign. This is due to an important discontinuity; the existence of the Irish Republic whose stated constitutional objective was the removal of Northern Ireland from being an integral part of the United Kingdom. To this can be added the actions of civil servants, and elements of the British intelligence community. Were their actions merely a reflection of the sentiments of the policy makers they served? Or were they, as Sir John Anderson said of Alfred Cope, working for themselves.⁷³⁷ In addition, the effect of Brendan Duddy, a Londonderry businessman, who acted as an intermediary⁷³⁸ with PIRA, has to be taken into consideration. Did he fulfil the same function as the Ballina businessman Patrick Moylett did for Collins and de Valera?

The academic Naill O'Dochartaigh has claimed the whole period of Operation Banner: 'provides a revelatory case of back-channel negotiation'.⁷³⁹ What he failed to understand and appreciate was that the deniable contacts and the subsequent interactions were a product of

---

736 This included Eamon de Valera, Erskine Childers and Patrick Moylett.
737 See Chapter 4 p. 28.
738 Aaron Edwards in his book *Agents of Influence: Britain's Secret Intelligence War Against the* IRA (Dublin: Merrion Press, 2021) has claimed that Duddy was an Irish Republican activist.p.122–123.
739 O' Dochartaigh, N., *Deniable Contact: Back Channel Negotiation in Northern Ireland* (Oxford: Oxford University Press, 2021), p. 1.

the 'operating codes'. This crucial omission makes his arguments insufficiently correct.

What has been left unstated in the Banner Analysis and the literature has been the tendency of these operational codes to create political deficits with respect to United Kingdom as a whole. The policy elite displayed no awareness of the most fundamental challenge of statesmanship: there is no such thing as a natural state. The eternal problem is how to bind together disparate regions often with diverse ethnic populations. Furthermore, the European tradition that the state defends itself unconditionally from internal and external threats gained little traction in British political culture. In June 1984, Margaret Thatcher told her cabinet: 'Ten thousand British soldiers could not be left in Northern Ireland forever, nor could the very considerable cost of subsidising the province be sustained, without continuing the search for possible forward movement'.[740] The trajectory had been set for what was to emerge seventeen months later, the Anglo-Irish Agreement. Apart from citing its date, 15th November 1985, no comment was made in the Banner Analysis about the motives of the Thatcher Government in agreeing to this initiative. Instead, it was asserted that 'it can be seen as a useful stepping stone towards normalisation'.

This conditional culture was compounded by another deficit. The failure to articulate a counter narrative that related Northern Ireland to the rest of the United Kingdom. Henry Kissinger accurately identified the consequences this would have: 'She (Mrs Thatcher) never developed her own distinct vision for Northern Ireland, allowing the negotiations (for the Anglo-Irish Agreement) to be led by Robert Armstrong, the Cabinet Secretary to whom she delegated the task'.[741] The opportunity for this civil servant to pursue political initiatives subject to little restraint or supervision resulted in the operating codes of Cope demonstrating a surprising persistence.

---

740 CAB 128/80. Most Confidential annex to cabinet minutes, 28th June 1984, Quoted in O' Dochartaigh, N., *Deniable Contact: Back Channel Negotiation in Northern Ireland* (Oxford: Oxford University Press, 2021), p. 196.
741 Kissinger, H., *Leadership* (Allen Lane: London, 2022), 362.

George Chester Duggan had observed the changes in personnel that took place in Dublin Castle from May 1920, and the critical function the incoming civil servants played: 'it was they (the civil Servants) who filled the picture, who decided what was to its foreground and background, what figures sinister, commonplace or mystical were to fill the canvas'.[742] The key function Armstrong also dispensed was political stage management. First, nemesis for the sin of representational democracy was not long in coming. All the Unionist MPs elected to represent constituencies in Northern Ireland were excluded from the political stage. Into the foreground stepped the Irish government by invitation of Armstrong.

The desire for increased cross-border security was traded at the price of introducing a consultative dimension into Anglo-Irish relations. It was accepted that Irish governments would, in the future, put forward proposals rather than acknowledging they have the right do so. It was expressed in the weasel words of Whitehall: 'The United Kingdom Government accepts that the Irish Government will put forward views and proposals on matters relating to Northern Ireland within the field of activity of the Conference in so far as those matters are not the responsibility of a devolved administration in Northern Ireland'.[743] The territorial integrity of the United Kingdom was thereby qualified. It was akin to a German government accepting that Denmark would put forward proposals on a range of issues with respect to the German state of Schleswig-Holstein.[744]

PIRA while not invited onto the stage, ascribed different motives for the Anglo-Irish Agreement: 'The catalyst for the Hillsborough Treaty was undoubtedly a combination of the Brighton bomb and the electoral rise of Sinn Fein'.[745] The Agreement was opposed by Sinn Fein, yet Adams's

---

742 See Chapter 3, p. 10.
743 Quoted in Connolly E., and Doyle, J., Ripe moments for exiting Political Violence: An Analysis of the Northern Ireland Case. Irish Studies in International Affairs.
744 Schleswig-Holstein is the most northern most of the sixteen states of Germany. In the nineteenth century, it was subject to a long-term political and territorial dispute. In 1848, Denmark tried to annex it and was victorious in a war that ended in 1852. War broke out again in 1864 and it was absorbed into Prussia in 1867. Finally, it was subject to a plebiscite in 1920.
745 Quoted in Smith, M. L. R., *Fighting for Ireland* (London: Routledge, 1995), p. 189.

interpretation of what it represented strategically was accurate. It 'gave Dublin, for the first time, a foot in the door in the Six Counties'. It would not be the last time the citizens of Northern Ireland had a qualification of the 'rights' of British citizenship imposed on them. The academic Arthur Aughey argued unionists were expected to recognise their duty of accepting a role for the Irish Republic in the good government of Northern Ireland: 'In terms of reciprocal rights and duties, it may be claimed that such an acceptance would infringe a higher duty – the maintenance of the fundamental integrity of the United Kingdom'.[746]

Widespread rejection of the agreement was expressed by the Unionist community: 'The Unionist campaign of opposition involved co-operation across the entire unionist spectrum from the mainstream UUP to the illegal loyalist paramilitary groups – using massive public protests, resignations from parliament to force by-elections and a major escalation of loyalist paramilitary attacks. In this case, it failed to force a formal British change of policy'.[747] The Unionist protests failed because they were unable to gain any traction on the institutional governance of Northern Ireland. However, without Unionist support, further political progress, in terms of setting up a devolved administration, was impossible.[748]

The litmus test for the Anglo-Irish Agreement was whether it would bring about an improvement in cross-border security, and an ending the use of the territory of the Irish Republic as an active sanctuary for PIRA. The reality was that for the remaining five years of the 1980s and 3 years of the 1990s, none of the assumptions the British made about improved security co-operation were realised. Thatcher recognised in her memoirs the folly of the Agreement but remained wedded to its transactional assumptions: 'Our concessions alienated the Unionists without

---

746 Aughey, A., *Under Siege* (London: Hurst & Company, 1989), p. 23.
747 Connolly, E., and Doyle, J., 'Ripe moments for Exiting Political Violence: An Analysis of the Northern Ireland Case', *Irish Studies in International Affairs* 26 (2015), 155.
748 For 2 years after the agreement Unionist leaders refused to even talk to British ministers.

gaining the level of security co-operation we had a right to expect'.⁷⁴⁹ She concluded 'in the light of this experience it is surely time to consider an alternative approach'. She never elucidated what she had in mind. Going 'down the main drain' would again be assessed as a viable pathway for the policy elite to take.

Slip Sliding Away

The Israeli historian Martin van Creveld was cited in the Banner Analysis. He gave a summary of the operational outcome of the British Army's campaign in Northern Ireland and its success against an irregular force: 'it should be recognised that the Army did not 'win' in any recognisable way; rather it achieved its desired end-state, which allowed a political process to be established without unacceptable levels of intimidation'.⁷⁵⁰ The report stated the violence was reduced to an extent that made it clear to PIRA that they could not win by arms alone.

The Banner Analysis left unexamined the bridging process, which enabled political legitimacy to be conferred on both PIRA and its political party Sinn Fein. This process would entail a sustained engagement with all three of the operating codes. The first steps were taken while Thatcher was still Prime Minister: 'In the winter of 1989–1990, Northern Ireland Secretary of State Peter Brooke, working with a core group of senior civil servants in the Northern Ireland Office, made a calculated move to re-engage with the Provisionals. It marked a significant shift in British Government policy, a decision to explore, for the first time since the mid-1970s, the possibility of a political settlement that included the Provisionals'.⁷⁵¹ John Chilcot one of the civil servants involved designated

---

749 Thatcher, M., *The Downing Street Years* (London: Harper Collins, 1993), 415.
750 Op cit, p. 8–15.
751 O'Dochartaigh, N., *Deniable Contact: Back Channel Negotiation in Northern Ireland* (Oxford: Oxford University Press, 2021), p. 203.

this as 'Political Movement'. This ran in parallel with engagement with the constitutional parties and the Irish government.[752]

These separate political initiatives resulted in a decision in 1991 to reactivate secret channels of communications with PIRA. This involved personnel from MI6 and MI5. It was given the codename CHIFFON.[753] The aim was to bring about a ceasefire and negotiations with this terrorist group.[754] The 'challenge of currency conversion' had been abandoned. The relationship between strategy and its enabling tactics, as identified by Colin Gray, had been broken.[755] The political choices would provide neither legitimacy nor practical guidance for the Army or the RUC. In one sense, it rendered redundant the integrated approach to counterterrorism and would remain so until the announcement of an armed truce by PIRA.

In the early 1990s, PIRA was still a lethal terrorist organisation but increasingly constrained by intelligence-driven counter-terrorism efforts.[756] This had the effect of disrupting planned attacks, stemming the flow of recruits and funding and reluctance by members in many areas to risk their lives. It was no coincidence that South Armagh PIRA led the fight to the end, as they were geographically proximate to the safe haven of the Irish Republic.

MI5 is now engaged in its own exercise of 'currency conversion'. This would take a very different trajectory from the one Colin Gray had articulated. How was PIRA going to be helped to resolve the generic problem of terrorism as a strategy? This has been summarised by the academic Lawrence Freedman: 'terrorism is an interesting problem in strategy, as the gap between available capacity and desired ends is often very

---

752 Ibid, p. 206.
753 See Taylor, P., *Operation Chiffon* (London: Bloomsbury, 2023).
754 See Andrew, C., *The Defence of The Realm: The Authorized History of MI5* (London: Penguin, 2010), 783.
755 See Chapter 1, p. 2.
756 For a book that has an intelligence focus see Edwards, A., *Agents of Influence: Britain's Secret Intelligence War Against the IRA* (Dublin: Merrion Press, 2021).

wide indeed'.[757] He identified a generic typology of strategy: controlling, consensual and coercive. Terrorism can only reside in the last category. This was the challenge John Deverell faced as the MI5 officer who was Director and Co-ordinator of Intelligence in Northern Ireland.

The first step was an unauthorised meeting between an MI6 Officer called Michael Oatley, and the Londonderry businessman Brendan Duddy. It took place in late 1990 or early 1991, although Oatley had meet intermediaries of the Irish Republican movement since the 1970s, he was to retire soon, and together they decided to mount a final attempt to establish a channel for pursuing separate political initiatives. The result was a meeting with Martin McGuiness. He had been given a 'listening brief' by the leaders of PIRA.[758] Oatley's subsequent report, and impending retirement brought to a head the need for a decision. Should he be replaced with another serving intelligence officer? Deverell, Chilcot and Brooke as Secretary of State, with the knowledge of the Prime Minister John Major, made a choice to commit to a replacement.

The name of the MI6 officer appointed was Robert McLaren.[759] He was seconded to MI5 to work under John Deverell. This constituted, according to O'Dochartaigh: 'the sole official channel between the IRA Army Council and the British Prime Minister'.[760] What was remarkable about McLaren, was how his actions demonstrated a congruence with Alfred Cope, in that he passed to Duddy official documents that ultimately ended up in republican hands.[761] Progress was slow, and McLaren in February 1992 send Duddy a note expressing the sentiment that neither side seems to have any ideas about how to bring peace closer.[762]

---

757 Freedman, L., 'Terrorism as a Strategy', *Government and Opposition* 42/3 (summer 2007) 319.
758 Op cit, p. 224.
759 When he first contacted Brendan Duddy, it was under the alias of Colin Ferguson from Euroassets, a London based company.
760 Op cit, p. 228.
761 Op cit, p. 229.
762 Note from R McL[Robert McLaren], 18th February 1992, POL35/242 and POL35/592 Quoted in Dochartaigh, N., *Deniable Contact: Back Channel Negotiation in Northern Ireland* (Oxford; Oxford University Press, 2021) 230.

By April 1992, Patrick Mayhew had replaced Peter Brooke as Secretary of State for Northern Ireland. At the end of 1992, a British Government was committed to a political initiative.

The discontinuity from the first campaign was that public signalling became an integral part of the process. Patrick Mayhew, in December 1992, gave a speech at the University of Ulster which outlined how a British government might respond to a ceasefire from PIRA. There was an emphasis on a willingness to include a strong 'All Ireland' dimension. In essence, a new narrative had been crafted by civil servants. Implicit in this was the assumption that a British government would not counter the strategic narrative of Irish Republicanism.

The leaders of PIRA knew there was a mismatch between their capability for bombing and murder, and the political demands they desired. The academic M. L. R. Smith has argued there emerged by the early 1990s, what he characterised as 'neo-realism' in the Republican movement.[763] This had two dimensions: PIRA became willing to be specific about what measures were necessary to bring their terrorist campaign to an end; second, there was a recognition of the limits of their coercive strategy, and their interests would be best served by a 'broader nationalist alliance'. The first step was taken by PIRA. Successive Irish Governments had been regarded as: 'a Vichy-like regime lacking legitimacy and actively frustrating Sinn Fein's attempts to secure Irish unity'.[764] This changed in 1992 with the launch of a new policy document titled: *Towards a lasting peace*. This recognised the legitimacy of Irish governments and their centrality, along with the SDLP, in helping PIRA achieve their objectives. This document made a reference to: 'Fianna Fail and the SDLP have considerable influence in world power centres. They could and should reject the British propaganda view of 'Britain as an honest broker'.[765] Where these 'world power centres' were located was not specified. Their attitude to the Unionist population of Northern Ireland was unchanging and

---

763 See Smith, M. L. R., *Fighting for Ireland?* (London: Routledge, 1995), 197.
764 Op cit, p. 156.
765 For a full text of this document see <www.sinnfein.ie/contents15210>, assessed 21/4/23.

entombed in geographical determinism; geography was still political destiny: 'Unionists make up 20 per cent of the people of Ireland and therefore are a minority not a majority in Ireland'.[766]

The new 'All Ireland' narrative of the British state, and the emergence of a republican neo-realism were not enough to increase the tempo of political movement. On 22nd February 1993, a fake message was drafted by Robert McLaren, Brendan Duddy and Noel Gallagher, an Irish Republican closely associated with the leadership of PIRA.[767] This document stated: 'The conflict is over, but we need (British) advice on how to bring it to a close. We wish to have an unannounced ceasefire in order to hold dialogue leading to peace'.[768] The British response was to be a nine-paragraph statement which would be handed over at a meeting between the relevant parties.

This would take place in a hotel near Belfast on the 20th March. The three attendees were McLaren, Duddy and Deverell. The objective was to hand over the British government's response. On the same day PIRA exploded a bomb in Warrington that killed two boys aged 3 and 12. This event underlined yet again the conceit that accompanied these separate political initiatives. There was still no commitment by PIRA to show restraint or reciprocity when it came to the use of political violence. Deverell had been told by John Major's office not to hand over the written response and call off a proposed meeting with Martin McGuiness. Although according to O'Dochartaigh the handover had already taken place.[769] Undeterred by a Prime Ministerial instruction, 3 days later, a meeting took place between Robert McLaren, Martin McGuiness and Gerry Kelly, two senior members of PIRA. Brendan Duddy and two other people were there as observers.[770] What was communicated

---

766 Ibid.
767 Op cit, p. 234.
768 Bredan Duddy Papers NUI Galway. Quoted in Dochartaigh, N., *Deniable Contact: Back Channel Negotiation in Northern Ireland* (Oxford: Oxford University Press, 2021) 236.
769 Op cit, p. 240.
770 Op cit, p. 244.

was a calculated repudiation of Northern Ireland's place in the United Kingdom by a member of the British intelligence community: 'The final solution is union. It is going to happen anyway. The historical train – Europe-determines that. We are committed to Europe. Unionists will have to change. This island will be as one'.[771] Despite the different geographical context the political objective differed little from the one cited by Alfred Cope in his meeting in Dublin Castle with the Ballina businessman Patrick Moylett on the 30th May 1921: 'We are willing to acknowledge that we are defeated … We are willing to withdraw our whole establishment, from the lowest policeman to the highest judge'.[772]

The response came from PIRA on the 19th May. The offer was an armed truce for two weeks on the condition of secret talks starting with British officials, the assumption being these would lead to a complete end of PIRA's campaign. The limits of what a British government could agree to was defined by the reliance on the votes in the House of Commons of nine Ulster Unionist MPs, there was also a proposed change in the timeline of a ceasefire: 'Major now decided British officials would not have any meeting with Sinn Fein until an IRA ceasefire had held for three months, a much more restrictive position than had been suggested in the contacts up to this point'.[773]

John Hume, as leader of the SDLP, also had secret talks with Gerry Adams. These had begun in April 1993, and the contents of the dialogue were presented to the Irish government on 7th October 1993. The Irish government of Albert Reynolds concluded that the policy of isolating Sinn Fein was not producing political progress towards weakening Northern Ireland's position in the United Kingdom. Nor was it undermining Sinn Fein. As Connolly and Doyle have remarked by acknowledging the legitimacy of Sinn Fein's representation of a section of the catholic population of Northern Ireland this marked a crucial shift in the position of the Irish government.[774] More importantly a ceasefire by

---

771   Setting the Record Straight, Dublin: Sinn Fein 1994.
772   See Chapter 4, p. 23.
773   Op cit, p. 250.
774   Op cit, p. 158.

PIRA had still not been announced. M. L. R. Smith has suggested this represented a high noon of the organisation's ability to forge a united nationalist agenda without having to forgo the use of violence.[775] By late October 1993, the British Government had moved to abandon the idea of a joint declaration based on these secret talks. The human cost of this bridging process was underlined in the same month by the bombing of a fishmongers shop on the protestant Shankill Road in Belfast that killed ten people, including the bomber.

This atrocity provided the British government with a pretext for backing away from the Hume–Adams plan. The Prime Minister John Major went so far as to state in November 1993 that the prospect of including PIRA in any peace talks would 'turn my stomach'.[776] John Major now presented the Irish Government with a new text that stressed the need to secure Unionist support for any declaration.

Cope had been successful in keeping secret his negotiations with Collins and de Valera out of the public domain until after the announcement of the armed truce in July 1921. It was not until 1924 that a serious attempt was made, in the House of Lords, to have Cope's activities investigated. Operation Chiffon fell victim to the disaggregated world of late twentieth-century journalism. Major's government was unable to keep these talks a secret. The journalist Eamon Mallie in an article in the Observer[777] exposed the pursuit of separate political initiatives. Inconsistent results were to follow quickly. John Major was now hoisted by the petard of his own perfidy. In a 'tete-a-tete' meeting that took place in Dublin Castle on the 3rd December 1993, the minutes made clear how vulnerable the British government had made itself: 'The Irish Government had felt let down on learning of exchanges between HMG

---

775   Op cit, p. 198.
776   Quoted in Smith, M. L. R., *Fighting for Ireland?* (London: Routledge, 1995), 198.
777   Mallie, E., 'Ministers covered up Sinn Fein Dialogue', *The Observer* (28th November 1993).

and PIRA, and wondering if it was caught in a Dutch auction'.[778] John Major refuted any allegation of a Dutch auction.[779] Political pressure from the Irish manifested itself quickly: 'With almost three years of secret British communication with the IRA now exposed, the Irish government pressed the British as hard as they could to issue a joint declaration'.[780] Just 12 days later, the British and Irish governments issued the Downing Street Declaration on the 15th December.

The Irish Government argued that PIRA wanted to negotiate an end to their campaign. Furthermore, they insisted that the British government acknowledge publicly Northern Ireland's membership of the United Kingdom had become conditional, a major concession to a central pillar of Irish Republican ideology. The fourth paragraph of the Declaration stated:

> The role of the British Government will be to encourage, facilitate and enable the achievement of such agreement over a period through a process of dialogue and co-operation based on full respect for the rights and identities of both traditions in Ireland. They accept that such agreement may, as of right, take the form of agreed structures for the island as a whole, including a united Ireland achieved by peaceful means on the following basis. The British Government agree that it is for the people of the island of Ireland alone, by agreement between the two parts respectively, to exercise their right of self-determination on the basis of consent, freely and concurrently given, North and South, to bring about a united Ireland, if that is their wish. They reaffirm as a binding obligation that they will, for their part, introduce the necessary legislation to give effect to this, or equally to any measure of agreement on future relationships in Ireland which the people living in Ireland may themselves freely so determine without external impediment.[781]

---

778 Minutes of a Tete-a-Tete Meeting between the Prime Minister and the Taoiseach, Dublin Castle 3rd December 1993. <www.nationalarchives.gov.uk/education/resources>, assessed 6th November 2024.
779 A Dutch auction begins with a high asking price which is quickly lowered. Most commonly used for goods that are required to be sold quickly.
780 O'Dochartaigh, N., *Deniable Contact: Back Channel Negotiation in Northern Ireland* (Oxford: Oxford University Press, 2021), 259.
781 <www.cain.ulster.ac.uk/events/peace.docs> assessed 15/10/24.

A British government now endorsed the narrative of an organisation which had been committing acts of political violence for 23 years at this point. The business-like tradition of imputing norms of transaction to a terrorist organisation had produced a thin gruel for the British state. This was acknowledged in the clear-eyed judgement of a senior civil servant, Roderic Lyne in a draft letter to the Private Secretaries of members of the Cabinet: 'This is more than a hope, but less than a firm prediction'.[782] A heavy price had been paid for this dish. A British government had placed on record a willingness to accept a united Ireland as a possible result of any negotiations. It had now adopted a position of neutrality in terms of the maintenance of the integrity of a part of the United Kingdom.

The gap between PIRA's declining military capability and their political demands had been bridged. They now had choices that had previously eluded them. If the art of strategy is to shape the choices of others; be they allies or enemies, PIRA now had now achieved this courtesy of John Major's government. To paraphrase Colonel French's memo of July 1921 a British government had now created a way for everyone to think and talk about these issues from an Irish Republican point of view.

Despite all the declarations of intent their military campaign continued apace[783] M. L. R. Smith summarised this approach: 'the Provisional's were prepared to entertain an end to their violence, but their willingness to discuss the terms under which they would renounce violence was itself contingent on opening up a direct line of dialogue with the British'.[784] The ability to have established a dialogue before ending the violence was of pivotal concern to PIRA. This was exactly what Cope had facilitated for Lloyd George in July 1921.

The announcement on the 31st August 1994 by PIRA of a 'complete cessation of military operations' was an armed truce. However, there was no reference to a permanent end to violence. PIRA continued to attempt to

---

782 <www.national archives.gov.uk/education/resources> assessed 6th November 2024.
783 For example, there were three mortar bomb attacks on Heathrow airport in the space of 5 days in March 1994.
784 Op cit, p. 207.

procure weapons from overseas, and to target individuals and locations for attack.[785] British demands for clarification failed to illicit a clear response from PIRA. There is still incomplete clarity surrounding this period. For example, a letter dated 15th September 1994 has been retained by the Cabinet Office until 2094.[786] There were important discontinuities with the first campaign. Unlike Collin's organisation, whose networks were broken and whose campaign was suffering from a dearth of weapons and ammunition, PIRA's networks in the Irish Republic were largely intact. It was not short of weapons, ammunition, or explosives. It was increasingly difficult to use them to achieve their stated political objectives.

The ceasefire cannot in any sense of the word be interpreted as surrender. Importantly nor does the narrative of a military stalemate stand up. A former senior RUC officer has given a more accurate assessment: 'By this time the organisation (PIRA) was experiencing very significant rates of attrition in terms of arrests and conviction of its members, and very significant seizures by security forces of its armaments, as well as experiencing serious recruiting difficulties. It is my view that these factors were crucial in bring about a realisation on their part that it was time to 'take a different path'.[787] PIRA's military capability was in relative decline. It was facing what Smith has called 'strategic failure'.[788] Attaining its ends by the sole means of political violence was no longer a strategic option.

The Long Goodbye to Political Violence

The Banner Report characterised the period between the first ceasefire in 1994, and the formal closure of Operation Banner in 2007 as 'the long tail to the campaign'.[789] The four paragraphs devoted to this period

---

785 Interview with a former member of the RUC Special Branch, 13th March 2022.
786 See PREM 19/47884/1.
787 Interview with a former senior officer of the RUC, 3rd December 2024.
788 Op cit, p. 215.
789 Op cit, p. 216.

consisted of an extended narrative of events. There was no analysis of the choices made by the policy elite and their consequences. In addition, recognition of why and how Irish republicanism now had choices which did not entail repudiating any of its political principles was not addressed. Policy makers and civil servants failed to understand the analysis made by the academic Richard English; Irish Republican ideology has as its focus an endless struggle to transform the political and economic relationship between the whole of Ireland and the United Kingdom.[790] This is endorsed by a former member of the Irish diplomatic service: 'Irish nationalism is like a shark. It must keep moving or it dies'.[791]

Between August 1994 and November 1995, PIRA withdrew from negotiations with the British government. This was largely a consequence of policy makers, changing the parameters of engagement. In March 1995, the Secretary of State for Northern Ireland 'announced in Washington DC that Sinn Fein would not be allowed to take part in all-party talks until the PIRA had decommissioned at least some weapons'. Sinn Fein made it clear that they would not surrender any weapons before a political settlement. Secondly, Sinn Fein had a long list of demands on the Irish language, economic development, the release of prisoners, and the future of the RUC. Added to this, they were still engaged in criminal activities designed to raise money for both PIRA and Sinn Fein. For example, they killed a post-office employee in a robbery in Newry which went wrong. These activities went on until at least 2004.[792] These crimes were ignored by the British government.

On 9th February 1996, PIRA exploded a massive bomb in Canary Wharf which killed two people, injured many others, and cost 800 million pounds in compensation claims which the British state had to pay.

---

790 See English, R., *Irish Freedom: The History of Nationalism in Ireland* (London: Pan, 2007).
791 See Delaney, E., *Accidental Diplomat: My Years in the Irish Foreign Service* (Dublin, 2001), p. 305. Quoted in Bew, P., *Ireland: The Politics of Enmity 1789–2006* (Oxford: Oxford University Press, 2006), p. 580.
792 For an insight to the extent of this criminality, see Bradley, G., and Feeney, B., *Insider* (Dublin: The O'Brien Press, 2009), 303–310.

This response had not been expected. Subsequent bombs were exploded in the centre of Manchester,[793] and a bomb attack inside the Army's Headquarters in Northern Ireland. PIRA killed Lance Bombardier Stephen Restorick on 12th February 1997. The murder weapon was a Barrett 0.50 heavy calibre rifle supplied from the United States. This weapon had been used in South Armagh since 1990.[794]

The proper response of the Major government, according to Jonathan Powell, should have been to inform PIRA that there would be no more negotiations until the use of violence was permanently ended.[795] Despite these bombings and the killing of a British soldier, in less than a month later two former civil servants met with three members of PIRA on the 6th March 1996 in West Belfast.[796] This resulted in the worst imaginable outcome. Their credibility with Irish Republicans was terminally damaged by insisting that the British state would not negotiate with them while their violent campaign was on going, yet this was exactly what they were doing. The conclusion drawn by PIRA was that they could remain consummate actors if they fused the threat of political violence and political negotiations together.

The motive for these terrorist attacks was to convince the British public that the government had been responsible for the breakdown of negotiations and put pressure on the government to make concessions to the PIRA position that hitherto they had been unwilling or unable to make. However, in terms of public opinion in England 89 per cent blamed PIRA for walking away from the ceasefire. The British government now found itself subject to political violence that PIRA still had the capability to undertake: 'until the change of government in May 1997, the

---

793 After the bombing of the Arndale Centre in Manchester, Stephen Lander, Director General of MI5 recommended to John Major that 'the government should continue with its current strategy', which included 'providing reassurance to the Provisional leadership about the nature of the talks process which is on offer'.
794 According to the Banner report PIRA snipers had killed seven soldiers before effective countermeasures were found. See 2–16 para 247.
795 See Powell, J., *Great Hatred, Little Room* (London: Vintage Books, 2009) 85.
796 Op cit, p. 263.

IRA was resorting to the naked use of terrorism as a means to coerce the government back to the negotiating table'.[797] The thin gruel described by Roderic Lyne had turned out to be an inedible dish.

New Labour – New Cope?

The landslide electoral victory of New Labour and its leader, Tony Blair, in May 1997 had a dramatic effect on the choices a British government was prepared to make with respect to Northern Ireland. This new government was no longer dependent on the support of Ulster Unionist MPs in the House of Commons to survive. Furthermore, the native political intelligence of James Molyneaux, the leader of the Ulster Unionists, had been replaced in September 1995, by a surprise winner in the leadership contest, the former law lecturer from Queens University Belfast, David Trimble. Prior to becoming leader, he had been cultivated by civil servants in the Northern Ireland Office over a number of years.[798]

Before the General Election, a secret dinner had been held at the Travellers' Club in Pall Mall between the New Labour team and the Permanent Under Secretary of the NIO, John Chilcott. He brought along a selected number of civil servants to discuss policy, when New Labour took over. The message communicated to the civil servants was a New Labour government would move to bring Sinn Fein into talks if there were a ceasefire.[799] During the subsequent election campaign Mo Mowlem, who was to become the new Secretary of State for Northern Ireland, went so far as to declare that a New Labour government would require only 6 weeks between a ceasefire and the beginning of talks.

---

797 Hoffman, B., *Inside Terrorism* (London: Victor Gollancz, 1998) 148.
798 For and extensive insight to his activities, see the Thatcher Foundation files on Trimble.
799 See Powell, J., *Great Hatred, Little Room* (London: Vintage Books, 2009), 88.

This begs the question of what changes in the methods of governance took place to achieve this objective?

The most important appointment for the governance of Northern Ireland was the appointment of Jonathan Powell as Tony Blair's Chief of Staff. His appointment was an imitation of the chief of staff position in the White House which dated back to 1946. This had been an initiative of President Harry Truman: 'Powell became the person Blair saw first thing in the morning ... and became the figure who decided which people and what paperwork Blair saw, monitoring closely the flow of information through the Prime Ministers boxes ... Whitehall quickly learned that if they wanted Blair to see someone, or something, they should first contact Powell'.[800] There has been an attempt to place Powells' *modus operandi* in the historical context of the Prime Minister's Private Office, but his activities with respect to Northern Ireland were largely omitted from this account.[801] His social and educational background was closer to Sturgis than Cope.[802] Blair himself could not explain why Powell became so central to Northern Ireland: 'I was never entirely sure why or how Jonathan became so important on the issue, but he did ... Without him there would be no peace'.[803]

Like Cope he had brought into the 'business like tradition': 'it is very hard for democratic governments to admit to talking to terrorist groups while those groups are still killing innocent people. But on the basis of my experience, I think it is right to talk to your enemy however badly they are behaving. And luckily for this process, the British government's back

---

800 Hytner, S., *Consiglier: Learning from the Shadows* (London: 2014), 68.
801 Evans, A., *A History of Private Office 1964–2010*, PhD thesis, Queen Mary College, University of London, 2020. Chapter 4, pp. 192–236 examines Powell's role in Blair's government.
802 Powell was a graduate of Oxford University. He worked for the BBC and Granada TV before joining the Foreign and Commonwealth Office in 1979. In 1994, he met Blair in Washington DC where he was serving as a diplomat. He left the FCO in 1997 and he joined Blair's opposition 'kitchen cabinet' as his Chief of Staff. When Blair was elected Prime Minister in 1997, Powell was his Chief of Staff until 2007, and was at the heart of the Downing Street machine.
803 Blair, T., *A Journey* (London: Hutchinson, 2010), p. 160.

channel to the Provisional IRA had been in existence whenever required from 1973 onwards'.[804] The RUC and the Army were catapulted into the same context Major General Simpson had identified with respect to the first campaign.[805] 'used as dogs in a dog-fight, not to win, but to produce concessions to those who kill their friends'.

Powell took the negotiations on a whole new trajectory. Downing Street took complete control of all relations with the Irish Republic and PIRA. He kept interaction with the Northern Ireland Office to a bare minimum. Mo Mowlem the new Secretary of State for Northern Ireland and her advisors compounded the problem by making clear their initial lack of trust in the briefings they received from the Army.[806]

Second, Powell appeared uninterested in the tactical and operational dimensions of the ongoing campaign the RUC and the Army were responsible for. There were no formal meetings with either the GOC or the Chief Constable of the RUC. To their credit, the holders of both posts resisted pressure to downgrade surveillance capacity on the border. Although Powell received intelligence inputs, there was no guarantee he would adhere to the professional recommendations made to him. It has been suggested that Powell like Alfred Cope, shared sensitive material with PIRA.[807] Third, political communications were confined to London, Dublin, and PIRA whose key operational networks in the Irish Republic were intact. The security forces in Northern Ireland were seen as part of the problem. The Army's HQ at Lisburn was simply informed by London of what decisions had been agreed. Just how far Powell had moved from the normative parameters of counterterrorism is illuminated by a paragraph in Chapter 8 of the Banner Analysis titled: Major Findings, Overview and Conclusions. It stressed the importance of a: 'pan-government comprehensive approach, but also a single campaign authority so

---

804 Op cit, p. 66.
805 See Chapter 1, p. 8.
806 Interview with an unnamed former Army officer who had served at Army HQ in Lisburn.
807 Interview with a former member of RUC Special Branch 2nd April 2023.

that responses are coordinated effectively'.[808] Powell's actions represented the antithesis of this principle.

The granular details of Powell's actions, and interactions with Gerry Adams and Martin McGuinness remain largely hidden. There are a total of twenty-five files titled: 'Ireland: Situation in Northern Ireland' which covered the period from the 2nd of May 1997 to the 12th April 1998, which remain closed.[809] Interestingly, one file which covered the period 1st February 1999 to 7th June 2001 was opened in 2024.[810] However, one insight was provided by what could be described as a happy accident of surveillance: 'On one occasion, one of our surveillance teams was following Siobhan O'Hanlon, who was a senior Belfast member of the PIRA and worked directly for Gerry Adams. O'Hanlon led the team to the airport and, much to the team's surprise, she collected Jonathan Powell, who had been on a commercial flight and was travelling alone. She took him directly to West Belfast to meet senior members of PIRA'.[811] O'Dochartaigh quotes an interview with John Chilcot, a former Permanent Under Secretary at the Northern Ireland Office to illustrate how a New Labour government facilitated a profound change in the way PIRA interacted with an elected democratic government: 'the British government and Sinn Fein, in certain ways and on certain occasions would come to cooperate and coordinate more closely with each other than either of them did with any of the other parties to negotiation'.[812]

This relationship manifested itself in many ways. A good example was the deception of elected politicians and the public, mutually agreed by Tony Blair and Gerry Adams, over the release of convicted terrorists as part of the Good Friday Agreement: 'I did something very 'Tonyish' and he did something very 'Gerryish': I privately assured him we would do it in one year if the conditions allowed, but publicly and officially, it would

---

808 Op cit, para 856, p. 8–15.
809 These are all in the PREM 49 series of files held at the National Archives.
810 Prem 49/2076. There are also two accompanying files PREM 49/918 and PREM 49/403.
811 Interview with a former member of the RUC Special Branch, 21 March 2023.
812 Op cit, p. 265.

be two. He agreed and what's more, never called in the promise or used it publicly to embarrass me'.[813] The journalist Jenny McCartney has provided one of the best summaries of the consequences of these operating codes: 'In their efforts to bring a settlement to Northern Ireland, Blair and Powell did everything within their power to appease the terrorist leaders. They overturned the law; they ruthlessly sacrificed the political moderates of the nationalist SDLP and the Ulster Unionist party; and they presided over a system that handed the top government jobs to Ian Paisley's DUP and Sinn Fein, the two groups that had done the most to inflame the vicious conflict in the first place. The peace came at a very steep price'.[814]

Conclusions

In the latter half of Operation Banner, there was a critical continuity from the first half, and indeed from the first campaign; an inability and unwillingness of both the policy elite and their civil servants to set out a counter-narrative to Irish Republicanism. This omission was of critical importance as its utility and necessity have long been recognised in the academic literature. The strategist Beatrice Heuser has argued: 'propaganda is a tool in COIN and the insurgents' box that predates the invention of the term by centuries'.[815]

Before the end of Operation Banner in July 2007, ongoing campaigns in Iraq and Afghanistan underlined the salience of a strategic-level narrative. The Australian Army officer Colonel David Kilcullen, a former advisor to General Petraeus, developed a three-pillar model[816] for an interagency approach that ISAF was aiming to follow in Afghanistan.

---

813   Blair, T., *A Journey* (London: Hutchison, 2010), p. 172–173.
814   McCartney, J., 'Mr Powell's Talking Cure', *The Spectator* (21st August 2010).
815   Heuser, B., and Shamir E. eds., *Insurgencies and Counterinsurgencies* (Cambridge: Cambridge University Press, 2016), p. 360.
816   These pillars consisted of: security, economics and politics.

He argued that 'information', as it is now referred to, was the plinth on which all these pillars stood: 'Substantive security, political and economic measures are critical but to be effective they must rest upon and integrate with a broader information strategy. Every action in counterinsurgency sends a message; the purpose of the information campaign is to consolidate and unify this message'.[817] Given the evidence that has been examined it is impossible to see, even in a nascent form, anything resembling a sustained information campaign during Operation Banner.

The Irish border represented an enduring challenge to both the Army and the RUC. The constitutional and subsequent political stance of successive Irish Governments created a real geostrategic impediment. This was a deliberate political choice: 'the Irish government's rhetorical constitutional claim remained in force – an ideological provocation to unionists'.[818]

The actions of the RUC and the Army resulted in political violence failing to facilitate PIRA's strategic objectives. Thence their emphasis on building a pan nationalist alliance. Successive generations of the British policy elite, plus elements of the intelligence community, gave PIRA choices they did not have at a time when their electoral support was small.[819]

---

817   Kilcullen, D., Three Pillars of Counterinsurgency, 28 September 2006, Remarks delivered at the US Government Counterinsurgency Conference, Washington DC.
818   Bew, P., *Ireland, The Politics of Enmity 1789–2006* (Oxford: Oxford University Press, 2007), 533.
819   At this point their share of the vote was 12 per cent.

CHAPTER 7

Conclusions

The American journalist David Greenberg, in an article for The New York Times, published in 2011, coined an arresting rhetorical strap line: 'Why Last Chapters Disappoint'.[820] He argued almost anyone who has written a book attempting to analyse a social or political problem has fallen into the same elephant trap: 'Practically every example of that genre, no matter how shrewd or rich in its survey of the question at hand, finishes with an obligatory prescription that is utopian, banal, unhelpful and out of tune with the rest of the book'.[821] His lament was that few writers have an exit strategy. Furthermore, those who give the most nuanced diagnoses often do not have the problem-solving talent to develop concrete, practical recommendations.

The Operational Codes – And Echoes

This book has an exit strategy: to evaluate the impact of the 'operating codes' on the two counter-insurgency campaigns the British Army fought in Ireland and Northern Ireland. One of the most important questions posed in the preface was the relationship between the independent variables of counter-insurgency and the 'operating codes'. In particular, how they have affected both the successes the Army achieved and the failures they had to confront.

A characteristic common to both campaigns was the persistence of these codes. They manifested themselves at the strategic level in three

---

820 See *New York Times* (18 March 2011).
821 Ibid.

ways. First an unwillingness of the policy elite and their civil servants to craft a counter narrative to Irish Republicanism. Second, this was compounded by continual attempts to pursue separate political initiatives which usually produced inconsistent results. Finally, political–military integration was a mirage; chased but never realised. In the first campaign, these codes frustrated and antagonised both junior and senior Army commanders and undermined a carefully planned military offensive designed to defeat the IRA in the summer of 1921.

Between 1969 and 2007, these operational codes had a similar effect on the different tactical and operational context of Operation Banner. Specifically, the geostrategic and political challenge presented by the United Kingdom's land border. Little was done over the decades this campaign lasted to craft a narrative that would give legitimacy and guidance to the actions of the Army and the police. When there was controversy such as the killings in Londonderry the Army was ordered to lower its profile. This was not helpful in the deterring of further terrorist attacks and reassuring the public. Critically, the narratives of an outright defeat and a stalemate remain today the accepted historical judgements with respect to these campaigns.

The persistence of these codes, over a period of 85 years is a cultural phenomenon that has attracted little attention. The price paid in casualties by the Army, the RIC, DMP and the RUC was not insignificant. Major General Simpson's characterisation of law enforcement organisations and the army being used as 'dogs in a dogfight' remains a pertinent and apt phrase. The siren calls for normative solutions have been resisted. No attempt will be made to outline a strategy to mitigate the dysfunctional consequences these operational codes will have on future conflicts and wars the British state could find itself engaged in or supporting.

A New Anglo-Irish Relationship

A consequence of the first campaign was the emergence of a new Anglo-Irish relationship that was defined by a paradox and has persisted to the present. It was a product of the nature of the political settlement engineered by Alfred Cope and Lloyd George. On the Irish Republican side, it produced an absence of a sense of obligation with respect to reciprocity, and the sanctity of agreements once entered into would be kept; this has co-existed with an inability by successive generations of the Irish political elite to ascribe any salience to the geographically conditioned human associations that have existed between the south of Ireland and England for hundreds of years. The Irish Free State, as it became known, was and is located in the most anglicised part of Ireland. A shrewd observer of the consequences of the decision-making habits of Lloyd George was James Craig, the leader of the Ulster Unionists: 'Lloyd George would always rather make a bad bargain in five minutes than a good one in five hours'.[822]

The Anglo-Irish relationship that emerged can be characterised as close but tortuous. The first quality was often obscured by the twists and turns of the second. It had nothing to do with Northern Ireland. The academic John Wilson Foster has summarised this phenomenon: 'Northern Ireland, in reality, is the veronica[823] that distracts the Irish Bull from his real problem which is the British Irish relationship itself. This schizophrenic relationship would rankle even if the Northern Irish disappeared'.[824]

Another manifestation of this schizophrenic relationship is the number of organisations, spread across a range of disparate activities, which retained after 1922, the Royal prefix. An incomplete list includes: The Royal Dublin Society, The Royal College of Surgeons in Ireland, The Royal Irish Academy, The Royal Cork Yacht Club and The Royal Curragh Golf Club. These organisations represent a paradox that is rarely commented on or acknowledged.

It can be discerned briefly in the transitional period between the armed truce in July 1921 and January 1922, when the Dail ratified the Anglo-Irish treaty. Surprisingly, The Irish Times stated in December 1921, the

---

822 Strugis Diary, p. 202.
823 This is a manoeuvre of the red cape in bull fighting used to divert a charging bull.
824 Foster, J. W., *Ireland out of England?* In J. W. Foster, and W. B. Smith (eds.) *From the Idea of the Union* (Belcouver Press, 2021), 109.

withdrawal of the British Army would be a source of profound regret.[825] The same article went on to underline the loss of trade to business houses and farmers in the garrison towns of southern Ireland. Newbridge and Naas would be hard hit unless there was some form of compensation.[826] Farmers from different parts of Ireland had asked if it were possible for some detachments of the British Army to be left in the country.[827]

This proposal would have been viable if the conditions of peace had stipulated the Irish Free State would be recognised as a recruiting area. However, as Cope had intimated to Moylett on the 30th May 1921, the British policy elite and their civil servants were intent on embracing a narrative of defeat. Cope offered to withdraw their whole establishment, including the Army. Dominion Home Rule status brought about a profound change in the political, administrative and military arrangements in what had been an integral part of the United Kingdom for over 120 years.

Business-Like Traditions in Counter-Insurgency

Huge changes took place in British society between the beginning of the first campaign in 1919 and the end of the second in 2007. These changes impacted many aspects of British culture. The American academic Louis Menand has correctly observed: 'Cultures get transformed not deliberately or programmatically but by the unpredictable effects of social, political and technological change, and by random acts of cross-pollination'.[828] Despite this process, the close similarity in the behaviour of different generations of British policy elites and civil servants when dealing with political violence aimed at the British state is remarkable.

825 Irish Times (9th December 1921).
826 See Costello, C., *A Most Delightful Station* (Cork: The Collins Press, 1996), 325.
827 It is also important to note that by 1838, 42 per cent of soldiers in the British Army were Irish. By 1878, one-fifth of the officer corps of the British Army were Irish.
828 Menand, L., *The Free World* (New York: Picador, 2021), 13.

Conclusions

There have been numerous examples, cited in previous chapters, of the trade-offs – so favoured by the political elite and their civil servants yet inappropriate to the conduct of an unconventional war. Central to this was a feeble conceit which assumed that by negotiating, they would become 'more like us'. It was assumed they could square political violence with the conduct of a business-like transaction. This often had lethal consequences which they struggled to comprehend. On 28th June 1921, the day Cope contacted Sinn Fein to get a response to Lloyd George's offer of an armed truce and talks, Sturgis was forced to confront the price the police continued to pay: 'Another RIC man in plain clothes shot in Dublin this evening – whoever commands the IRA in Dublin ought to be fried in boiling oil by us, "approved" by Dail Eireann'.[829]

The Army achieved success with respect to two of the three independent variables in both campaigns. Strategic failure pivoted around the absence of what modern political philosophers describe as a counter-narrative.[830] This was compounded by the unaccountable power wielded by both Alfred Cope and Jonathan Powell. Their assumptions and actions went unchecked and hidden from both parliament and the public domain. Furthermore, there was no internal debate. Powell issued written instructions to the intelligence assessments staff to make the reports they produced more upbeat prior to the Good Friday Agreement.[831] Both Lloyd George and Cope, Tony Blair[832] and Powell bought into the same narrative, albeit one separated by nearly 85 years.

Cope was responsible for creating a dysfunctional relationship between Dublin Castle, the Army and the police. By the start of the

---

829 Sturgis diary entry 28th June 1921 (p. 194).
830 I am grateful to my colleague at the University of Reading, Dr Maxime Lepoutre for this insight. See Lepoutre, M., 'Narrative Counter Speech', *Political Studies* 72/2 (2024), 570–589.
831 Interview with a former member of the Royal Ulster Constabulary Special Branch, 23rd March 2023.
832 It emerged in 2006 that Tony Blair had asked the junior common room of his Oxford College, St Johns to subscribe to Republican news in the early years of the Troubles, See Bew, P., *Ireland the Politics of Enmity 1789–2007* (Oxford: Oxford University Press, 2007), 555.

armed truce on 11th July 1921 it had reached a critical stage. He had no compunction about placing the Army in an increasing invidious position which undermined the original parameters of the armed truce negotiated by General Macready on the 8th July. In September 1921, Cope wrote to Thomas Jones[833] demanding Prime Ministerial support for a further erosion of the Army's already delicate position: 'I hope that the Military people here have clear instructions from the PM to do nothing in the way of rounding up Sinn Fein Courts or drilling and if we fail to stop these amicably with Sinn Fein, to wink at them during the present critical period'.[834] This invocation of Prime Ministerial power needs to be understood in the context of a collapse of relations with the Army. Just days[835] after the armed truce came into effect Strugis gave a compelling insight to the low ebb it had sunk to: 'GHQ regard Andy as a complete Shinn and believe him no more or less than they would believe Michael Collins, so anything he asks for they regard as ipso facto something to be resisted and yielded if at all only after a struggle'.[836] Senior army commanders had intelligence concerning Cope's secret negotiations with Collins and other leading Irish Republicans. Winter's organisation had captured documents in the organised searches which indicated he had been passing confidential information to known members of Sinn Fein.

The Irish historian Paul McMahon has summarised the challenge the Army faced with respect to this 'illogical compact'[837] it found itself in: 'From the British point of view, the truce was supposed to freeze the situation as of July 1921, and the IRA was to refrain from recruiting, training, raising funds and importing arms. But IRA units comprehensively broke all these terms. Most obviously the IRA swelled in size as

---

[833] Thomas Jones was Deputy Secretary to the Cabinet.
[834] Middlemas, K., ed., *Whitehall Diary* (Vol. III) (London: Oxford University Press, 1971) 99.
[835] This is Sturgis's diary entry for 13th July 1921.
[836] Sturgis, M., *The Last Days of Dublin Castle* (Dublin: Irish Academic Press, 1999), 203.
[837] See Chapter 4, p. 33.

it drew in thousands of new recruits'.[838] In addition, Sinn Fein used its international contacts to obtain arms and ammunition. This had been a key vulnerability identified by Winter's intelligence organisation in May 1921. McMahon confirmed this intelligence assessment was accurate: 'the greatest handicap for the IRA before the truce had been the lack of essential armaments ... The British Authorities had some success in detecting and preventing this gun-running, (after the armed truce) even though significant quantities of munitions did get through to Ireland'.[839] Sturgis met with Collins during the armed truce, and discussed its shortcomings, and interpreted the meeting in a manner that was redolent of a business culture: 'I was with him (Collins) and Finton Murphy for more than two hours and we went pretty thoroughly into the weaknesses of the truce as a business proposition'.[840]

Jonathan Powell, as Blair's Chief of Staff, wielded far greater institutional power than Alfred Cope. This was underlined by his proclivity, in tandem with Gerry Adams, to create and use a narrative that disparaged the security forces. It was encapsulated in one word: 'securocrat'.[841] Its origin goes back to the Apartheid era in South Africa where it was originally used to label members of the police and security services that dominated the South African government in the 1980s. This narrative had a clear intent. The Army and the police in Northern Ireland were perceived as a problem or obstacle which put the achievement of peace at risk, and therefore they had to be circumnavigated. The assumption being that both these institutions were an impediment to a resolution of the conflict.

In one sense this was not new; similar narratives like the Black and Tans[842] were employed in the first campaign and gained a wide

---

838   McMahon, P., 'British Intelligence, and the Anglo-Irish Truce, July–December 1921', *Irish Historical Studies* 35/140 (November, 2007) 530.
839   Ibid, p. 530.
840   Strugis Diary, p. 222.
841   Powell, J., *Great Hatred, Little Room* (London: Vintage Books, 2009), 310.
842   The term had its origins in the mixed army and police uniforms issued to the new reinforcements of the RIC. It was also the name of a famous pack of hunting hounds in the south of Ireland.

currency. In fact, this narrative gained a traction that took it up to the end of the twentieth century: 'The Tans were the dogs of war disguised as policemen'.[843] In the first campaign Irish Republican propaganda produced leaflets claiming British soldiers serving in Ireland between 1919 and 1921 were the direct decedents of British soldiers who had allegedly indulged in acts of cannibalism during the 1798 Irish rebellion.[844] Negative portrayal of both the Army, the RIC and the RUC represented a common and persistent narrative in both campaigns.

Powell like Sturgis and Cope indulged in the same feeble conceit assuming by negotiating with PIRA they would become 'more like us'. Powell like his predecessors thought he could square political violence with the parameters of a business transaction. The most infamous example was the bank robbery that occurred on the 21st of December 2004 at the headquarters of the Northern Bank in Belfast. A total of £26.5 million was stolen. This robbery was conducted by PIRA after clearance at an Army Council meeting.[845] Subsequently there was a fanciful accusation by Sinn Fein that the PSNI[846] and the British had staged the robbery. The effect on Powell was devastating as he realised PIRA did not conform to his assumptions of reciprocity: 'I was dumbstruck. It was a huge betrayal of trust, and I felt like a complete idiot coming over for talks with Adams and McGuiness when the IRA had been planning a major crime like this'.[847]

The reason Powell was flying into Belfast was to discuss a possible bilateral approach, whereby the British Government and Sinn Fein would move forward together without agreement from the Unionists and the Irish government.[848] This robbery caused Powell to wonder if Adams and McGuinness ever intended to deliver an end to the IRA or was it

---

843 Geraghty, T., *The Irish War* (London: Harper Collins, 1998), 332.
844 See the personal papers of General Strickland, GOC sixth Division, Imperial War Museum.
845 Interview with a former member of the RUC Special Branch 21 March 2021.
846 Police Service of Northern Ireland.
847 See Powell, J., *Great Hatred, Little Room* (London: Vintage Books, 2009) 262.
848 Ibid, p. 264.

just a model of an unceasing negotiation[849] as indicated by RUC Special Branch intelligence at the time.[850]

The Challenge of the Irish Border

There was one critical discontinuity between the two campaigns. At the strategic, operational and tactical levels, the Irish border had a profound and enduring effect. A permeable border was one of four criteria[851] cited by the former French soldier, David Galula as necessary for insurgent success. It was a consequence of the succession of the south of Ireland from the rest of the United Kingdom in 1922. At a stroke, the Irish Free State was freed from any obligations with respect to the population of Northern Ireland. This marked the beginning of a long-term propaganda campaign against the devolved government in Northern Ireland, without the risk of having to take responsibility for, or deal with any of the practical consequences. The Irish historian A. T. Q. Steward has illuminated the scope of this campaign: 'The unionist government in the North was vilified on every occasion, and both moderate nationalists and republicans gave their fullest support to, and expressed solidarity with, the northern catholic community in its grievances. By contrast the government of Northern Ireland never interfered after 1922 in the affairs of independent Ireland'.[852] It is hard to think of another modern European state behaving in this manner over such a long period of time. For example, French government co-operated with the Spanish government to end the sanctuary that ETA enjoyed in the Basque region of France. This meant that eventually the viability of its campaign in Spain was fatally compromised.

---

849 Ibid, p. 265.
850 Interview with a former member of RUC Special branch, 13th October 2023.
851 The other three were a cause, weak governmental administration by the counter-insurgent, outside support.
852 Stewart, A. T. Q., *The Shape of History* (Belfast: Blackstaff Press, 2001), 172.

The most important strategic advantage PIRA enjoyed was its ability to use the territory of the Irish state with little or no hindrance. It was this factor that enabled their campaign to be sustained over decades. As stated in the preface of this book,[853] Gerry Adams claimed the ceasefire of 1994 was a product of a stalemate, and in particular the Army's inadequate strategy of containment. He naturally omitted to comment on the achievements of the Army and the RUC despite the advantages conferred on PIRA by the accessibility of the territory of the Irish Republic. General Sir Rupert Smith, GOC Northern Ireland at the time of the Good Friday Agreement, has stated:

> Stalemate, from the PIRA's point of view, is probably correct: they could always initiate an attack from their sanctuary (the Irish Republic), but it was either disrupted before execution, defeated in execution, or the reaction led to the arrest of the terrorists and loss of weapons etc. So, they decided the primacy of the armed wing of their strategy was lost to the political wing and called a cease fire. I, as GOC NI, thought that the IRA had been neutralised as an armed factor in what followed and led to the Agreement, but not as an organisation, they could have started again.[854]

Another dimension of the Irish border manifested itself when it came to the decommissioning of weapons between July and September 2005. This process took place exclusively in the sovereign territory of the Irish Republic, not in Northern Ireland. The quantity and the quality of the weapons and explosives revealed underlined the scale of these inaccessible networks: 'the Provisional's are thought to have decommissioned 1,000 rifles, 3 tons of Semtex, about twenty-five medium machine guns, seven surface–air missiles, seven flame throwers, twenty RPGs and about 100 grenades, figures that compared favourably with Security Forces statistics'.[855]

---

853 See Preface, p. 4.
854 Interview with General Sir Rupert Smith, 21st September 2023.
855 van der Bijl, N., *Operation Banner, The British Army in Northern Ireland 1969–2007* (Barnsley, Pen and Sword, 2009), 225.

Searching for Success and Confronting Failure: Continuities and Discontinuities

Between 1919 and 1921, there were no sanctuaries where the IRA could be confident their networks were beyond attack. On 26th May 1921, four days before Cope proposed a narrative of defeat to Moylett, an organised search, based on timely and accurate intelligence, destroyed a key network, and gained access to what can be described, in contemporary terms, as real time data: 'O[856] is in high glee having had a most successful raid this afternoon and cleared out Michael Collins' new headquarter office. Among the captured documents a letter written *this morning* saying what a bloody business it was "that we lost all those gallant fellows yesterday at the Custom House"'.[857]

These successes were not confined to Winter's Combined Intelligence Service. General Sir Alexander Godley, as Military Secretary to the War Office,[858] visited Ireland during the armed truce. He gave a compelling and clear-eyed view of the success the Army had achieved overall: 'I saw practically every Brigadier and every commanding officer in the country. They all without exception said that the rebels were beaten, and that if, instead of agreeing to an armistice, the Government had stuck it out for another fortnight, they would have been glad to surrender'.[859]

The operating codes were a product of assumptions and choices about the conduct of counter-insurgency campaigns. The choices made at the strategic level shaped the political outcomes and were presented and accepted as achieving a resolution of the conflict. They were not a product of the different social, cultural or economic backgrounds of successive generations of policy elites. The disparate backgrounds of these men

---

856 O is the code word for Brigadier Winter the head of the Combined Intelligence Service.
857 Sturgis Diary, p. 182.
858 He was appointed by Winston Churchill then Secretary of State for War.
859 General Sir Alexander Godley, *Life of an Irish Soldier* (London: John Murray, 1939), 275.

made no difference. In addition, any expectation of institutional learning over a span of 85 years was unrealistic. Learning of this kind can only take place over a shorter period.[860] In addition, what has been discernible in both campaigns were two phenomena: an unwillingness to sustain a counterinsurgency campaign to a finish; second, a proclivity for indirectness and a blurring of issues.

Did Insurgency and Terrorism Work?

This is a controversial issue that has its own literature.[861] The failure in both campaigns at the strategic level had consequences as to how the protagonists viewed the peace settlements they were part of. The former PIRA Chief of Staff Joe Cahill has provided an insight to this: 'The Good Friday Agreement is not a settlement. It's not perfect, it has faults, but it's a basis for progress. It could be a stepping stone to a thirty-two-county republic. I see it as a new line of strategy'.[862] There is no doubt the cause of independence for the 'island of Ireland' received sustained attention from the British policy elite and their civil servants because of PIRA violence. The academic Richard English has argued: 'A stronger claim can be made that in relation to Irish self-determination PIRA's violence did drive politics further in their direction than things would have otherwise

---

860 For an insight to the requirements of institutional learnings in a military context, see Sloan, G. R., 'The Royal Navy and Organizational Learning', *Naval War College Review* 72/4 (2019) 1–24.

861 This literature is extensive and has an international flavour. See Alonso, R., *The IRA and Armed Struggle* (London: Routledge, 2007). Burleigh, M., *Blood and Rage: A Cultural History of Terrorism* (London: Harper Press, 2008). Sanders, A., *Inside the IRA: Dissident Republicans and the war for Legitimacy* (Edinburgh: Edinburgh University Press, 2011). English R., *Does Terrorism Work? A History* (Oxford: Oxford University Press) 2016.

862 Anderson, B., *Joe Cahill: A life in the IRA* (Dublin: O'Brien Press, 2002), 367.

have moved'.[863] He has also argued that due to the sustained threat and the use of political violence PIRA were able, during the peace process, to extract more concessions 'than otherwise would have been probable'.[864]

During the armed truce in the first campaign the judgements about the effects and achievements of the insurgency were finely balanced. General Macready was in no doubt about the negative consequences of the operational codes, and who should shoulder responsibility:

> The whole situation has changed since the Prime Ministers surrender on the 10th July, ... because during the five months which intervened between the truce and the treaty the rebel forces had been recruited and reorganized, quantities of arms and ammunition imported, and above all, the military and police intelligence services had been reduced (on Cope's instructions) and had lost touch with their objective.[865]

The circumstances of the armed truce and Cope's key role in bringing it about left Collins with a compromised narrative of victory. This is underlined by the fact that: 'Collins was always quick to deny negotiating with Andy Cope before the truce'.[866] There was also an acute paradox for Collins at a tactical and operational level. Despite breaking all the terms of the armed truce the IRA, even in its newly expanded form, did not have the capability to sustain another insurgency campaign: 'In private, Collins warned his colleagues that the IRA would be "slaughtered" if it had to face the might of the British Army'.[867]

The theorist of war Carl von Clausewitz argued for the vital necessity of both the policy maker and the military commander to respect the contemporary realities of each other's realms of behaviour and competence,

---

863 English, R., *Does Terrorism Work? A History* (Oxford: Oxford University Press, 2016), 116.
864 Ibid, p. 133.
865 Macready, Annals of An Active Life (Vol. II), London, p. 562.
866 Michael Collins to Kelly, S. T., 2nd May 1922, Irish National Archives DE2/514, quoted in Hopkinson, M., 'Negotiation: The Anglo-Irish War and Revolution', in J. Augusteijn, ed., *The Irish Revolution 1913–1923*, (Basingstoke: Palgrave, 2002), 125.
867 Quoted in Hart, P., *Mick: The Real Michael Collins* (London, 2005), 316–322.

notwithstanding the ultimate authority of the political. In both campaigns, the integration of the strategic with the operational and tactical levels was either largely absent or subject to serial abuse. Writing in 1811, Clausewitz forged a metaphor which gave an understanding about these relationships, of which irregular war is a subset: 'battle equals money and goods; strategy is the commercial transaction. The latter only gains its importance through the former'.[868] Evidence from both campaigns suggests a cultural allure for commercial transactions isolated from the money and goods -the battle. This disconnect goes some way to explaining the political settlements that were reached. The attainment of tactical and operational success and confronting strategic failure by the British Army in both campaigns reveals a paradox that has remained largely hidden. The failure to identify and acknowledge the impact of these operational codes, with one or two exceptions, in the vast literature both campaigns have produced a deficit this book has attempted to address.

---

868 Heuser, B., *Strategy Before Clausewitz* (Abingdon: Routledge, 2018), 193.

Bibliography

Primary Sources

A Record of the Rebellion in Ireland 1920–1921. *The British Army* (1922).

A Report on the Intelligence of the Chief of Police from May 1920 to July 1921, *National Archives*, CO904/156B.

Adams, R. J. C., Shadow of a taxman; how, and by whom, was the Republican government financed in the Irish War of Independence, PhD thesis (University of Oxford, 2018).

An Officer's Wife in Ireland (London: Parkgate Publications, 1984).

Bureau of Military History (Dublin: Cathal Brugha Barracks).

Documents on Irish Foreign Policy.

Capturing the Lessons of Northern Ireland, Seminar held at the University of Reading, 30th January 2013.

Documents on Irish Foreign Policy (Royal Irish Academy).

Evans, A., *A History of Private Office 1964–2010*, PhD thesis, Queen Mary College (University of London, 2020). Foulkes papers 7/24. *Basil Liddell Hart Archives* (London: King's College).

Government of Ireland Act 1920, c.1.4.

Gray, C. S., *Tactical Operations for Strategic Effect:* The Challenge of Currency Conversion, JSOU Report (November 2015).

Interview with a former senior military intelligence officer.

Interview with former RUC Special Branch Officers.

Interview with General Sir Rupert Smith.

Imperial War Museum Archives.

Irish Foreign Policy (Dublin: Royal Irish Academy).

Irish Times.

O'Connor, J. J., Witness Statement 1214, Bureau of Military History (Dublin: Cathal Brugha Barracks).

Jarman, N., *Managing Violence and Building Peace from Below* (Belfast: Northern Ireland Community Relations Council, 2013).

Jones, T., in K. Middlemas, ed., *Whitehall Diary* (Vol. 3), Ireland 1918–1925 (Oxford: Oxford University Press, 1971).

Kilcullen, D., *Three Pillars of Counterinsurgency*, Remarks delivered at the US Government Counterinsurgency Conference, Washington DC (28 September 2006).

Lloyd George Papers, House of Lords Library.
National Archives, UK. National Archives of Ireland.
National Archives, Washington, DC.
New York Times.
Operation Banner: An Analysis of Military Operations in Northern Ireland, Army Code 71842. (The British Army, 2006).
Papers of Field Marshall Sir Henry Wilson (Imperial War Museum).
Parliamentary Debates, House of Commons.
Pocket Diary, Lieutenant General Strickland, *Strickland Papers Imperial War Museum*.
PREM FILES on Northern Ireland.
Record of the Rebellion (Vol. 1), A3. Papers of General, Sir Hugh Jeudwine (Imperial War Museum).
Rust, Tactics, Politics, and Propaganda in the Irish War of Independence, 1917–1921, (MA Georgia State University, 2011).
The Amman Valley Chronicle and East Carmarthen News.
The Future of Northern Ireland: a paper for discussion (London: HMSO, 1972).
The Guardian, 18th October 2013.
The Spectator.
The British Presence, speech by Rt Hon Peter Brooke MP, Secretary of State for Northern Ireland, 1990.
The Papers of Captain Robert Jeune Imperial War Museum.
The Saville Inquiry (2010).
The Times.
The Papers of Field Marshal Sir Henry Wilson (Imperial War Museum).
Wilson, A., *PR Urban Elections in Ulster 1920* (London: Electoral Reform Society, 1972).
<www.sinnfein.ie/contents15210>, assessed 21/4/23.
<www.bloodysunday.co.uk>, accessed 23 April 2022.

Secondary Sources: Books

Adams, G., *Selected Writings* (Dingle: Brandon Press, 1997).
Aiken, N., *Reconciliation, and Transitional Justice* (New York: Routledge, 2014).
Alexander, Y., and Day, A., eds., *The Irish Terrorism Experience* (Aldershot: Dartmouth, 1991).
Alonso, R., The *IRA and Armed Struggle* (London: Routledge, 2007).

Bibliography

Anderson, B., *Joe Cahill: A Life in the IRA* (Dublin: O'Brien Press, 2002).
Andrew, C., *The Defence of the Realm: The Authorized History of MI5* (London: Penguin, 2010).
Aughey, A., *Under Siege* (London: Hurst & Co, 1989).
Baldy, T., *The Battle for Ulster* (Washington DC: National Defense University Press, 1987).
Bennett, H., *Uncivil War, the British Army and the Troubles 1966–1975* (Cambridge: Cambridge University Press, 2024).
Bew, P., *Ireland, the Politics of Enmity 1789–2006* (Oxford: Oxford University Press, 2007).
Bew, P., and Patterson, H., *The British State and the Ulster Crisis* (London: Verso Books, 1985).
Blair, T., *A Journey* (London: Hutchinson, 2010).
Bradley, G., and Feeney, B., *Insider: Gerry Bradley's Life in the IRA* (Dublin Press, 2009).
Briollay, S., *L'Irlande Insurgee* (Paris: Plon-Nourrit, 1921).
Burleigh, M., *Blood and Rage: A Cultural History of Terrorism* (London: Harper Press, 2008).
Coogan, T. P., *Michael Collins* (New York: Palgrave, 1990).
Costello, C., *A Most Delightful Station* (Cork: The Collins Press, 1996).
Cox, M., Guelke, A., and Stephen, F., eds., *A Farewell to Arms? From 'Long War' to Long Peace in Northern Ireland* (Manchester: Manchester University Press, 2000).
Cunliffe, P., *The New Twenty Years' Crises* (Montreal: McGill-Queens University Press, 2020).
Dictionary of National Biography 1951–1960 (Oxford: Oxford University Press, 1971).
Dulles, A., *The Craft of Intelligence* (London: Weidenfeld and Nicolson, 1963).
Edwards, A., *Agents of Influence: Britain's Secret Intelligence War Against the IRA* (Dublin: Merrion Press, 2021).
Egnell, R., and Ucko, D., True to Form? Questioning the British Counter-insurgency Tradition, in Heuser, B., and Shanir, E., eds., *Insurgencies and Counterinsurgencies* (Cambridge: Cambridge University Press, 2016) 32.
English, R., *Irish Freedom: The History of Nationalism in Ireland* (London: Pan, 2007).
English, R., *Does Terrorism Work? A History* (Oxford: Oxford University Press, 2016).
Foster, J. W., and Smith, W. B., eds., *From the Idea of the Union* (Belcouver Press, 2021).
Foy, M., *Michael Collin's Intelligence War* (Stroud: Sutton Publishing, 2006).

French, D., *The British Way in Warfare, 1688–2000* (London: Unwin Hyman, 2000).
Gallagher, F., *The Anglo-Irish Treaty* London: Hutchinson, 1965).
Gallagher, T., and O'Connell, J., eds., *Contemporary Irish Studies* (Manchester: Manchester University Press, 1983).
Galula, D., *Counterinsurgency Warfare: Theory and Practice* (Westport: Praeger Security International, 2006).
Geraghty, T., *The Irish War* (London: Harper Collins, 1998).
Gleeson, J., *Bloody Sunday* (London: Peter Davies, 1962).
Godley, A., *Life of an Irish Soldier* (London: John Murray, 1939).
Gray, C. S., *Another Bloody Century: Future Warfare* (London: Routledge, 2005).
Gray, C. S., *War, Peace and International Relations* (Abingdon: Routledge, 2012)
Gray, C. S., *Modern Strategy* (Oxford: University of Oxford Press, 1999).
Hamill, D., *Pig in the Middle: The Army in Northern Ireland 1969–1984* (London: Methuen, 1985).
Hart, P., *Mick: The Real Michael Collins* (London: Macmillan, 2005).
Hart, P., *British Intelligence in Ireland, 1920–1921. The Final Reports* (Cork: University of Cork Press, 2002).
Headlam, M., *Irish Reminiscences* (London: Robert Hales, 1947).
Heney, M., *The Arms Crisis of 1970*, London: Head of Zeus, 2020.
Heslinga, M. W., *The Irish Border as a Cultural Divide* (Assen: Van Gorcum, 1962).
Heuser, B., *Strategy Before Clausewitz* (Abingdon: Routledge, 2018).
Hoffman, B., *Inside Terrorism* (London: Victor Gollancz, 1998).
Holt, E., *Protest in Arms: The Irish Troubles 1916–1923* (London: Putnam, 1960).
Hopkinson, M., ed., The *Last Days of Dublin Castle* (Dublin: Irish Academic Press, 1999).
Hytner, R., Consiglieri: Learning from the Shadows (London, 2014).
Jones, T., in K. Middlemas, ed., *Whitehall Diary* (Vol. 3) (London: Oxford University Press, 1971).
Kennedy, L., *Who Was Responsible for the Troubles?* (Montreal: McGill-Queen's University Press, 2020).
Kennelly, I., *The Paper Wall: Newspapers and Propaganda in Ireland 1919–1921* (Cork: The Collins Press, 2008).
Kent, S., *Strategic Intelligence for American World Policy* (1965).
Kilcullen, D., in T. Rid, and T. Keaney, eds., *Intelligence, from Understanding Counterinsurgency* (Abingdon: Routledge, 2010).
Kissinger, H., *Leadership* (Allen Lane: London, 2022).
Kitson, F., *Bunch of Five* (London: Faber and Faber, 1977).
Kitson, F., *Low Intensity Operations* (1971).

Lawrence, R. J., *The Government of Northern Ireland* (Oxford: Clarendon Press, 1965).
Leites, N., *A Study of Bolshevism* (Glencoe, Illnois: The Free Press, 1953).
Liddell-Hart, B., *The British Way in Warfare* (London: Penguin Books, 1932).
Macready, N., *Annals of an Active Life* (Vol. 2) (London: Hutchinson & Co., 1926).
Madgwick, P., and Rose, eds., *The Territorial Dimension in United Kingdom Politics* (London: Macmillan Press, 1982).
Menand, L., *The Free World* (Picador: New York, 2021).
Middlemas, K. ed., *Whitehall Diary* (Vol. III).
Moloney, E., *A Secret History of the IRA* (London: Penguin Books, 2002).
McCann, E., *New Left Review*, 55 (1969).
McCleery, M., *Operation Demetrius and Its Aftermath: A New History of the Use of Internment without Trial in Northern Ireland 1971–1975* (Manchester: Manchester University Press, 2015).
Mc Colgan, J., *British Policy and Irish Administration* (London: George Allen and Unwin, 1983).
Meyer, C., *DC Confidential* (London: Weidenfeld and Nicolson, 2005).
Mockaitis, T. R., *British Counterinsurgency, 1919–1960* (London: Macmillan, 1990).
Mockaitis, T. R., *British Counterinsurgency in the Post Imperial Era* (Manchester: Manchester University Press, 1995).
Morrison, J., *The Ulster Cover-Up* (Belfast: Ulster Society, 1993).
Mumford, A., *The Counterinsurgency Myth: The British Experience of Irregular Warfare* (London: Routledge, 2011).
Neibhur, R., *Nations and Empires* (London: Faber and Faber, 1959).
Neumann, P., *Britain's Long War: British Strategy in the Northern Ireland Conflict 1969–1998* (Basingstoke: Palgrave Macmillan, 2003).
O'Dochartaigh, N., *From Civil Rights to Armalites: Derry and the Birth of the Irish Troubles* (Basingstoke: Palgrave MacMillan, 2005).
O'Dochartaigh, N., *Deniable Contact: Back Channel Negotiation in Northern Ireland* (Oxford: Oxford University Press, 2021).
O'Faolean, G., *A Broad Church, The Provisional IRA in the Republic of Ireland 1969–1980* (Newbridge: Merrion Press, 2019).
O'Halpin, E., *Head of the Civil Service: A Study of Sir Warren Fisher* (London: Routledge, 1989).
O'Neill, E., *Insurgency and Terrorism* (Washington: Brassey's, 1990).
Paget, J., *Counter Insurgency Campaigning* (London: Faber and Faber, 1967).
Patterson, H., *Ireland's Violent Frontier: The Border and Anglo-Irish. Relations During the Troubles* (Basingstoke: Palgrave Macmillan, 2013).
Peck, J., *Dublin from Downing Street* (Dublin: Gill and Macmillan, 1978).

Porch, D., *Counterinsurgency: Exposing the Myths of the New Way of War* (Cambridge: Cambridge University Press, 2013).
Powell, J., *Great Hatred, Little Room: Making Peace in Northern Ireland* (London: Vintage Books, 2009).
Ring, J., *Erskine Childers* (London: John Murray, 1996).
Rose, R. *Is the United Kingdom a State? Northern Ireland as a Test Case.*
Sanders, A., *Inside the IRA: Dissident Republicans and the War for Legitimacy* (Edinburgh: Edinburgh University Press, 2011).
Seliktar, O., *Politics, Paradigms, and Intelligence Failures: Why So Few Predicted the Collapse of the Soviet Union* (Routledge, 2015).
Sheehan, W., *A Hard-Local War: The British War and the Guerrilla War in Cork. 1919–1921* (Stroud: The History Press, 2011).
Simpson, H. J., *British Rule and Rebellion* (London: W. Blackwood, 1938).
Sloan, G. R., *The Geopolitics of Anglo-Irish Relations in the 20th Century* (London: Leicester University Press, 1997).
Smith, M. L. R., *Fighting for Ireland* (London: Routledge, 1995).
Smith, M., *The Spying Game: The Secret History of British Espionage* (London: Politico, 2016).
Stewart, A. T. Q., *Michael Collins: The Secret File* (Black Staff Press, 1997).
Stewart, A. T. Q., *The Shape of History* (Belfast: Blackstaff Press, 2001).
Storr, J. 'Irish Republican Insurgency and Terrorism', in B. Heuser, and E. Shamir, eds. *Insurgencies and Counterinsurgencies* (Cambridge: Cambridge University, 2016), p. 215.
Strachan, H. ed., *Big Wars and Small Wars in the 20th Century* (Abingdon: Routledge, 2006).
Strachan, H., *The Direction of War* (Cambridge: Cambridge University Press, 2013).
Strachan, H., *The Politics of the British Army* (Oxford: Clarendon Press, 1997).
Sturgis, M., *The Last Days of Dublin Castle* (Dublin: Irish Academic Press, 1999).
Sun Tzu, The Art of War (Oxford: Oxford University Press), 1963.
Taylor, P., *Operation Chiffon* (London: Bloomsbury, 2023).
Taylor, R., *Michael Collins* (London: Hutchinson, 1958).
Thatcher, M., The *Downing Street Years* (London: Harper Collins, 1993).
Townsend, C., *The British Campaign in Ireland 1920–1921* (Oxford: Oxford University Press, 1975).
Trask, D. F., *The AEF & Coalition Warmaking, 1917–1918, Lawrence* (Kansas: University Press of Kansas, 1993).
Van der Bijl, N., *Operation Banner: The British Army in Northern Ireland 1969–2007* (Barnsley: Pen and Sword Books, 2017).

Watkins, M., *State: The Concept, International Encyclopedia of the Social Sciences* (Vol. 15) (New York: Macmillan, 1967).
Winter, O., *Winter's Tale* (London: The Richards Press, 1955).
Wright, F., *Northern Ireland a Comparative Analysis* (Rowman & Littlefield, 1988).
Younger, C., *Ireland's Civil War* (London: Fontana Books, 1970).

Secondary Sources: Articles

Burton, B., and Nagl, J., 'Learning as We Go: The US Army Adapts to Counterinsurgency in Iraq, July 2004–December 2006', *Small Wars and Insurgencies*, 19/3.
Callan, P., 'Recruiting for the British Army in Ireland During the First World War', *Irish Sword* 17 (1990).
Cohen, E., Crane, C., Horvath, J., and Nagl, J., 'Principles, Imperatives, and Paradoxes of Counterinsurgency', *Military Affairs* March–April (2006).
Connolly, E., and Doyle, J., 'Ripe Moments for Exiting Political Violence: An Analysis of the Northern Ireland Case', *Irish Studies in International Affairs*.
Craig, T., 'From Backdoors to Back Lanes to Backchannels: Reappraising British Talks with the Provisional IRA, 1970–1974', *Contemporary British History* 26/1 (2012).
Denning, B. C., 'Modern Problems of Guerrilla Warfare', *Army Quarterly* 13 (1927).
Dochartaigh, N. O., 'Bloody Sunday: Error or Design', *Contemporary British History* 24/1 (2020).
Dolan, A., 'Killing and Bloody Sunday', *The Historical Journal* 49/3 (September 2006).
Edwards, A., 'Deterrence, Coercion and Brute Force in Asymmetric Conflict: The Role of the Military Instrument in Resolving the Northern Ireland "Troubles"', *Dynamics of Asymmetric Conflict* 4/3 (November 2011).
Edwards, A., 'A Whipping Boy If Ever There Was One? The British Army and the Politics of Civil–Military Relations in Northern Ireland', *Contemporary British History*, 28/2 (2014).
Freedman, L., 'Terrorism as a Strategy, Government and Opposition', 42/3 summer (2007).
Galtung, J., 'An Editorial', *Journal of Peace Research* 1/1 (1967).
Galula, D., 'Counterinsurgency Warfare' (Westport: Praeger Security International, 2006).

George, A. L., 'The Operational Code: A Neglected Approach to the Study of Political Leaders and Decision-Making', *International Studies Quarterly*, 13/2 (1969).
Hall, A., 'In complete Peace and Social Stagnation: Shortcomings of Good Friday Agreement', *Open Library of Humanities* 4/2 (7 August 2018).
Handel, M. J., *Intelligence and the Problem of Strategic Surprise* 7/3 (1984).
Hart, P., ed., *British Intelligence in Ireland, 1920-1921: The Final Reports* (Cork: Cork University Press, 2002).
Hewitt, C., 'Grievances, Catholic Nationalism and Violence in Northern Ireland During the Civil Rights Period: A Reconsideration', *British Journal of Sociology* 33/3 (1981).
Howard, M., and Paret, P., 'Carl von Clausewitz, On War, Princeton' (New Jersey: Princeton University Press, 1976).
Larsen, N. D., 'British Signals Intelligence and the 1916 Easter Rising in Ireland', *Intelligence and National Security*, 33 (2017).
Lepoutre, M., 'Narrative Counter Speech', *Political Studies* 72/2 (2024).
Matthes, J., 'Framing Politics: An Integrative Approach', *American Behavioural Scientist* 56/3 (2012).
McMahon, P., 'British Intelligence and the Anglo-Irish Truce, July-December 1921', *Irish Historical Studies* 35/140 (November 2007).
Morrison, J., *The Ulster Cover-up* (Belfast: Ulster Society Publications, 1993).
Mumford, A., 'Covert Peacemaking: Clandestine Negotiations and Backchannels with the Provisional IRA During the Early Troubles, 1972-1976', *The Journal of Imperial and Commonwealth History* 39/4 (2011).
Myers, K., 'An Irishman's Diary', *Irish Times* (16 September 2003).
Neumann, P., 'The Bullet and the Ballot Box: The Case of the IRA', *Journal of Strategic Studies* (28/6) (2005).
Patterson, H., 'The British State and the Rise of the IRA, 1969-1971: The View from the Conway Hotel', *Irish Political Studies* 23/4 (2008).
Pearse, P., 'Political Writings and Speeches', Quoted in Alexander Y., and Day, A., eds., *The Irish Terrorism Experience* (Aldershot: Dartmouth, 1991), p. 17.
Putkowski, J., 'The Best Secret Service Man We Had – Jack Byrnes, A2 and the IRA'. *Lobster* 28 (28th February 1995).
Richardson, D., 'The Royal Air Force and the Irish War of Independence 1918-1922'. *Air Power Review* 19/3 Autumn/Winter (2016).
Sloan, G. R., 'Hide Seek and Negotiate: Alfred Cope and Counterintelligence in Ireland 1919-1921'. *Intelligence and National Security* 33/2 (2017).
Sloan, G. R., 'The British State and the Irish Rebellion of 1916; An Intelligence Failure or a Failure of Response?' *Intelligence and National Security* 28/4 (August 2013).

Sloan, G. R., 'The Royal Navy and Organizational Learning', *Naval War College Review* 72/4 (2019).
Smith, M. R. L., 'The Intellectual Internment of a Conflict: The Forgotten War in Northern Ireland', *International Affairs* 75/1 (1999).
Sonderland, W., 'An Analysis of Guerilla Insurgency and Coup d'Etat as Techniques of Indirect Aggression', *International Studies Quarterly* (December 1970).
Thornton, R., 'Getting it Wrong: The Crucial Mistakes Made in the Early Stages of the British Army's Deployment to Northern Ireland (August 1969 to March 1972)', *Journal of Strategic Studies*, 30/1 (February 2007).
Tonge, J., Shirlow, P., and McAuley, J., 'So Why Did the Guns Fall Silent? How Interplay, not Stalemate Explains the Northern Ireland Peace Process', *Irish Political Studies* 26/1 (2011).
Wendt, A., 'Anarchy Is What States Make of It: The Social Construction of Power Politics', *International Organization* 46/2 (1992).
Whyte, J., 'How Much Discrimination Was There Under the Unionist Regime? 1921–1968, in T. Gallagher, and J. O'Connell, eds., *Contemporary Irish Studies* (Manchester: Manchester University Press, 1983).

Index

1st Battalion 'Parachute Regiment' 159, 160
1st Battalion The Prince of Wales Own Regiment of Yorkshire 146–7
3rd Battalion The Light Infantry 150
4th Royal Irish Dragoon Guards 30
5th Division 34, 42, 50, 106
5th Royal Irish Lancers 30
6th Division 34
6th Inniskilling Dragoons 30
8th Infantry Brigade 159
8th King's Royal Irish Hussars 30
9/11 (US) 191
10th (Irish) Division 29
16th (Irish) Division 29–30
36th (Ulster) Division 29–30
1916 Revolutionary wing 41

Active Service Units 166, 172–3, 182, 190
Adams, Gerry xiii, 163, 164, 181, 195–6, 202, 203, 212, 221, 222, 224
Aden 175
aerial photography 116
Afghanistan 213
agriculture 42
air-ground integration 116
'All Ireland' 200, 201
all-party talks 207
ambush prevention 116
amnesties 38, 41, 56
An Phoblacht 184
An T Oglac 63, 64, 116
Anderson, Sir John 69, 72, 73, 74, 76, 78, 80, 86, 87, 92, 117, 120, 123, 124, 129, 130, 193
'Andy Cabinet' 120, 130
Angleton, James Jesus 91n332
Anglo-Irish Agreement 1985 194–7, 200, 201, 202
Anglo-Irish Treaty 1921 7, 141n537, 217
anti-personnel devices 154
appeals 83

appeasement 35, 61–70, 213
Apprentice Boys march 149
Archdale, Edward 17
archives 139, 141
area searches 152
Argentina 54
armed truces 198, 203, 205, 219, 220, 221, 225, 227
Armistice 43
armoured car squadrons 116
arms and ammunition networks
    British Army 51, 52
    Collins, Michael 52
    Germany 27, 32
    IRA 100, 109, 131, 221
    IRB (Irish Republican Brotherhood) 52
    Irish Volunteers 51, 52
    January-May 1920 65
    Moylett 92n336
    PIRA 173, 189–91, 206
    Royal Navy deterrence 112
    Sinn Fein 51, 221
    smuggling 51
    United States 51, 208
arms dumps 116, 173, 190
arms raids 52–3
arms trials 171
Armstrong, Robert 194, 195
army training 116
Arndale Center, Manchester bombing 208
arrests
    Bloody Sunday 159, 188
    conditions of ceasefire 163
    de Valera 118–19
    immunity for leaders of insurgency 75
    IRA 98–9, 133
    January-May 1920 62–3, 66
    PIRA 166
    as response to marches 158
    and Winter's intelligence organisation 88

arson 96–7
Ashour, Nasser 190
Asquith, Herbert 28
Assistant Under Secretaries 5, 60, 67, 74, 78, 135
Athlone 81–2
Attlee, Clement 7
Attorney General of Ireland 56
attrition strategy 189, 190
Aughey, Arthur 144–5, 196
Auxiliary Forces 111

back-channel negotiation 193–4
Baggot Lane 109
Bailey, Daniel Julian 27
Baldy, T. 145
Balkan Street search 188
Ballykinlar Camp Co. Down 98, 128
Ballymurphy estate, Belfast 152
bank robberies 222
Banner Analysis 139–76, 177–214
  1971 as key year 154
  Anglo-Irish Agreement 1985 194
  attribution of intent 151
  Bloody Sunday 158–60, 161
  bridging process 197
  counter-terrorism 165
  decision points 192
  declassification of x
  evolution of Operation Banner 180–3
  Foreword 141
  incomplete picture 151
  information operations 3–4, 183–4
  intelligence 18–19
  on the IRA and PIRA 153, 167, 177
  land border 170–4
  Londonderry 147, 159
  long tail to the campaign 206–7
  on nature of conflict 188
  New Labour 211
  NICRA (Northern Ireland Civil Rights Association) 149, 158–9
  operating codes 5, 194
  Operation Motorman 165
  organisational learning 142, 187
  origins of the 'Troubles' 143–4, 145, 148, 150–1
  PIRA 167, 177
  political arrests 166
  public housing discrimination 147
  publication of 141
  reference to 1920–1921 campaign (lack of) 143–4
  review of military decision-making 188
  RUC 149
  social conditions in Northern Ireland 146–7
  tactical doctrine 158
  Tasking and Coordination Groups (omitted) 169
  terrorists killed 181–2
  United States 191
  wider context 153
Bantry Bay 26
barracks, attacks on 45
barricades 157, 159, 160, 161, 165
Barrier 12 159
Barrier 14 159
Barton, R.C. 124, 125
Belfast
  Ballymurphy estate, Belfast 152
  'Bloody Friday' bombs 164
  British Army response 152–3
  confrontations with Catholic community 152
  Conway Hotel, Belfast 155
  deprivation levels 147
  elections 1921 109
  expulsion of protestants from New Barnsley estate, Belfast 152
  Local Intelligence Centres 81, 82
  Lower Falls, Belfast 152
  Northern Bank, Belfast 152
  PIRA 165
  Shankill Road, Belfast 203
  violence in 152–3
Belfast Agreement *see* Good Friday Agreement
Belgium 189
Bell, Ivor 164
Bench Warrant at Assizes 42
Bennett, Hew 158
Bere Island 128
Bew, Paul 15, 149, 151

Index

bilateralism 222
Bills of Indictment 42
Bishop of Killaloe 54
Black and Tans 221–2
Blackhall Place 109
Blair, Tony 159, 186, 209, 210, 212, 213, 219, 221
'Bloody Friday' bombs 164
Bloody Sunday 188
Bloody Sunday (1920) 89, 91–138
Bloody Sunday (1972) 157–65
body guards 181
Bogside, Londonderry 147, 158, 159, 168
Boland, Harry 43, 51
Bolsheviks 51, 55
bombs 154, 158, 160, 164, 165, 166, 178, 189, 195, 201, 203, 205n783, 207
border x, 17, 142, 170–5, 182–3, 192, 211, 216, 223–4
border crossing points 142
boundaries of Northern Ireland 7
Bourn Committee 167–8
boycotts 44, 61
Boyd, Lieutenant General 76, 100, 102, 103, 121, 124
Bradley, Gerry 181, 182
bribery 108
bridging process 197, 203
Brighton bomb 195
Brind, Brigadier General 103, 117–18, 131
Briollay, Sylvain 12
British Army *see also* Irish Volunteers
   arms and ammunition networks 51, 52
   attacks on 76
   Bloody Sunday attacks 91, 97, 103–4, 161
   and the border 171
   Combined Intelligence Service 89
   confrontations with Catholic community 152
   and Cope 220
   counter-insurgency 64, 83, 91, 106–7
   counter-narratives 219
   deserters 75
   divisional action committee to liaise with 143
   economic effects of withdrawal 217–18
   first soldier's death in 'Troubles' 154
   history of 5th Division 42
   illogical compact 220
   intelligence 18, 19, 26–8, 33, 35–7, 64, 76–7, 79–89, 152
   and intensifying insurgency during 'Troubles' 154–5
   in Ireland 1916–1919 26–37, 56
   in Ireland January-July 1921 104–5
   Londonderry protests 159
   low-key approach 164
   military support for Irish police 150, 168–9
   narrative of defeat 118, 126, 216, 225
   and New Labour 211
   Operation Motorman 165–6
   organisational learning xiii, 153, 187
   and police primacy 176
   policy changes 103–4
   powers 62, 66
   regular battalions 180
   response in Belfast 152–3
   Restoration of Order in Ireland Act 1920 75
   Roulement Tours 180
   and the RUC 167–8
   Special Branch 74, 76–7, 89, 91, 104
   television coverage of Operation Banner 142
   truce period 127
British Cabinet
   Alfred Cope as information conduit for 6
   attitude to Bloody Sunday 101
   Bloody Sunday 161
   Cabinet committee for Ireland 92
   and de Valera 127–8
   information leakages 114–15
   law and order in Northern Ireland 162–3
   legal context for military campaigns 122
   meeting after de Valera's release 120
   response to 'Bloody Friday' 165
   and Sinn Fein 109
   troop deployments 113–16
British citizenship 196
British Government
   assistance to Stormont 149
   and Bloody Sunday 101, 159, 161, 163

convening of Irish Convention 41
declaration of Dail Eireann as illegal 46
inability to have secret negotiations 203
and the IRA 175
narrative of defeat 137, 140, 218, 225
New Labour 209
and PIRA 180, 197–8, 199–200, 204, 205, 206, 207, 208, 210, 212, 222
prisoner releases 38, 41
reluctance to engage with Irish Republicanism 3
security under the rule of law 118
security vetting failures 95
and Sinn Fein 202, 212, 213
strategic narratives (absence of) 183, 185, 193
and the 'Troubles' 151–2
truce agreement 51
and the 'unknown will of the enemy' 113
British intelligence community 49–50
Brooke, Peter 9, 197, 199
Broy, Eamonn 33, 44, 45, 66, 86
bugging 180
Bunting, Ronald 151
Bureau of Military History 74, 137
Burroughs, Ronnie 155n591
Burton, Major Stratford 95
business-like traditions 2–3, 179, 205, 218–23, 228 *see also* transactional reciprocity
Byrne, Vincent 38
Byrnes, Jack 49–50, 51, 57

Cahill, James 100
Cahill, Joe 157, 190, 226
'Cairo Gang' 92–3
Callaghan, James 151
Cameron, David 159
Cameron Commission (1969) 150–1
Canary Wharf bomb 207–8
capital convictions 128
captured documents 83–4, 86, 87–8, 93, 121, 220, 225
car bombs 165, 178
Carr, E. H. 13
cars 133
Carson, Sir Edward 17, 144–5
Casamara 190

Casement, Sir Roger 27
casualty rates 109, 132, 142, 150, 159, 164, 166
Catholics
  confrontation with British Army 152
  conscription 32
  deprivation levels 147
  housing 147
  intelligence work 98
  and the IRA 165
  removal of safeguards 144
  and the RUC 150
  Sinn Fein 202
  voting franchise 7–8
  Westminster as guarantor of rights of 145
cavalry regiments 30
ceasefire (1994) xiv, 192, 206, 208
ceasefire negotiations 163–4, 166, 198, 200, 201, 202, 205, 209, 224
censuses 147
Central Hotel, Dublin 92
Central Office of Intelligence 80–1
Central Raid Bureau 80–1, 82, 83
Chamberlain, Austen 114, 120
Channon, Paul 164
charities 40
Chesney, Father James 165
Chester 102
Chief of Police 99, 123, 124
Chief Secretary of Ireland 5, 38, 68, 74, 111
CHIFFON 198, 203
Chilcot, John 197–8, 199, 209, 212
Childers, Erskine 47, 86, 87, 88, 121
Childers, Molly 120–2
ciphers 79, 135
civic contract 113
Civil Rights Association 7, 8
civil rights movement 149 *see also* NICRA (Northern Ireland Civil Rights Association)
civil service *see also* Cope, Alfred
  Anglo-Irish Agreement 1985 194–5
  assumptions 178
  counter narratives 216
  intelligence 70–3, 74, 78–9
  January-May 1920 67–9

Index

legal context for military campaigns 122
long tail to the campaign 207
named personnel in Record of Rebellion 5–6
narrative of defeat 218
in negotiations 92, 103, 105, 108, 118
New Labour 209
Office of the UK Representative (UKREP) 155
and PIRA 208
security policy changes 142
strategic narratives 185, 200
withholding of information 115
civilian population
   civilian casualties xviii, 56, 57, 152, 159, 160, 164
   counter-insurgency effects on 63, 106, 113
   divisional action committee to liaise with 143
   intimidation 61
   military aid 152
civilian-military integrated approaches 142, 157
Clan na Gael 40
Clarke, Basil 129, 153n582, 184, 193
Clarke, Tom 40
Clarke, Trooper 178
class solidarity 18
Claudy 165
clerical services personnel 80, 95
CLF (Commander of Land Forces) 157n602, 172
Clonmel 81–2
Coalition Government 68, 75, 102, 105, 110, 132
Cobain, Ian 139
code breaking 28
coercion 7, 74, 130, 157
Cold War 171
Collins, Michael
   and Alfred Cope 6, 21, 70, 85, 108, 220, 227
   Anglo-Irish Treaty 1921 141n537
   armed truces 221
   arms and ammunition networks 52
   Bill of Indictment 42–3
   Bloody Sunday 89, 91, 93, 96
   cross-channel 'spectacular' 96–7
   death of 141n537
   and the DMP 48, 86
   dropping of case against 56
   and Eamon Broy 33n131, 86
   election campaigns 39–40, 43
   'forward policy' from 1917 68
   general election 1918 43
   imprisonments 38–9
   insurgency 24, 42, 44
   intelligence 19–20, 39, 40, 44, 47, 48, 50–1, 57, 80, 91, 94, 95–6
   intelligence 'squad' 47–8, 49, 52, 97
   IRB (Irish Republican Brotherhood) 24
   legitimacy 101
   and Lily Mernin 95
   and Lloyd George 105, 110
   logistics 97
   'Minister of Finance' 53
   narrative of victory 227
   operational networks 44–5, 57, 76, 94
   organisational changes 100
   private secretary 86
   raids 225
   and the RIC 46
   secret negotiations 102
   Secretary of the Irish National Aid Fund 40
   self-independence 42
   Sinn Fein 40
   'twelve apostles' 97
colonialism 175
colony, Ireland as 30
Combined Intelligence Service 80, 88
communism 151
compensation claims 135
Competent Military Authority 66, 103
Comprehensive Approach 142
concessions 11, 60, 109, 126, 128, 196, 204, 211
conciliation policy 9–10, 67, 71, 73, 74
conditionality 204
Connaught division 34
Connaught Rangers (Galway), 30
Connolly, E. 202
conscription 25, 30–4, 37, 41, 43
Conscription Bill 32

constitution 14, 15 n84, 122, 162
Continuity IRA 178n678
Conway Hotel, Belfast 155
Coogan, Tim Pat 69, 70
Cope, Alfred
  acknowledgement of impact of actions 136–7
  activities in public domain 134, 135
  appointment as Assistant Under Secretary 5–6, 69
  armed truces 227
  and British Army 220
  and de Valera 70, 86, 87, 111, 119–20
  Direct Rule period 163
  dysfunctional relationship between Dublin Castle, the Army and the police 219–20
  and Erskine Childers 86, 87–8
  and the 'illogical compact' 133
  and the intelligence machine 6, 74–9
  investigations 135, 203
  knighthood 136
  as Lloyd George's 'dirty man' 6, 21, 60, 70–3, 78, 107, 110, 135, 136
  and Macready 71–2, 74, 76, 111–13, 133–4, 192
  and Michael Collins 6, 21, 70, 85, 108, 220, 227
  named in Record of Rebellion xviii, 21
  negotiations 92, 103, 107–12, 118, 203
  not present at opening of parliament 123
  organised searches 130
  and Patrick Moylett 118, 119, 202, 218, 225
  prisoner releases 124
  public allegations against 134, 135–6
  report on functioning of Dublin Castle 68
  and the RIC 134, 135, 136
  role in truce 125
  similarities with Jonathan Powell 211
  and Sinn Fein 6, 71, 72, 73, 74, 77–8, 87, 105, 107, 111, 121, 123, 131, 134–6, 137, 219, 220, 222
  special representative of the British Cabinet xviii, 6, 21, 60, 70, 85
  truce agreement 126
  in truce period 133
  unchecked power 219
  undermining of security effort 131–2, 133–4
Cork 12, 105
Cosgrave, W.T. 40
counter-insurgency
  Banner Analysis 142
  Bloody Sunday 98, 160
  British Army 103
  business-like traditions 2, 218–23
  coherent responses to 25
  criteria for victory 170
  end of 126
  information operations 183–6, 214
  integrated approaches to 3, 142, 157, 165
  intelligence 17–20
  operating codes 5, 10–12, 215–28
  Operation Banner 142, 143
  principles 5, 59, 83, 131–2, 153
  secret negotiations 132–3
  undermining of 131
  as unfair fight 153
counter-intelligence 47, 50, 51, 77–8, 89, 91n332
counter-narratives 65, 114, 194, 216, 219
counter-terrorism 142, 165, 177, 188, 198, 211
Courts Martial 83, 94, 103, 128
covert intelligence 180–2
Craig, Sir James 17, 124, 144, 145, 217
Creasey, Sir Timothy 169
Creggan, Londonderry 147, 158, 168
cross-border security 171, 175, 182, 195, 196
cross-channel 'spectacular' 96–7
Crossley Motors 109
Crow Street, Dublin 53
crowd control doctrine 157, 158, 160
Crown legal appointments, Irishmen holding 108, 111
Cubbon, Brian 148
Cullen, Tom 48, 94
Cuman-na-Ban 76
Cunliffe, Philip 13
curfews 152, 188
Curragh Camp 29, 106, 107, 128
currency conversion 198

Index

Curzon, Lord 92
Cyclists 34

'D' branch 37, 99
Dail Eireann 17, 23, 46, 53, 56, 76, 101, 103, 110, 114, 217, 219
Darling, Captain 184
Dawson Street 86
De Valera, Eamon
   and Alfred Cope 70, 86, 87, 111, 119–20
   arrest and release 118–20, 121
   and the British Cabinet 117, 127–8
   Bureau of Military History 137n52
   on conscription 32
   and David Lloyd George 105
   by-election (1917) 40
   finance networks 55
   fundraising 54
   General Elections 43
   guarantees 125
   immunity 130
   island of Ireland 14
   and Molly Childers 121
   President of Sinn Fein 41
   response to Prime Minister's letter 124
   truce agreement 125
death sentences 128
declaration of independence 1919 14, 23
decommissioning of weapons 207, 224
deep interrogation techniques 154
defeat narrative 118, 126, 137, 140, 216, 218, 225
Defence of the Realm Act 34, 44, 62, 65, 69, 83
Democratic Unionist Party (DUP) 179n682, 213
demonstrations 41, 65, 148, 149, 151, 158–9
   see also protest marches
Denning, Major 185
'Department of Publicity' 47
deportations 37, 41
deprivation levels 145, 147
Deputy Chief of Police 80
deserters 75
detention camps 100
'Detention Orders' 62
detention policies 103–4

deterrence 179, 183, 216
Deverell, John 199, 201
Devlin, Joseph 17
devolved governments
   after GFA 179
   and Bloody Sunday 161
   elections 1921 109
   failure to meet 115, 122
   inter-war period 145
   Northern Ireland 144
   Office of the UK Representative (UKREP) 155–6
   suspension (1972) 8, 163
   Ulster Unionists 196
dialectical struggles 131–2, 188, 189
diasporas 185–6
Direct Rule 157–65
'dirty man' 21, 60, 70–3
Disclosure Unit 139
Dissent IRA 178n678
doctrine xiii
documentary evidence 83–5, 93, 121, 220
dog-fights 6, 60, 211, 216
Dominion Home Rule 74, 108, 218
Douglas-Home, Sir Alec 161
Dowling, Corporal Joseph 32, 33n132, 34
Downing Street Declaration 1969 161
Downing Street Declaration 1993 204
Doyle, J. 202
'Draft Circular' 184–5
Dromkeen 109
Dublin
   Central Hotel, Dublin 92
   Central Office of Intelligence 81, 82
   Crow Street, Dublin 53
   elections 1921 109
   IRA HQ 53
   Mary Street, Dublin 87, 109
   Shanahan's public house, Dublin 102
   Shelbourne Hotel, Dublin 117
   South Frederick Street, Dublin 85
   St Andrew Street, Dublin 53
   Trinity College Dublin 110
   Upper Pembroke St, Dublin 97
Dublin Castle
   civil service 5, 28, 60, 68, 72, 73–4
   media censorship 119

official statement on Bloody Sunday 99
peace negotiations 103, 118, 203
political choices 105
political crime detection 85–6
press 184
provision of immunity 86
secret negotiations 92
unauthorised access to 78
witholding of information 115
Dublin Metropolitan Police (DMP)
  'G' division 33, 39, 40, 44, 48, 49, 68, 77, 85, 86
  intelligence 24, 36, 39, 40, 44, 49, 56, 57
  prisoner releases 41
  security vetting failures 96
  Sinn Fein attacks on 61
Duddy, Brendan 193, 199, 201
Duggan, Eamonn 107n399, 124, 125
Duggan, George Chester 67, 69, 72, 195
Duggan, J.E. 85
Duke, Henry 38
Dulanty, Mr 136–7
Dumont, Mr (US Consul) 117
Dundalk 81–2

East Clare election 40, 43
East Tyrone elections 42
Easter rebellion 37, 38, 40
east-west axis Dublin-Cheshire Gap 17
Eaton Place 141n537
Edwards, Aaron xiii, xiv, 193n738
elections 39–40, 41–2, 43–4, 109–11, 144, 146, 209
electoral law 144
Eliot, T.S. 91n332
English, Richard 207, 226
entry controls 34
epitomes 83, 84, 88
escapes from internment camps 128
Europe 172, 202
executions 40, 115
explosives clearance operations 177
External Loan 54

Faulkner, Brian 154, 162, 163
felony 94
fences 172

Fermoy 46
Fianna Fail 200
finance networks 53–5, 93
First Dail Loan 54
First World War 1–2, 3, 25, 29–30, 43
Fisher, Guardsman 178
Fisher, H.A.L. 92
Fisher, Sir Warren 68–9, 74, 75
Fitzgerald, Desmond 47
flags 113
Flying Columns 123
Fogarty, Michael 54
food prices 42
Foot, Michael 70, 71
Ford, Major General 157
Foreign and Commonwealth Office 9, 155
Foulkes, Colonel 105n389, 129, 184
Foy, Michael 19–20, 36
framework operations 180
France 26, 190, 223
franchise 146
Free State Executive Council 54
Freedman, Lawrence 188, 198
Freeland, Lieutenant General Sir 174
French, David xi–xii
French, Field Marshal Viscount 33, 34, 65, 184, 205
Frongoch prisoner of war camp 37–8, 56

Gaddafi, Colonel 189, 190
Gaelic League 76
Gallagher, Frank 107
Gallagher, Noel 201
Galtung, John 179
Galula, David xvii, 42, 153, 170, 182, 223
Galway 81–2
Garda 172, 183
general elections 43–4, 209
geographical determinism 14–16, 201
geography 113, 142, 152, 170, 173–4, 182–3, 187, 189, 216
George, Alexander xvi, 10, 11
George V, King 46, 56
geostrategics 9
Germany 26, 27, 28, 29, 32, 33–4, 189
GHQ 36, 37, 49, 53, 64, 105, 129, 133, 184, 220

Index

Gibraltar 189
Gingrich, Newt 186
Glesson, James 98
GOC (General Officer Commanding) 169, 172, 174, 211, 224
GOC Dublin District 76, 100, 102
GOC-in-C, Irish Command 34, 62, 67, 129
Godley, General Sir Alexander 225
Good Friday Agreement 15, 177, 178–9, 188, 212, 219, 224, 226
Government of Ireland Act 109–10, 111, 144, 145
Government of Ireland Bill 75
Gray, Colin xviii, 2, 36, 59, 105, 115, 137, 198
Greenberg, David 215
Greenwood, Lady 120
Greenwood, Sir Hamar 5, 68, 111, 115, 119, 120, 122, 134–5, 193
Griffith, Arthur 43, 70, 92, 101, 107, 124, 125
guerrilla warfare 19, 35, 79, 104
Guildhall Square, Londonderry riot 151

Hall, Amanda 179
Harris, Lieutenant General Sir Ian 148
Harrison, George 191
Hart, Peter 19, 61, 79, 96, 97, 99
Hartshorne, Richard 16
Harwood, R. E. 68
Hawes, Major General 12
Headlam, Maurice 44, 73
Heath, Edward 154, 156, 157, 162
Heathrow airport bombs 205n783
Heslinga, M. W. 16, 17
Heuser, Beatrice 213
Hill Dillon, Major 36
Hillsborough Treaty 195
hilltop observation posts 183
HMS Bluebell 28
Hoche, Lazare 26
Hoey, Daniel 46
Holland 189
Holohan, Brian 51, 52
Holt, Edward 87
Home Rule 74, 108, 143–4, 218
Home Rule Act 108
Hopkinson, M. 71

Houlihan, Patrick 53
housing 146–7
HQ Northern Ireland 183, 186, 188, 211
human associations 15–16
humanitarianism 172
Hume, John 202, 203
Hume-Adams plan 203
Humint 180, 181, 187
hunger strikes 37, 65, 191
Hunt report 169

identity 20
immunity 6, 75, 86, 124, 130
imprisonments 37, 38, 65, 98 *see also* internments; prisoner releases
incitement charges 42–3
independent variables xiv–xvi
India 80, 89
infantry regiments 30
information campaign 3–4, 153
Information Corporate Memory Analysis branch 141
information leakages 114
information operations 183–6, 214
Information Policy Unit, HQNI 183
informers 18, 83, 100, 181
INLA 178n678
institutional learning *see* organisational learning
insurgency
  and civil war: triggers 148–53
  did it work? 226–8. *see also* counter-insurgency
  intensification 154–7
  social conditions as cause of 147
integrated approaches to counter-insurgency 3, 142, 157, 165
integrated political-military approaches xvii, xix, 57, 111, 174, 216
intelligence
  as aid to force 130
  and Alfred Cope 74–9
  Alfred Cope as information conduit for 6
  assessing effectiveness of 79–80
  Banner Analysis 18–19
  Bloody Sunday 160

British Army 18, 19, 26–8, 33, 35–7, 64, 76–7, 79–89, 152
British intelligence community 49–50
building a new intelligence community 79–89
Catholics 98
clerical services personnel 81
collation of 88–9
counter-insurgency 17–20
counter-intelligence 47, 50, 51, 77–8, 89, 91n332
counter-terrorism 177, 198
covert intelligence 180–2
cross-border cooperation 182–3
'D' branch 99
Dublin Metropolitan Police (DMP) 24, 36, 39, 40, 44, 49, 56, 57
evolution of Operation Banner 180
failure to prevent arms supplies 191
Germany 32
and guerrilla warfare 79
hilltop observation posts 183
Humint 180, 181, 187
and insurgency 64
IRA 20, 37, 64, 76, 94–5, 158, 225
Irish Volunteers 36, 47–8, 49, 52, 56, 94–5, 97
Jonathan Powell 211
leading to arrests 63
Libya 190
local intelligence hubs 80–1
modern approaches to 89
Molly Childers 120
'operating codes' 17–20
Operation Banner 155
Operation Demetrius 154–5
operational networks 46–55
organisational learning 187
Parallel Diplomacy 156–7
PIRA 177
police 24–5, 35, 36, 56, 76, 81
'radical embedding' 37–46
Record of the Rebellion 18, 28, 36–7, 48, 49, 50, 89, 92, 99, 193
recruitment of intelligence personnel 81
reduction in bombs 189
restrictions of First World War 56

Royal Irish Constabulary (RIC) 24, 33, 36, 37, 42, 45–6, 56, 57, 81, 82, 85, 89
Royal Ulster Constabulary (RUC) 89, 154–5, 168
SAS 167
Sinn Fein 28, 36, 48, 77, 120–2, 123–4
Special Branch 76–7
successes 225
Troubles 89
and uncertainty 158
interceptions 181
Internal Loan 54
international law 9–10
international treaties 14
internments 98, 106, 128–9, 154, 158, 166
interrogation 154
intimidation 18, 44, 61, 66
IRA (Irish Republican Army)
aborted/failed operations 181, 182, 189
armed truces 227
arms and ammunition networks 100, 109, 131, 221
arms raids 52–3
attack on Lord Muskerry's property 135
Bloody Sunday attacks 93, 98, 104, 160
ceasefire negotiations 166
central council meeting January 1970 153
Central Raid Bureau 83
criminal activities 222
cross-party consensus to engage in dialogue 174–5
death of Collins 141n537
death of Wilson 141n538
dialogue with 157
documentary evidence 84–5
elections 110
elimination of Courts Martial officers 94
finance networks 93
HQ in Dublin 85
imprisonments 106
informers in British government service 18
intelligence 20, 37, 64, 76, 94–5, 158, 225
intimidation 66
January–July 1921 105
and the land border 142

Index

Londonderry 158
major offensives against 105
motor car restrictions 133
murders in 1922 141n537
murders in period leading up to July 21 truce 126
'operating codes' 13
operational networks 109, 142
order of battle (lack of) 28
organisational changes 100–1
peace negotiations 102
psychological effects of raids on 84
raids 84, 98, 100
rebellion within 103
Roman Catholics 165
sanctions for arrests of 98
secret negotiations 199
structural changes 153, 167
An T Oglac 63, 64, 116
technology 181
truce agreement 220
UKREP (Office of the UK Representative) 156
undercover agents 181
Iraq 213
IRB (Irish Republican Brotherhood)
arms and ammunition networks 52
Fintan Lalor Circle 38
'forward policy' from 1917 68
Irish National Aid Fund 40
and Irish Republicanism 39
and Michael Collins 24
prisoner releases 38
rebellion 1916 (failed) 14
Sinn Fein Convention 1917 41
'Ireland: Situation in Northern Ireland' files 212
Irish Bulletin 47
Irish Command 105
Irish Convention 41, 56
'Irish Dimension' 173
Irish Executive 33, 67, 102, 123
Irish Free State x, 14, 54, 217, 218, 223
Irish Government *see also* devolved governments
Anglo-Irish Agreement 1985 195, 200
and the border 171, 182

isolation of Sinn Fein 202
PIRA 173, 204
Irish Labour Party 32, 144n549
Irish language 207
Irish National Aid Fund 40
Irish National League 41
Irish nationalist mythology 92
'Irish Net' 156
Irish Office 66, 102, 119, 134
Irish Parliamentary Party (IPP) 17, 32, 39, 41, 43
Irish Republicanism
and artifice 16
assumption of moderate faction open to negotiation 68
Bloody Sunday (1920) 96
and the British government 3, 8, 15
civil service 208
claims on another state's territory 15
counter-narratives 65, 114
Courts Martial 94
declared illegal 75–6
Downing Street Declaration 1993 205
forced underground 46
'forward policy' from 1917 39, 68
Good Friday Agreement 178
ignition of the 'Troubles' 148
island of Ireland 15
long tail to the campaign 207
neo-realism 200–1
and a new Anglo-Irish relationship 217
and NICRA 151
'operating codes' 13–17
paranoia 108
propaganda 47, 152, 222
propaganda against 105
strategic narratives 114, 200
Irish Revolutionary Headquarters 26–7
Irish Sea 16
Irish Situation Committee 86, 114n433, 115
Irish Times 151, 217
Irish Volunteers
Active Service Unit 100
arms and ammunition networks 51, 52
arms raids 52–3
attacks on command networks 98
attacks on police 66

Bloody Sunday 96
capabilities 126
civilian security 63
conscription 33
Courts Martial 94
declaration of illegal organisations 76
depleted capacity of 131
disruption of command network 64
effect of deportations on 38
First World War 28–30
'G' division DMP 44
general elections (1918) 43
imprisonments 65
intelligence 36, 52, 56, 94–5
intelligence 'squad' 47–8, 49, 52, 97
internments 128–9
Irish Republicanism 23–4
January-July 1921 104–5
and Martial Law 106
murder of soldier 46
operational networks 88, 130
organisational changes 100
peace negotiations 102, 118
and the policy elite's choices 104
premises networks 53
Regulation 14B 128
and the RIC 45
sanctions for arrests of 98
social composition 50
strategic narratives 127, 129
threat presented by 35
truce agreement 125
island of Ireland 14–15, 16, 226
Italy 27

Jackson, General Sir Mike 141
Jeudwine, Lieutenant General Sir Hugh 50, 102–3, 106, 130
Jeune, Lieutenant Robert 77–8, 93, 94, 97, 99
joint declarations 203, 204
Jones, Thomas 65, 120, 127, 220
judicial inquiries 159, 160

Kavanagh, Detective 86
Keenlyside, Captain 97
Keeping Peace 143

'keeping the door open' policy 75
Kelly, Gerry 201
Kelly, John 157
Kennedy-Pipe, Caroline 180
Kent, Sherman 79
Kerry 105
Kilcullen, Colonel David 213
Kilkenny elections 40
Kissinger, Henry 194
Kitchener's New Army 29
Kitson, General Sir Frank 17–18, 143
Kula 191

Lagan, Chief Superintendent 158
land border *see* border
land mine attacks 118
Land Operations Volume III: Counter-Revolutionary Operations 143
Laneside 156
Law, Bonar 41, 109
leases 53
legitimacy 2, 92, 101, 103, 105, 113, 122, 127, 133, 173, 188, 197, 202, 216
Leites, Nathan xvi, 10
Lewes Jail 40, 41
Libya 170, 173, 189, 190, 192
Liddell Hart, Basil 1, 157
Limerick 81–2, 109
Liverpool 96–7
Lloyd George, David
  absence of counter-narrative 219
  and Alfred Cope 6, 21, 60, 70–3, 78, 107, 135, 136
  ambivalence 105
  and the Army 3
  assumptions 110
  and Craig 144
  and de Valera 119, 120, 127
  decision-making habits 217
  Government of Ireland Bill 75
  information leakages 115
  Irish elections 1921 109
  letter of 25th June 123–4
  and Macready 67, 71, 127
  private secretary 110, 122
  secret negotiations 92, 101, 102, 103
  and Sinn Fein 131

Index

loans 54
local election franchise 7–8
Local Intelligence Centres 81, 82
local intelligence hubs 80–1
London attacks on timber yards 96
Londonderry
    Bloody Sunday 147, 148, 149, 150, 151, 157–65, 216
    Guildhall Square riot 151
    Michael Collins 42
    PIRA 165
long war, aspirations of 189, 190
Longford County elections 40
Lord Chancellor 122
Lord Lieutenant 33
Loughgall 181
'Low Intensity Operations' 143
Lower Falls, Belfast 152
Lucas, Colonel 133
Lyne, Roderic 205, 209
Lynn, Robert 134, 135

MacCorkell, Colonel and Mrs 163n621
MacEoin, Sean 55
MacLellan, Brigadier 158, 159, 160
MacNeill, Eoin 107n399
Macpherson, Sir Ian 69
Macready, General Sir Nevil
    and Alfred Cope 71–2, 74, 76, 111–13, 133–4, 192
    appointment as GOC 67–8
    and Basil Clarke 153n582
    building a new intelligence community 83, 86
    and David Lloyd George 67, 71, 127
    on elections 110
    and Field Marshal Sir Henry Wilson 114, 115, 116, 117
    and the IRA 102, 103, 105
    peace negotiations 122–3, 124–5, 126, 129, 130, 220, 227
    prisoner releases 65
    Record of the Rebellion 140–1
MacStiofain, Sean 164
magistrates 62
Mahon, Lieutenant General Sir Bryan T. 29

Major, John 199, 201, 202, 203, 204, 205, 208
Malaya 143
Mallie, Eamon 203
Manchester 96, 208
Mannix, Patrick 96
manpower shortages 30–1
Mansion House 125
Martial Law 62, 98, 106, 112, 115, 122, 133
Mary Street, Dublin 87, 109
Maskey, Paul 15
Mason, Roy 168
Mayhew, Patrick 200
McCann, Eamonn 8
McCarten, Dr 51
McCartney, Jenny 213
McClean, Captain 96
McGarrity, Joe 51
McGrane, Eileen 33n131, 86
McGuiness, Joseph 40
McGuiness, Martin 159, 164, 199, 201, 212, 222
McKee, Dick 52, 96
McLaren, Robert 199, 201
McMahon, Paul 220, 221
McNamara, Detective 48
McNeill, Professor 124
media 4, 119, 152, 183, 184, 193 *see also* press
Memo A 113
Memo B 114
Menand, Louis 218
Mernin, Lily 95–6
Mespil Road 109
Metropolitan Police 169
MI5 169, 198, 199
MI6 156, 198, 199
Middleton, Lord 124
Midland division 34
military aid 152
Military Aid to Civilian Power (MACP) 149–50
military arsenals, attacks on 52–3
Military Courts 128
military deployment onto streets of Northern Ireland 148 *see also* troop deployments
military ring 91, 93

Military Service Bill (1918) 31
military support for Irish police 150, 168–9
military vehicles 109, 116
Minister of Finance post 53
Ministers of Justice 171
Ministry of Defence 139, 141, 148
missiles 191, 224
Mitchell, Senator George 178
mobile troop units 114
Mockaitis, T.R. 154
moderates, negotiations with 105
Moloney, Ed 191
Molyneaux, James 209
Monteith, Robert 27
Morning Post 134
Morrison, John 146, 150, 163
motor car restrictions 133
mountainous districts 113
Mountbatten, Lord 169
Mountjoy Jail 124
Mountjoy Square arms dump 109
Mowlem, Mo 209, 211
Moylett, Patrick 51, 92, 101, 102, 103, 117, 118, 119, 131, 137, 202, 218, 225
Mulcahy, Richard 76, 85, 93, 96, 100, 104
Mulley, Fred 168
Mumford, A. 132–3, 157
murders
   Bloody Sunday 91–2, 94–5, 96, 97
   border 172n655
   Dail Eireann untouched 114
   Lord Mountbatten 169
   murder campaigns 46, 48, 49
   police 56, 68
   policemen 61
   of soldiers 169
   Special Branch 92
   Youghal attacks 118
Murphy, Finton 221
Muskerry, Lord 135–6
mutual deterrence 179
MV Eksund 190
Myers, Kevin 61, 151

Nagl, Lt Col John 153
narrative of defeat 118, 126, 137, 140, 216, 218, 225

Nationalism 149
nationalist ideology 13, 15, 152
NATO 9
naval service 42
negative peace 179
neo-realism 200, 201
Neumann, P. 168
New Labour 209–13
Newman, Sir Kenneth 169
newspapers 47
NICRA (Northern Ireland Civil Rights Association) 8, 146, 148, 149, 151, 158
Niebuhr, Reinhold 16
night-time raids 160
NIHT (Northern Ireland Housing Trust) 147
NORAID 170, 191
North Irish Horse (HQ Belfast) 30
North Roscommon by-election 39
Northern Bank, Belfast 222
Northern division 34
Northern Ireland Cabinet, resignation of 163
Northern Ireland Office 173
Notes on Guerrilla Warfare in Ireland 106–7
no-warning bombs 164, 165
Noyk, Michael 53

'O' 80, 85, 225 *see also* Winter, Brigadier Ormonde
Oatley, Michael 199
O'Brien, Art 108
observation posts 183
occupation 158
O'Concubair, Seamus 111
O'Connell, David 157, 163
O'Connor, Joseph 38, 60n220
O'Connor, Lord Justice 108, 111
O'Daly, Paddy 38
O'Dochartaigh, Naill 193–4, 199, 201, 212
Office of the UK Representative (UKREP) 155–6
official documents, leaking of 87, 199
Official IRA 160, 166
O'Flanagan, Father 108
O'Halpin, Eunan 99

Index

O'Hanlon, Siobhan 212
Omagh bomb 178
O'Mara, James 54
'on the run,' men 76
'one man, one vote, one value' 7, 146
O'Neill, Lord 150
'operating codes,' definitions xvi, xviii, xix, 1–22, 215–28
Operation Banner
  back-channel negotiation 193–4
  continuity with first campaign 142
  ending of 177
  evolution of 180–3
  first half 139–76
  Good Friday Agreement 178
  incomplete nature of assessment 139
  information operations 214
  intelligence infrastructure 155
  latter half 177–214
  military assessments 140–5
  operating codes 216
  Operation Banner: An Analysis of Military Operations in Northern Ireland, Army Code 71842 x
  SAS 167
  television coverage 142
Operation Banner: An Analysis of Military Operations in Northern Ireland, Army Code 71842 see Banner Analysis
Operation Chiffon 198, 203
Operation Demetrius 154
Operation Forecast 158–9
Operation Motorman 165–70, 173–4, 175
operational networks 44–5, 46–55, 57, 76, 86, 129–30, 142, 173
operational security maintenance 114
Orange Order 145, 148
organisational learning xiii, 141, 142, 187, 226
organised searches 83, 86, 109, 118, 123, 130, 152, 220

Paisley, Ian 151, 213
Palestine 143, 175
'paper wall' 47
Parachute Regiment 159, 160
Parallel Diplomacy 156–7
paramilitary activity 155, 181, 186, 196

paratroopers 158–9
parliament, opening of 122–3
Patterson, H. 151, 189
peace negotiations *see also* ceasefire negotiations; truce agreements
  in 1920s 107, 108, 117–26, 226
  Good Friday Agreement 15, 177, 178–9, 188, 212, 219, 224, 226
  Operation Banner 141n537, 157, 163–4, 178, 201, 210–11, 218, 221, 227
Pearse, Patrick 14
Peck, Sir John 16
perfidy 162
permanent ceasefire 163–4, 205–6
personal freedoms, restrictions on 105–6
petrol bombs 160
Phillips, C.J. 92, 101, 102
photographic units 116
PIRA (Provisional Irish Republican Army)
  aborted operations 177–8, 181
  Active Service Units 166, 172–3, 182, 190
  and the Anglo-Irish Agreement 1985 195, 200, 201, 202
  armed truces 198, 205
  arms and ammunition networks 173, 189–91, 206
  Army Council 173
  becoming terrorist organisation 192
  and the border 172–3
  and Brendan Duddy 193
  British Government's goal to destroy 180
  broadening of campaign scope 187, 189
  ceasefire negotiations 166, 203
  cellular structure 166
  criminal activities 207, 222
  declining military capabilities 205, 206, 224
  engineering department 173
  estimates of strength in 1980s 188–9
  evolution of threat 168
  hilltop observation posts 183
  Humint 181
  independence from Catholic nationalist community 192
  information campaign 4
  intelligence 19
  key decision points 192

and Libya 190
long tail to the campaign 207–8
Martin McGuiness 159
meeting with Secretary of State 163–4
New Labour 212
no-warning bombs 164
'operating codes' 13
Operation Motorman 166
operational networks 206
outside support 170
political legitimacy 197
political violence 226–7
reorganisation 165
robberies 207, 222
safe havens 165, 171, 196, 198, 224
secret negotiations 199
split from IRA 153
stalemate narrative 224
standing down of units in 2005 177
support for 170–1
'turning' of operatives 181–2
UKREP (Office of the UK Representative) 156
undercover agents 181
and the US 191
withdrawal from negotiations 207
Plunkett, Count 39, 41
police *see also* Dublin Metropolitan Police (DMP); Royal Irish Constabulary (RIC); Royal Ulster Constabulary (RUC)
    attacks on 44–5, 56, 66–7, 85, 109, 126, 132
    blacklists 28
    casualty rates 132
    Central Office of Intelligence 81
    cross-border security 171, 182–3
    divisional action committee to liaise with 143
    injuries during public disorder 150
    intelligence 24, 35, 36, 76, 81
    January-July 1921 104–5
    lack of support from non-Irish 150
    manpower shortages 148
    military support for Irish police 150, 168–9
    peace negotiations 103

    police primacy from late 1970s 176
    re-establishment of abandoned police posts 113
    Sinn Fein attacks on 61–2
    in sub-war 11
    transfer of powers 62
policy elites
    assumptions 2, 68, 105, 173, 178
    Bloody Sunday 161
    consistency over time 218
    counter narratives 173, 216
    Irish Republicanism 8–9
    long tail to the campaign 207
    narrative of defeat 218
    and the (non) existence of a natural state 194
    operating codes 2, 59, 137
    Record of the Rebellion 5
    secret negotiations 101–2
    and the threat of guerrilla warfare 35–6
policy reversals 66–7
political crime detection 85
political prisoner status 163
political stage management 195
'political treatment' of prisoners 65
political violence 155, 179, 201, 205–9, 214, 218, 219, 226–7
political-military integration xvii, xix, 57, 111, 174, 216
population fluidity 20
Porch, Douglas xiii
Portland Prison 124
poverty 145, 147
POW camps 38
Powell, Enoch 9
Powell, Jonathan 208, 210, 211–12, 213, 219, 221, 222
PREM FILES 139n534
premises networks 53
press 114, 127, 129, 134, 183, 203 *see also* media
Prince of Wales Leinster Regiment (Birr) 30
prisoner releases
    and Alfred Cope 70, 87, 124
    British Government 38, 41, 56, 125
    Dublin Metropolitan Police (DMP) 41

Index

Duggan and Staines 125
Good Friday Agreement 178, 212
IRB (Irish Republican Brotherhood) 38
and Macready 65
Record of the Rebellion 130
Secretaries of State for Northern Ireland 4, 21
Sinn Fein 56, 207
propaganda
  border 223
  Britain as an 'honest broker' 200
  British Army 129
  conscription 37–8
  guerrilla warfare 185
  information operations 184–5
  and insurgency 213
  Irish Republicanism 47, 105, 152, 222
  lack of anti-rebel 114
  Wilson's operational plan 112
  Winter's intelligence 89
proportional representation 144n549
prosecutions 83, 128, 181
protest marches 149, 158–9, 196
Protestants 7–8, 152
Province Executive Committee 142
PSNI 222
public housing discrimination 146–7
public order, and the concept of a 'state' 7

'qualified states' 9
'quick lifts' 160

'radical embedding' 25, 37–46
RAF Collinstown 52–3
raids 52–3, 83–4, 86–7, 93–4, 98, 100, 160, 163, 225
'Rape of the Falls' 152–3
Reagan, Ronald 191
Real IRA 178n678
re-arrests 4
rebellion 1916 (failed) 14, 26, 143
reciprocity 35–6, 121, 205, 210, 217, 219, 222, 228
Record of the Rebellion (*Record of the Rebellion in Ireland 1920–1921*)
  and Alfred Cope 74
  arrests of IRA officers 63–4

Bloody Sunday 98, 104
British Army 56
business-like traditions 3
counter-insurgency principles 60–1
counter-intelligence 50
declassification of ix
immunity for leaders of insurgency 75
intelligence 18, 28, 36–7, 48, 49, 89, 92, 99, 193
Irish Volunteers' capabilities 126
January-May 1920 61–2, 63, 65
naming of policy elites 5–6, 21
'operating codes' 5
organisational learning 142
origins of 140–1
prisoner releases 130
prisoners 65
in public domain 140
publicity 129
Regulation 14B 128
'release of extremists' 124
restricted distribution of 132
RIC Crimes Special Branch 45
Sinn Fein tactics 61
strategic narratives 127
troop deployments 1921 116
recruitment of intelligence personnel 81
Redmond, Assistant Commissioner 48, 52
Redmond, Captain 17
Regulation 14B 128
reimbursement of funds 54
religious conflict 152
Republican Bonds 54
research operations of intelligence organisations 79–80, 88
Reserve units 34
Restoration of Order in Ireland Act 1920 75, 76, 94, 103, 128
Restorick, Lance Bombardier Stephen 178, 208
Reynolds, Albert 202
rioting 147, 150, 151, 160–1, 168
Roberts, Colonel 160
Rose, Richard 6, 7, 8, 9–10
Ross, Sir John 122
Rossville St, Londonderry 159
Roulement Tours 180

Royal Dublin Fusiliers (Naas) 30
Royal Dublin Horseshow 73
Royal Engineers 116
Royal Inniskilling Fusiliers (Omagh) 30
Royal Irish Constabulary (RIC)
  and Alfred Cope 71, 78, 134, 135, 136
  ambushes in February 1921 109
  attacks on 44–5, 66–7, 85, 109
  Black and Tans 221–2
  Bloody Sunday 104
  Central Office of Intelligence 81, 82
  Combined Intelligence Service 89
  Crimes Special Branch 42, 45, 46, 49
  'D' branch 37, 99
  and 'G' division DMP 46, 57
  intelligence 24, 33, 36, 37, 42, 45–6, 56, 57, 81, 82, 85, 89
  raids 86
  re-establishment of abandonded police posts 113–14
  Restoration of Order in Ireland Act 1920 75
  Sinn Fein attacks on 61
  Special Branch 42, 92–4, 96, 97–8, 99
  transactional reciprocity 219
Royal Irish Fusiliers (Armagh) 30
Royal Irish Regiment (Clonmel) 30
Royal Irish Rifles (Belfast) 30
Royal Marines 116
Royal Munster Fusiliers (Tralee) 30
Royal Navy 28, 112
Royal prefix, retention of 217
Royal Ulster Constabulary (RUC)
  Banner Analysis 149
  and British Army x, 167–8
  cooperation with Irish police 172
  cross-border security 172
  intelligence 89, 154–5, 168
  internment policy 154
  latter half of Operation Banner 177
  Londonderry 149–50, 158
  manpower shortages 148
  military support for Irish police 150, 168–9
  operational primacy 169
  organisational learning 187
  and PIRA 176

  and Powell 211
  and protestant paramilitaries 186
  Sinn Fein's demands about 207
  Special Branch 84, 155, 167, 169, 182
  use of force 148, 150
rural areas 142, 167, 183
Russia 51, 55

safe permits/passes 134–5
SAS 167, 189
Saurin, Frank 95
Saville Inquiry 159, 160
Saville of Newdigate, Lord 159
Scotland, proximity to 16–17
Scotland House 49, 51
Scotland Yard 81
SDLP (Social Democratic and Labour Party) 200, 202, 213
search powers 62, 66
searches 83–8, 109, 118–19, 123, 130, 160, 163, 166, 189, 220
secession xiv, 10, 54
Second Dail 110
secret negotiations 91–2, 101–2, 107–12, 118, 123, 132–3, 163, 198–9, 202–3, 209, 220
secret rooms 53
Secret Service 49
Secretaries of State for Northern Ireland 4, 9, 163, 200, 207, 209, 211
'Secrets of Crew House' memorandum 184
sectarianism 8
Security Information Group 185
security policy changes 142
security under the rule of the law 5, 59, 83, 118
security vetting 95–6
'securocracy' 221
self-determination 226
Seliktar, Ofira 147n564
semi-structured interviews xvi
Semtex 191, 224
Shanahan's public house, Dublin 102
Shankill Road, Belfast 203
Shantallow 168
Shaw, Lieutenant-General Sir Frederick 34, 35, 65, 67, 129, 153n582
Shelbourne Hotel, Dublin 117

shootings 164, 166
Shortt, Edward 34, 120
signals 26–8, 116
Simpson, Major General 10–11, 60, 211, 216
Single Transferable Vote 144
Sinn Fein
   and Alfred Cope 6, 71, 72, 73, 74, 77–8, 87, 105, 107, 111, 121, 123, 134–6, 137
   all-party talks 207
   arms and ammunition networks 51, 221
   arrest of leaders 34
   and the border xn4
   and the British Cabinet 109
   and British Government 202, 212, 213
   camouflaged rebels 63
   campaign 1920–1921 as sub-war 11
   challenges to British legitimacy 61
   civil service reports on 69
   conscription 25, 32
   criminal activities 207
   Crown legal appointments, Irishmen holding 108
   declaration of illegal organisations 76
   declaration of independence 1919 14, 23
   Eamonn de Valera as President of 41
   effects of IRA internments on 106
   by-election defeats 41–2
   elections 1918 43–4
   elections 1921 110
   electoral rise in 1980s 195
   in England 77
   Good Friday Agreement 179n682
   hunger strikes 65
   immunity 130
   and Imperial Germany 33
   impossibility of compromise 121
   informers 21
   intelligence 28, 36, 48, 77, 120–2, 123–4
   intimidation 66
   legitimacy 103, 122, 202
   meeting with US Consul 117
   and Michael Collins 40, 50
   Military Service Bill (1918) 32
   Molly Childers 120–1
   MPs 40, 56, 110
   and New Labour 209, 212, 213
   'operating codes' 12
   other parties subordinate to 17
   peace negotiations 186
   propaganda 129, 186
   and the RIC 45–6
   searches of offices 63
   secret negotiations 92
   truce agreement 51, 105, 125
   undercover agents 181
   voice-overs of media statements 183
Sinn Fein Convention 1917 41, 57
Sinn Fein Publicity Department 3
SIS 156, 163
Smith, General Sir Rupert xi, xv n24, 175, 224
Smith, Howard 155n591
Smith, Michael 156
Smith, M.L.R. xii, 188, 200, 203, 206
smuggling 51, 112, 171, 173
Smyth, Patrick 46
social authority 23, 55, 61, 62, 92, 113, 133
social conditions in Northern Ireland 146–7
social origins of 'Troubles' 143–5
social security benefits 145, 147
Soloheadbeg murder 23
Sonderland, W. 25, 55
South Africa 221
South Armagh 41, 167, 168, 183, 198
South Frederick Street, Dublin 85
South Irish Horse (HQ Dublin) 30
Southern Irish Unionists 124
Spain, similarities with xiv, 223
'Spearhead Battalion' - 3rd Battalion The Light Infantry 150
Special Branch of Dublin Military District 37, 74, 76, 91, 93
Special Forces 182
Special Military Areas 34–5
Special Reconnaissance Regiment 167
special representative of the British Cabinet 60, 70–3, 85
Special Reserves 30
Spike Island 128
Spindler, Karl 27
SS Castro 27
St Andrew Street, Dublin 53
Staines, Michael 107n399, 124, 125

stalemate narrative xiii–xiv, 180, 216, 224
stand-by battalions 150
states, qualities of statehood 6–10
Steele, Frank 156, 163, 164
stenographers 80, 81
Stevenson, Miss 110, 122
Steward, A.T.Q. 223
Stormont 144, 155, 157, 161, 163
Strachan, Hew xi, 3, 155
strategic narratives 127, 129, 161, 173, 183
Strickland, General 75, 105, 130–1, 133, 140n536
strikes 65 *see also* hunger strikes
Sturgis, Mark 69, 71, 72–3, 80, 85, 88, 91, 92, 93, 104, 108, 109, 110, 112, 118, 119, 120, 122–3, 124, 126, 137, 219, 220, 221, 222
'Sub-War' 10–11
succession 54, 57, 223
Support Company 159
Supreme Court (US) 54
surveillance 79, 88, 180, 183, 187, 211, 212

Tactical Doctrine Retrieval Cell 141n539
Tank Corps 116
Tasking and Coordination Groups 168–9
taxation 42
Taylor, Sir John 67
technology 180–1
television coverage 142
territorial conflict 152
territorial integrity 9, 195–6, 205
terrorism *see also* counter-terrorism
 casualty rates 164
 intelligence 181
 interceptions 181
 PIRA 167, 208
 Sinn Fein attacks on police and public 61
 social conditions as cause of 147
 as a strategy 198–9
terrorists, release of 178, 212
'Tet Offensive' 189–90
Thatcher, Margaret 183, 191, 194, 196, 197
Thompson, Sir Basil 57, 120
Thomson, Sir B 49
Thornton, Frank 48, 94

Times, The 23
Tipperary 94
Tobin, Liam 48, 94
Towards a lasting peace 200
Townshend, Charles xi, 19, 23, 26, 47, 66, 69, 79, 80, 126
train ambushes 119
Tralee Bay 28
transactional reciprocity 35–6, 121, 205, 210, 217, 219, 222, 228
Traynor, Oscar 137
Treacy, Sean 23
treason charges 86n318, 94
treasonable felonies 94
trials 70, 83, 128
tricolour 41
Trimble, David 209
Trinity College Dublin 110
troop deployments 113–14, 115, 116, 125, 129–30, 146, 150, 155, 165
truce agreements 71, 101, 102, 105, 109, 125–8, 198, 203, 205, 220 *see also* armed truces; peace negotiations
Truman, Harry 210
Tudor, General 124, 184
Tugwell, Lt Col Malcolm 183
'twelve apostles' 97
twin track approach 187–8
Twohig, John P. 46
Twomey, Seamus 164

Ucko, David xiii, 21
UKREP (Office of the UK Representative) 155–6
Ulster Defence Regiment 165, 180
Ulster Unionists
 and the Anglo-Irish Agreement 1985 196
 and the Catholic population 144–5
 constitutional change 162
 Enoch Powell 9
 general elections (1918) 44
 Heslinga 16
 minority status 201
 MPs 9, 17, 195, 202
 and New Labour 209, 213
Ulsterisation 168
unarmed civilians, firing on 159

Under Secretaries 5, 86
undercover agents 49–51
Unilateral Declaration of Independence (UDI) 46, 53, 55
unitary authority, lack of single 142, 172, 184, 211
United Kingdom of Great Britain and Ireland ix
United Kingdom of Great Britain and Northern Ireland x
United States
  arms and ammunition networks 51, 208
  British Embassy 185
  Clan na Gael 40
  Consul 117
  Eamonn de Valera 55
  External Loan 54
  First World War 29–30
  funding 191
  Irish diaspora 186
  Irish secret societies 77
  NORAID 170, 191
  support for PIRA 170
  terrorism 191
unity of effort 59, 60, 69, 114, 156–7
universal suffrage 7
unlawful incitement 42
Upper Pembroke St, Dublin 97
urban environments 142, 143, 152
use of force xvi, 59, 115, 148

van Creveld, Martin 197
van der Bijl, Nick 178
vetting procedures 95–6
Villa 191
voluntary recruiting campaign 32
von Clausewitz, Carl 2, 35, 132, 187, 227, 228

War Office 76
warnings before Bloody Sunday 93
warrants for arrests 62
Warrenpoint 169

Warrington bomb 201
Waterford elections 42
Watt, Samuel 73
Way Ahead 167–8
weapons *see also* arms and ammunition networks; arms dumps
  decommissioning of weapons 207, 224
  distribution centres 109
  Germany 27, 32
  PIRA 173, 189–91
West Cork as Special Military Area 34
"whisperers" 44
Whitelaw, William 163n622, 164
Wilderness of Mirrors 91–104
Wilford, Lieutenant Colonel Derek 159, 160–1
Wilson, Field Marshal Sir Henry 31, 68, 101, 110, 112, 114–17, 125–7, 131, 134, 140–1
Wilson, Harold 148, 151, 155, 157
Wilson, Lt Col Walter 77, 93, 103, 105
Wilson Foster, John 217
Winter, Brigadier Ormonde 19, 64, 66, 76, 80–9, 99, 119, 123, 130–2, 220–1, 225
women
  Army officers killed in front of wives 97
  clerical services personnel 81, 95
  private secretary 86
  suffrage 44
Wood, Mr 185, 186
Woodcock, Caroline 97–8
Woodcock, Lt Col 97–8
Woodfield, P.J. 163, 164
Worcester Regiment 119
Worthington-Evans, Sir Laming (Secretary of State) 115n435, 120, 132
Wright, Frank 179
Wright, Guardsman 178
Wright, Oliver 155–6
Wylie, W. E. 72, 74, 75

Yeomanry Regiments 30, 34
Young Soldiers 34

Reimagining Ireland

Series Editor: Dr Eamon Maher, Technological University Dublin

The concepts of Ireland and 'Irishness' are in constant flux in the wake of an ever-increasing reappraisal of the notion of cultural and national specificity in a world assailed from all angles by the forces of globalisation and uniformity. Reimagining Ireland interrogates Ireland's past and present and suggests possibilities for the future by looking at Ireland's literature, culture and history and subjecting them to the most up-to-date critical appraisals associated with sociology, literary theory, historiography, political science and theology.

Some of the pertinent issues include, but are not confined to, Irish writing in English and Irish, Nationalism, Unionism, the Northern 'Troubles', the Peace Process, economic development in Ireland, the impact and decline of the Celtic Tiger, Irish spirituality, the rise and fall of organised religion, the visual arts, popular cultures, sport, Irish music and dance, emigration and the Irish diaspora, immigration and multiculturalism, marginalisation, globalisation, modernity/postmodernity and postcolonialism. The series publishes monographs, comparative studies, interdisciplinary projects, conference proceedings and edited books.

Proposals should be sent either to Dr Eamon Maher at eamon.maher@ittdublin.ie or to ireland@peterlang.com.

Vol. 1	Eugene O'Brien: 'Kicking Bishop Brennan up the Arse': Negotiating Texts and Contexts in Contemporary Irish Studies ISBN 978-3-03911-539-6. 219 pages. 2009.
Vol. 2	James P.Byrne, Padraig Kirwan and Michael O'Sullivan (eds): Affecting Irishness: Negotiating Cultural Identity Within and Beyond the Nation ISBN 978-3-03911-830-4. 334 pages. 2009.
Vol. 3	Irene Lucchitti: The Islandman: The Hidden Life of Tomás O'Crohan ISBN 978-3-03911-837-3. 232 pages. 2009.
Vol. 4	Paddy Lyons and Alison O'Malley-Younger (eds): No Country for Old Men: Fresh Perspectives on Irish Literature ISBN 978-3-03911-841-0. 289 pages. 2009.

Vol. 5   Eamon Maher (ed.): Cultural Perspectives on Globalisation and Ireland
         ISBN 978-3-03911-851-9. 256 pages. 2009.

Vol. 6   Lynn Brunet: 'A Course of Severe and Arduous Trials': Bacon, Beckett
         and Spurious Freemasonry in Early Twentieth-Century Ireland
         ISBN 978-3-03911-854-0. 218 pages. 2009.

Vol. 7   Claire Lynch: Irish Autobiography: Stories of Self in the Narrative of a
         Nation
         ISBN 978-3-03911-856-4. 234 pages. 2009.

Vol. 8   Victoria O'Brien: A History of Irish Ballet from 1927 to 1963
         ISBN 978-3-03911-873-1. 208 pages. 2011.

Vol. 9   Irene Gilsenan Nordin and Elin Holmsten (eds): Liminal Borderlands in
         Irish Literature and Culture
         ISBN 978-3-03911-859-5. 208 pages. 2009.

Vol. 10   Claire Nally: Envisioning Ireland: W. B. Yeats's Occult Nationalism
         ISBN 978-3-03911-882-3. 320 pages. 2010.

Vol. 11   Raita Merivirta: The Gun and Irish Politics: Examining National History
         in Neil Jordan's Michael Collins
         ISBN 978-3-03911-888-5. 202 pages. 2009.

Vol. 12   John Strachan and Alison O'Malley-Younger (eds): Ireland: Revolution
         and Evolution
         ISBN 978-3-03911-881-6. 248 pages. 2010.

Vol. 13   Barbara Hughes: Between Literature and History: The Diaries and
         Memoirs of Mary Leadbeater and Dorothea Herbert
         ISBN 978-3-03911-889-2. 255 pages. 2010.

Vol. 14   Edwina Keown and Carol Taaffe (eds): Irish Modernism: Origins,
         Contexts, Publics
         ISBN 978-3-03911-894-6. 256 pages. 2010.

Vol. 15   John Walsh: Contests and Contexts: The Irish Language and Ireland's
         Socio-Economic Development
         ISBN 978-3-03911-914-1. 492 pages. 2011.

Vol. 16	Zélie Asava: The Black Irish Onscreen: Representing Black and Mixed-Race Identities on Irish Film and Television ISBN 978-3-0343-0839-7. 213 pages. 2013.
Vol. 17	Susan Cahill and Eóin Flannery (eds): This Side of Brightness: Essays on the Fiction of Colum McCann ISBN 978-3-03911-935-6. 189 pages. 2012.
Vol. 18	Brian Arkins: The Thought of W. B. Yeats ISBN 978-3-03911-939-4. 204 pages. 2010.
Vol. 19	Maureen O'Connor: The Female and the Species: The Animal in Irish Women's Writing ISBN 978-3-03911-959-2. 203 pages. 2010.
Vol. 20	Rhona Trench: Bloody Living: The Loss of Selfhood in the Plays of Marina Carr ISBN 978-3-03911-964-6. 327 pages. 2010.
Vol. 21	Jeannine Woods: Visions of Empire and Other Imaginings: Cinema, Ireland and India, 1910–1962 ISBN 978-3-03911-974-5. 230 pages. 2011.
Vol. 22	Neil O'Boyle: New Vocabularies, Old Ideas: Culture, Irishness and the Advertising Industry ISBN 978-3-03911-978-3. 233 pages. 2011.
Vol. 23	Dermot McCarthy: John McGahern and the Art of Memory ISBN 978-3-0343-0100-8. 344 pages. 2010.
Vol. 24	Francesca Benatti, Sean Ryder and Justin Tonra (eds): Thomas Moore: Texts, Contexts, Hypertexts ISBN 978-3-0343-0900-4. 220 pages. 2013.
Vol. 25	Sarah O'Connor: No Man's Land: Irish Women and the Cultural Present ISBN 978-3-0343-0111-4. 230 pages. 2011.
Vol. 26	Caroline Magennis: Sons of Ulster: Masculinities in the Contemporary Northern Irish Novel ISBN 978-3-0343-0110-7. 192 pages. 2010.
Vol. 27	Dawn Duncan: Irish Myth, Lore and Legend on Film ISBN 978-3-0343-0140-4. 181 pages. 2013.

Vol. 28   Eamon Maher and Catherine Maignant (eds): Franco-Irish Connections in Space and Time: Peregrinations and Ruminations
ISBN 978-3-0343-0870-0. 295 pages. 2012.

Vol. 29   Holly Maples: Culture War: Conflict, Commemoration and the Contemporary Abbey Theatre
ISBN 978-3-0343-0137-4. 294 pages. 2011.

Vol. 30   Maureen O'Connor (ed.): Back to the Future of Irish Studies: Festschrift for Tadhg Foley
ISBN 978-3-0343-0141-1. 359 pages. 2010.

Vol. 31   Eva Urban: Community Politics and the Peace Process in Contemporary Northern Irish Drama
ISBN 978-3-0343-0143-5. 303 pages. 2011.

Vol. 32   Mairéad Conneely: Between Two Shores/*Idir Dhá Chladach*: Writing the Aran Islands, 1890–1980
ISBN 978-3-0343-0144-2. 299 pages. 2011.

Vol. 33   Gerald Morgan and Gavin Hughes (eds): Southern Ireland and the Liberation of France: New Perspectives
ISBN 978-3-0343-0190-9. 250 pages. 2011.

Vol. 34   Anne MacCarthy: Definitions of Irishness in the 'Library of Ireland' Literary Anthologies
ISBN 978-3-0343-0194-7. 271 pages. 2012.

Vol. 35   Irene Lucchitti: Peig Sayers: In Her Own Write
ISBN 978-3-0343-0253-1. 328 pages. 2011.

Vol. 36   Eamon Maher and Eugene O'Brien (eds): Breaking the Mould: Literary Representations of Irish Catholicism
ISBN 978-3-0343-0232-6. 249 pages. 2011.

Vol. 37   Mícheál Ó hAodha and John O'Callaghan (eds): Narratives of the Occluded Irish Diaspora: Subversive Voices
ISBN 978-3-0343-0248-7. 227 pages. 2012.

Vol. 38   Willy Maley and Alison O'Malley-Younger (eds): Celtic Connections: Irish–Scottish Relations and the Politics of Culture
ISBN 978-3-0343-0214-2. 247 pages. 2013.

Vol. 39   Sabine Egger and John McDonagh (eds): Polish–Irish Encounters in the
           Old and New Europe
           ISBN 978-3-0343-0253-1. 322 pages. 2011.

Vol. 40   Elke D'hoker, Raphaël Ingelbien and Hedwig Schwall (eds): Irish
           Women Writers: New Critical Perspectives
           ISBN 978-3-0343-0249-4. 318 pages. 2011.

Vol. 41   Peter James Harris: From Stage to Page: Critical Reception of Irish Plays
           in the London Theatre, 1925–1996
           ISBN 978-3-0343-0266-1. 311 pages. 2011.

Vol. 42   Hedda Friberg-Harnesk, Gerald Porter and Joakim Wrethed
           (eds): Beyond Ireland: Encounters Across Cultures
           ISBN 978-3-0343-0270-8. 342 pages. 2011.

Vol. 43   Irene Gilsenan Nordin and Carmen Zamorano Llena (eds): Urban and
           Rural Landscapes in Modern Ireland: Language, Literature and Culture
           ISBN 978-3-0343-0279-1. 238 pages. 2012.

Vol. 44   Kathleen Costello-Sullivan: Mother/Country: Politics of the Personal in
           the Fiction of Colm Tóibín
           ISBN 978-3-0343-0753-6. 247 pages. 2012.

Vol. 45   Lesley Lelourec and Gráinne O'Keeffe-Vigneron (eds): Ireland and
           Victims: Confronting the Past, Forging the Future
           ISBN 978-3-0343-0792-5. 331 pages. 2012.

Vol. 46   Gerald Dawe, Darryl Jones and Nora Pelizzari (eds): Beautiful
           Strangers: Ireland and the World of the 1950s
           ISBN 978-3-0343-0801-4. 207 pages. 2013.

Vol. 47   Yvonne O'Keeffe and Claudia Reese (eds): New Voices, Inherited
           Lines: Literary and Cultural Representations of the Irish Family
           ISBN 978-3-0343-0799-4. 238 pages. 2013.

Vol. 48   Justin Carville (ed.): Visualizing Dublin: Visual Culture, Modernity and
           the Representation of Urban Space
           ISBN 978-3-0343-0802-1. 326 pages. 2014.

Vol. 49	Gerald Power and Ondřej Pilný (eds): Ireland and the Czech Lands: Contacts and Comparisons in History and Culture ISBN 978-3-0343-1701-6. 243 pages. 2014.
Vol. 50	Eoghan Smith: John Banville: Art and Authenticity ISBN 978-3-0343-0852-6. 199 pages. 2014.
Vol. 51	María Elena Jaime de Pablos and Mary Pierse (eds): George Moore and the Quirks of Human Nature ISBN 978-3-0343-1752-8. 283 pages. 2014.
Vol. 52	Aidan O'Malley and Eve Patten (eds): Ireland, West to East: Irish Cultural Connections with Central and Eastern Europe ISBN 978-3-0343-0913-4. 307 pages. 2014.
Vol. 53	Ruben Moi, Brynhildur Boyce and Charles I. Armstrong (eds): The Crossings of Art in Ireland ISBN 978-3-0343-0983-7. 319 pages. 2014.
Vol. 54	Sylvie Mikowski (ed.): Ireland and Popular Culture ISBN 978-3-0343-1717-7. 257 pages. 2014.
Vol. 55	Benjamin Keatinge and Mary Pierse (eds): France and Ireland in the Public Imagination ISBN 978-3-0343-1747-4. 279 pages. 2014.
Vol. 56	Raymond Mullen, Adam Bargroff and Jennifer Mullen (eds): John McGahern: Critical Essays ISBN 978-3-0343-1755-9. 253 pages. 2014.
Vol. 57	Máirtín Mac Con Iomaire and Eamon Maher (eds): 'Tickling the Palate': Gastronomy in Irish Literature and Culture ISBN 978-3-0343-1769-6. 253 pages. 2014.
Vol. 58	Heidi Hansson and James H. Murphy (eds): Fictions of the Irish Land War ISBN 978-3-0343-0999-8. 237 pages. 2014.
Vol. 59	Fiona McCann: A Poetics of Dissensus: Confronting Violence in Contemporary Prose Writing from the North of Ireland ISBN 978-3-0343-0979-0. 238 pages. 2014.

Vol. 60   Marguérite Corporaal, Christopher Cusack, Lindsay Janssen and
            Ruud van den Beuken (eds): Global Legacies of the Great Irish
            Famine: Transnational and Interdisciplinary Perspectives
            ISBN 978-3-0343-0903-5. 357 pages. 2014.

Vol. 61   Katarzyna Ojrzyn'ska: 'Dancing As If Language No Longer
            Existed': Dance in Contemporary Irish Drama
            ISBN 978-3-0343-1813-6. 318 pages. 2015.

Vol. 62   Whitney Standlee: 'Power to Observe': Irish Women Novelists in
            Britain, 1890–1916
            ISBN 978-3-0343-1837-2. 288 pages. 2015.

Vol. 63   Elke D'hoker and Stephanie Eggermont (eds): The Irish Short
            Story: Traditions and Trends
            ISBN 978-3-0343-1753-5. 330 pages. 2015.

Vol. 64   Radvan Markus: Echoes of the Rebellion: The Year 1798 in Twentieth-
            Century Irish Fiction and Drama
            ISBN 978-3-0343-1832-7. 248 pages. 2015.

Vol. 65   B. Mairéad Pratschke: Visions of Ireland: Gael Linn's *Amharc Éireann*
            Film Series, 1956–1964
            ISBN 978-3-0343-1872-3. 301 pages. 2015.

Vol. 66   Una Hunt and Mary Pierse (eds): France and Ireland: Notes and
            Narratives
            ISBN 978-3-0343-1914-0. 272 pages. 2015.

Vol. 67   John Lynch and Katherina Dodou (eds): The Leaving of
            Ireland: Migration and Belonging in Irish Literature and Film
            ISBN 978-3-0343-1896-9. 313 pages. 2015.

Vol. 68   Anne Goarzin (ed.): New Critical Perspectives on Franco-Irish Relations
            ISBN 978-3-0343-1781-8. 271 pages. 2015.

Vol. 69   Michel Brunet, Fabienne Gaspari and Mary Pierse (eds): George Moore's
            Paris and His Ongoing French Connections
            ISBN 978-3-0343-1973-7. 279 pages. 2015.

Vol. 70   Carine Berbéri and Martine Pelletier (eds): Ireland: Authority and Crisis
            ISBN 978-3-0343-1939-3. 296 pages. 2015.

| Vol. 71 | David Doolin: Transnational Revolutionaries: The Fenian Invasion of Canada, 1866
ISBN 978-3-0343-1922-5. 348 pages. 2016. |
|---|---|
| Vol. 72 | Terry Phillips: Irish Literature and the First World War: Culture, Identity and Memory
ISBN 978-3-0343-1969-0. 297 pages. 2015. |
| Vol. 73 | Carmen Zamorano Llena and Billy Gray (eds): Authority and Wisdom in the New Ireland: Studies in Literature and Culture
ISBN 978-3-0343-1833-4. 263 pages. 2016. |
| Vol. 74 | Flore Coulouma (ed.): New Perspectives on Irish TV Series: Identity and Nostalgia on the Small Screen
ISBN 978-3-0343-1977-5. 222 pages. 2016. |
| Vol. 75 | Fergal Lenehan: Stereotypes, Ideology and Foreign Correspondents: German Media Representations of Ireland, 1946–2010
ISBN 978-3-0343-2222-5. 306 pages. 2016. |
| Vol. 76 | Jarlath Killeen and Valeria Cavalli (eds): 'Inspiring a Mysterious Terror': 200 Years of Joseph Sheridan Le Fanu
ISBN 978-3-0343-2223-2. 260 pages. 2016. |
| Vol. 77 | Anne Karhio: 'Slight Return': Paul Muldoon's Poetics of Place
ISBN 978-3-0343-1986-7. 272 pages. 2017. |
| Vol. 78 | Margaret Eaton: Frank Confessions: Performance in the Life-Writings of Frank McCourt
ISBN 978-1-906165-61-1. 294 pages. 2017. |
| Vol. 79 | Marguérite Corporaal, Christopher Cusack and Ruud van den Beuken (eds): Irish Studies and the Dynamics of Memory: Transitions and Transformations
ISBN 978-3-0343-2236-2. 360 pages. 2017. |
| Vol. 80 | Conor Caldwell and Eamon Byers (eds): New Crops, Old Fields: Reimagining Irish Folklore
ISBN 978-3-0343-1912-6. 200 pages. 2017. |

Vol. 81	Sinéad Wall: Irish Diasporic Narratives in Argentina: A Reconsideration of Home, Identity and Belonging ISBN 978-1-906165-66-6. 282 pages. 2017.
Vol. 82	Ute Anna Mittermaier: Images of Spain in Irish Literature, 1922–1975 ISBN 978-3-0343-1993-5. 386 pages. 2017.
Vol. 83	Lauren Clark: Consuming Irish Children: Advertising and the Art of Independence, 1860–1921 ISBN 978-3-0343-1989-8. 288 pages. 2017.
Vol. 84	Lisa FitzGerald: Re-Place: Irish Theatre Environments ISBN 978-1-78707-359-3. 222 pages. 2017.
Vol. 85	Joseph Greenwood: 'Hear My Song': Irish Theatre and Popular Song in the 1950s and 1960s ISBN 978-3-0343-1915-7. 320 pages. 2017.
Vol. 86	Nils Beese: Writing Slums: Dublin, Dirt and Literature ISBN 978-1-78707-959-5. 250 pages. 2018.
Vol. 87	Barry Houlihan (ed.): Navigating Ireland's Theatre Archive: Theory, Practice, Performance ISBN 978-1-78707-372-2. 306 pages. 2019.
Vol. 88	María Elena Jaime de Pablos (ed.): Giving Shape to the Moment: The Art of Mary O'Donnell: Poet, Novelist and Short Story Writer ISBN 978-1-78874-403-4. 228 pages. 2018.
Vol. 89	Marguérite Corporaal and Peter Gray (eds): The Great Irish Famine and Social Class: Conflicts, Responsibilities, Representations ISBN 978-1-78874-166-8. 330 pages. 2019.
Vol. 90	Patrick Speight: Irish-Argentine Identity in an Age of Political Challenge and Change, 1875–1983 ISBN 978-1-78874-417-1. 360 pages. 2020.
Vol. 91	Fionna Barber, Heidi Hansson, and Sara Dybris McQuaid (eds): Ireland and the North ISBN 978-1-78874-289-4. 338 pages. 2019.

Vol. 92   Ruth Sheehy: The Life and Work of Richard King: Religion, Nationalism and Modernism
           ISBN 978-1-78707-246-6. 482 pages. 2019.

Vol. 93   Brian Lucey, Eamon Maher and Eugene O'Brien (eds): Recalling the Celtic Tiger
           ISBN 978-1-78997-286-3. 386 pages. 2019.

Vol. 94   Melania Terrazas Gallego (ed.): Trauma and Identity in Contemporary Irish Culture
           ISBN 978-1-78997-557-4. 302 pages. 2020.

Vol. 95   Patricia Medcalf: Advertising the Black Stuff in Ireland 1959–1999: Increments of Change
           ISBN 978-1-78997-345-7. 218 pages. 2020.

Vol. 96   Anne Goarzin and Maria Parsons (eds): New Cartographies, Nomadic Methologies: Contemporary Arts, Culture and Politics in Ireland
           ISBN 978-1-78874-651-9. 204 pages. 2020.

Vol. 97   Hiroko Ikeda and Kazuo Yokouchi (eds): Irish Literature in the British Context and Beyond: New Perspectives from Kyoto
           ISBN 978-1-78997-566-6. 250 pages. 2020.

Vol. 98   Catherine Nealy Judd: Travel Narratives of the Irish Famine: Politics, Tourism, and Scandal, 1845–1853
           ISBN 978-1-80079-084-1. 468 pages. 2020.

Vol. 99   Lesley Lelourec and Gráinne O'Keeffe-Vigneron (eds): Northern Ireland after the Good Friday Agreement: Building a Shared Future from a Troubled Past?
           ISBN 978-1-78997-746-2. 262 pages. 2021.

Vol. 100   Eamon Maher and Eugene O'Brien (eds): Reimagining Irish Studies for the Twenty-First Century
           ISBN 978-1-80079-191-6. 384 pages. 2021.

Vol. 101   Nathalie Sebbane: Memorialising the Magdalene Laundries: From Story to History
           ISBN 978-1-78707-589-4. 334 pages. 2021.

Vol. 102   Roz Goldie: A Dangerous Pursuit: The Anti-Sectarian Work of Counteract
            ISBN 978-1-80079-187-9. 268 pages. 2021.

Vol. 103   Ann Wilson: The Picture Postcard: A New Window into Edwardian Ireland
            ISBN 978-1-78874-079-1. 282 pages. 2021.

Vol. 104   Anna Charczun: Irish Lesbian Writing Across Time: A New Framework for Rethinking Love Between Women
            ISBN 978-1-78997-864-3. 320 pages. 2022.

Vol. 105   Olivier Coquelin, Brigitte Bastiat and Frank Healy (eds): Northern Ireland: Challenges of Peace and Reconciliation Since the Good Friday Agreement
            ISBN 978-1-78997-817-9. 298 pages. 2022.

Vol. 106   Jo Murphy-Lawless and Laury Oaks (eds): The Salley Gardens: Women, Sex, and Motherhood in Ireland
            ISBN 978-1-80079-417-7. 338 pages. 2022.

Vol. 107   Mercedes del Campo: Voices from the Margins: Gender and the Everyday in Women's Pre- and Post-Agreement Troubles Short Fiction
            ISBN 978-1-78874-330-3. 324 pages. 2022.

Vol. 108   Sean McGraw and Jonathan Tiernan: The Politics of Irish Primary Education: Reform in an Era of Secularisation
            ISBN 978-1-80079-709-3. 532 pages. 2022.

Vol. 109   Gerald Dawe: Northern Windows/Southern Stars: Selected Early Essays 1983–1994
            ISBN 978-1-80079-652-2. 180 pages. 2022.

Vol. 110   John Fanning: The Mandarin, the Musician and the Mage: T. K. Whitaker, Seán Ó Riada, Thomas Kinsella and the Lessons of Ireland's Mid-Twentieth-Century Revival
            ISBN 978-1-80079-599-0. 296 pages. 2022.

Vol. 111   Gerald Dawe: Dreaming of Home: Seven Irish Writers
            ISBN 978-1- 80079-655-3. 108 pages. 2022.

Vol. 112	John Walsh: One Hundred Years of Irish Language Policy, 1922–2022 ISBN 978-1-78997-892-6. 394 pages. 2022.
Vol. 113	Bertrand Cardin: Neil Jordan, Author and Screenwriter: The Imagination of Transgression ISBN 978-1-80079-923-3. 286 pages. 2023.
Vol. 114	David Clark: Dark Green: Irish Crime Fiction 1665–2000 ISBN 978-1-80079-826-7. 450 pages. 2022.
Vol. 115	Aida Rosende-Pérez and Rubén Jarazo-Álvarez (eds): The Cultural Politics of In/Difference: Irish Texts and Contexts ISBN 978-1-80079-727-7. 274 pages. 2022.
Vol. 116	Tara McConnell: "Honest Claret": The Social Meaning of Georgian Ireland's Favourite Wine ISBN 978-1-80079-790-1. 346 pages. 2022.
Vol. 117	M. Teresa Caneda-Cabrera (ed.): Telling Truths: Evelyn Conlon and the Task of Writing ISBN 978-1-80079-481-8. 228 pages. 2023.
Vol. 118	Alexandra Maclennan (ed.): The Irish Catholic Diaspora: Five Centuries of Global Presence ISBN 978-1-80079-516-7. 264 pages. 2023.
Vol. 119	Brian J. Murphy: Beyond Sustenance: An Exploration of Food and Drink Culture in Ireland ISBN 978-1-80079-956-1. 328 pages. 2023.
Vol. 120	Fintan Cullen (ed.): Ireland and the British Empire: Essays on Art and Visuality ISBN 978-1-78874-299-3. 264 pages. 2023.
Vol. 121	Natalie Wynn and Zuleika Rodgers (eds): Reimagining the Jews of Ireland: Historiography, Identity and Representation ISBN 978-1-80079-083-4. 308 pages. 2023.
Vol. 122	Paul Butler: A Deep Well of Want: Visualising the World of John McGahern ISBN 978-1-80079-810-6. 244 pages. 2023.

Vol. 123	Carlos Menéndez Otero: The Great Pretenders: Genre, Form, and Style in the Film Musicals of John Carney ISBN 978-1-80374-135-2. 258 pages. 2023.
Vol. 124	Gerald Dawe: Politic Words: Writing Women | Writing History ISBN 978-1-80374-259-5. 208 pages. 2023.
Vol. 125	Marjan Shokouhi: From Landscapes to Cityscapes: Towards a Poetics of Dwelling in Modern Irish Verse ISBN 978-1-80079-870-0. 260 pages. 2023.
Vol. 126	Pat O'Connor: A 'proper' woman? One woman's story of success and failure in academia ISBN 978-1-80374-305-9. 248 pages. 2023.
Vol. 127	Natalie Wynn: Community, Identity, Conflict: The Jewish Experience in Ireland, 1881–1914 ISBN 978-1-78707-483-5. 338 pages. 2024.
Vol. 128	Marie-Violaine Louvet: The Irish Against the War: Post-Colonial Identity & Political Activism in Contemporary Ireland ISBN 978-1-80079-998-1. 296 pages. 2024.
Vol. 129	Anne Rainey: Hiberno-English, Ulster Scots and Belfast Banter: Ciaran Carson's Translations of Dante and Rimbaud ISBN 978-1-80374-070-6. 338 pages. 2024.
Vol. 130	Nicole Volmering, Claire M. Dunne, John Walsh and Noel Ó Murchadha (eds): Irish in Outlook: A Hundred Years of Irish Education ISBN 978-1-80374-090-4. 348 pages. 2024.
Vol. 131	Grace Neville, Sarah Nolan and Eugene O'Brien (eds): 'Getting the Words Right': A *Festschrift* in Honour of Eamon Maher ISBN 978-1-80374-144-4. 382 pages. 2024.
Vol. 132	Hiroko Ikeda: Sweeney's Revival: Translating and transcending the liminal ISBN 978-1-80374-429-2. 194 pages. 2024.
Vol. 133	Maria Gaviña-Costero, Dina Pedro, and Dónall Mac Cathmhaoill (eds): 'Lost, Unhappy and at Home': The Impact of Violence on Irish Culture: Volume I: Literature ISBN 978-1-80374-321-9. 298 pages. 2024.

Vol. 134   Maria Gaviña-Costero, Dina Pedro, and Dónall Mac Cathmhaoill (eds): 'Lost, Unhappy and at Home': The Impact of Violence on Irish Culture: Volume II: Socio-Cultural Aspects
ISBN 978-1-80374-318-9. 312 pages. 2024.

Vol. 135   Graham Spencer: The SDLP, Politics and Peace: The Mark Durkan Interviews
ISBN 978-1-80079-940-0. 288 pages. 2025.

Vol. 136   Seán William Gannon and Natalie Wynn (eds): The Limerick Boycott in Context
ISBN 978-1-80079-899-1. 318 pages. 2025.

Vol. 137   Connal Parr and Stephen Hopkins (eds): Paving the Path to Peace: Civil Society and the Northern Ireland Peace Process
ISBN 978-1-80374-332-5. 330 pages. 2025.

Vol. 138   Germán Asensio Peral, Madalina Armie, Verónica Membrive (eds): A Nation, not A Parish: The Homewhere-s and Elsewhere-s of 1930s Irish Culture
ISBN 978-1-80374-848-1. 296 pages. 2025.

Vol. 139   Tom Inglis: Unbecoming Catholic: Being Religious in Contemporary Ireland
ISBN 978-1-80374-817-7. 210 pages. 2025.

Vol. 140   Conor Curran: Blue Chippers from the Emerald Isle: A history of Irish footballers and scholarships in the USA in the twentieth century
ISBN 978-1-80374-739-2. 326 pages. 2025.

Vol. 141   Flore Coulouma, Cornelius Crowley and Florence Schneider (eds): Strange Country: Ireland's Politics and Culture, 1998-2021
ISBN 978-1-80374-601-2. 330 pages. 2025.

Vol. 142   Eamonn Wall: Conocimiento: Writing Irish Borderlands
ISBN 978-1-80374-870-2. 212 pages. 2025.

Vol. 143   Ian Kennedy: Prime the Pump: Catholic Social Teaching, Arts Policy and the Post-war Irish Amateur Drama Movement 1949 to 1969
ISBN 978-1-80374-598-5. 348 pages. 2025.

Vol. 144   Seán Creagh: Republican Solipsist: The Life and Times of
           Joseph McGarrity, 1874–1940
           ISBN 978-1-80374-893-1. 268 pages. 2025.

Vol. 145   Geoffrey Sloan: Seeking Success and Confronting Failure: The British
           Army's campaigns in Ireland and Northern Ireland, 1919 to 2007
           ISBN 978-1-80374-816-0. 298 pages. 2025.

Vol. 146   James McAuley, Graham Spencer, Máire Braniff (eds): A Companion to
           Conflict and Peace in Northern Ireland
           ISBN 978-1-80079-867-0. 588 pages. 2025.

www.ingramcontent.com/pod-product-compliance
Ingram Content Group UK Ltd.
Pitfield, Milton Keynes, MK11 3LW, UK
UKHW022229230426
12048UKWH00016BA/1141